Ira S. Owens

Greene County Soldiers in the late War

Ira S. Owens

Greene County Soldiers in the late War

ISBN/EAN: 9783337133603

Printed in Europe, USA, Canada, Australia, Japan

Cover: Foto ©ninafisch / pixelio.de

More available books at **www.hansebooks.com**

GREENE COUNTY SOLDIERS

IN THE

LATE WAR.

BEING A HISTORY OF THE

SEVENTY-FOURTH O. V. I.,

WITH SKETCHES OF THE

TWELFTH, NINETY-FOURTH, ONE HUNDRED AND TENTH, FORTY-FOURTH, TENTH OHIO BATTERY, ONE HUNDRED AND FIFTY-FOURTH, FIFTY-FOURTH, SEVENTEENTH, THIRTY-FOURTH, ONE HUNDRED AND EIGHTY-FOURTH,

TOGETHER WITH A

LIST OF GREENE COUNTY'S SOLDIERS.

IRA S. OWENS,
COMPANY C, SEVENTY-FOURTH O. V. I.

DAYTON, OHIO:
CHRISTIAN PUBLISHING HOUSE PRINT,
1884.

TO MY

COMRADES IN ARMS,

THIS VOLUME IS

FRATERNALLY INSCRIBED

BY THE AUTHOR.

PREFACE.

In 1872 the author of this book wrote and published a small book the title of which was, "GREENE COUNTY IN THE WAR." But the supply being exhausted, a second edition has been published, similar to the first one, but enlarged and revised. In addition to the first book, sketches of other regiments have been added, together with anecdotes and incidents of the late war; also, a list of Greene County's soldiers, copied from muster-rolls in the Adjutant General's office at Columbus. In this, as well as the former work, the author does not attempt to give a general history of the rebellion, but simply a history of his own regiment — the Seventy-fourth Ohio — and parts of other organizations in which Greene County was represented. It is not, however, strictly confined to Greene County alone, but other counties in the state, as well. The author having spent considerable time and labor in getting out this book, offers it to the public, hoping that it may prove interesting and profitable to its readers.

IRA S. OWENS.

CONTENTS.

	PAGE.
INTRODUCTION	13

SEVENTY-FOURTH REGIMENT, O. V. I.

Organization and Rendezvous	17
Officers	17
Ordered to Nashville	18
A Strict Disciplinarian	18
March to Lebanon, Tennessee	19
The Star Spangled Banner	20
In Line of Battle	21
Prayer-meeting With Andrew Johnson	22
A Rebel Boaster	23
A Colored Social Meeting	25
A Skirmish With the Rebels	26
Rosencranz' Words of Cheer	27
March to Murfreesboro	28
Rosencranz' Address to the Army	29
Battle of Murfreesboro	30–39
Sanitary Commission-work	39–42
Official Report of General Rosencranz	43–53
Hospital Sufferings and Scenes	53
Seventy-Fourth Killed and Wounded	56–59
Colonel Josiah Given Succeeds Colonel Moody	61
Changes of Officers	62
In the Hospitals at Nashville	63
The Humane Colonel	65

CONTENTS.

	PAGE.
At Home on Furlough	66
The Great Atlanta Campaign	69
Trick on the Rebels	72
A Johnnie After Some Coffee.	73
The Killing of General Pope	75
Fixing a Rebel Sharpshooter	75
Leatherbreeches' Battery	76
Death of General McPherson	80
On the Skirmish Line	82
Method of Cooking Roasting-ears	83
Melville Davis Mortally Wounded	84
Death of William H. Hollenberry	85
Evacuation of Atlanta	86
The Negroes	91
In Front of Savannah	94
Capture of Fort McAllister	95
A Boat-load of Salt Beef.	97
Burning Property in South Carolina	98
Assassination of President Lincoln	104
Homeward March	106
Richmond and Belle Isle.	107
Citizens Once More	111
Recapitulation	111–113
Incidents	113–118
Campaign Songs	119–125

TWELFTH REGIMENT, O. V. I.

Organization	126
Battle of Scarey Creek	126
Death of Colonel Lowe at Carnifex Ferry	126
Rout of Rebel Cavalry	127

CONTENTS.

	PAGE.
Second Battle of Bull Run	127
South Mountain and Antietam	128
Battle of Cloyd Mountain	129
Muster-out	130
Reunion	130-139

NINETY-FOURTH REGIMENT, O. V. I.

Organization	140
Fight With a Scouting Party	141
Falling Back to Lexington	142
One Dollar a Drink for Water	143
Fighting at Stone River, Chickamauga, etc.	144
Mustered Out	145

ONE HUNDRED AND TENTH REGIMENT, O. V. I.

Organization	146
Pursuit of Lee	147
Fighting in the Wilderness	148
Battle of Monocacy	149
Battle of Winchester	150
Assault Before Petersburg	151
Mustered Out	151
Song — Keifer Leads the Van	152

FORTY-FOURTH REGIMENT, O. V. I.

Organized	154
Retreat to the Kanawha	155
Re-organized as Eighth Ohio Cavalry	157
Mustered Out	158

TENTH OHIO BATTERY.

Organized	159
Battle of Corinth	160

	PAGE.
A Clever Maneuver	161
Kennesaw Mountain	163
Officers	164
Mustered Out	164
Reunion	164–167

ONE HUNDRED AND FIFTY-FOURTH REGIMENT, O. V. I.

Organized	168
Skirmish With McNeil's Battalion	168
Battle of New Creek	169
Mustered Out	169

FIFTY-FOURTH REGIMENT, O. V. I.

Organized	170
Battle of Pittsburg Landing	170
Battle at Chickasaw Bayou	171
Engaged at Vicksburg	171
Pursuit of Hood	172
Mustered Out	173

SEVENTEENTH REGIMENT, O. V. I.

Dr. John Turnbull	174

THIRTY-FOURTH REGIMENT, O. V. I.

Organized	175
Battle of Fayetteville	176
Colonel Toland Killed at Wytheville	177
The Lynchburg Raid	179
Battle of Winchester	181
Pursuit of the Rebels	183
Attack on Beverly	184
Consolidated With the Thirty-Sixth Ohio	185

CONTENTS.

ONE HUNDRED AND EIGHTY-FOURTH REGIMENT, O. V. I.

PAGE.

Organized.. 186
Encounters With Guerrillas........................... 186

ROSTERS.

Seventy-Fourth 188–212
Twelfth.. 213–216
Ninety-Fourth... 217–222
One Hundred and Tenth................................. 223–224
Forty-Fourth... 225
Tenth Ohio Battery.. 226–230
One Hundred and Fifty-Fourth..................... 231–240
Fifty-Fourth.. 241
Thirty-Fourth... 242–243
One Hundred and Eighty-Fourth.................. 244–245
Third New York Cavalry................................ 246
First Ohio Regular Infantry.......................... 247
Errata—Officers of Seventy-Fourth............. 248
Anecdotes and Incidents............................... 249
Closing Scenes of the War............................ 291

INTRODUCTION.

In the fall of 1861, the people of Greene County, realizing to some extent the magnitude of the war in which the country was then engaged (the southern states, all save Maryland and Kentucky, marshaling their entire strength, fully equipped with arms stolen from the General Government, for the destruction of the Union; the North, without a single exception, meeting them with an equal force upon the bloody field of battle, in defense of the Union), and being anxious to show, at the end of the war, a bright chapter in its history, proposed to raise an entire regiment of volunteers, to be known as the "Greene County Regiment." Hardly had a day passed after the battle-cry had sounded from Sumter, when, at a war-meeting held in the old Firemen's Hall in the city of Xenia, the organization of two companies for the defense of the nation's capital was commenced. These being speedily completed and officered, with Captains John W. Lowe and Al. Galloway at their head, hastened to Columbus. The city of Washington having by this time become sufficiently guarded, they were sent to Camp Dennison, and were among the first to lay out the camp and begin the erection of camp-buildings. At the close of their three months' service they re-enlisted, and became a part of that well-known and hard-fighting regiment, the Twelfth Ohio, at the head of which fell the brave Colonel Lowe.

After the ever-memorable departure of these two noble companies, the work of enlistment continued. Other squads and companies, composed of men from shop, plow, and exchange, were continually leaving the county and joining regiments forming in other parts of the state, thus leaving this county without its proper credit. Hence at a meeting of half a dozen or more of the citizens of Xenia, held late one evening in the auditor's room of the court-house, it was resolved to form a Greene County regiment. A committee was appointed, consisting of Revs. R. D. Harper, P. C. Prugh, Judge Winans, and Hugh Carey, Esq., who were to proceed immediately to Jamestown, and, if possible, prevail upon a company, composed of the best men of that place and vicinity, organized under Captain Ballard, and chafing for the field, to remain in the county for the time, and take the post of honor in the new regiment. This company had already offered its services to General Fremont, then at the head of the army in Missouri.

The delegation proceeded, the next day, to Jamestown, held a consultation with the company, and proposed that they should immediately go into camp at Xenia and become the nucleus of the county regiment, the committeemen pledging themselves to use every possible effort in speedily filling it up.

After a few earnest speeches the company yielded, reconsidered their former purpose, and in a few weeks were in camp. The pleasant memories that still cluster around the scenes of that winter, in which soldiers and citizens happily mingled, meetings of prayer and praise, both in and out of camp, public days of fasting and feasting, speeches, parties, and concerts, will not soon be forgotten by those who, just as winter began to break, were "left behind."

No truer patriots than were these ever lived. No braver men ever fought. And Corporal Owens has done good service to both county and regiment in writing their history.

The readiness with which this regiment enlisted and marched to the field, the manner in which it fought, the many bloody battles it won in the great struggle of freedom for the nation and the world, its re enlistment of those who survived after having spent three long years of the most intense labor in marchings and fightings, imposing itself all the while as a wall of fire between our enemies and our homes, standing again and again in the very presence of death, should never be forgotten. The author of this little book has done much toward making all this a part of living history in the nation's struggle to free itself from the "accursed thing." In this he makes no attempt at display, but proposes, in a plain, simple way, to give a sketch of those scenes and actions in which his own regiment was engaged, together with a brief account of the other organizations to which Greene County contributed her men and means.

We bespeak for this little, unassuming companion a place, not only among the survivors and friends of the old Seventy-fourth, but in the families and homes of the county as well.

P. C. P.

HISTORY
OF THE
Seventy-Fourth Regiment, O. V. I.

CHAPTER I.

In October, 1861, the organization of the Seventy-fourth O. V. I. was commenced. Its rendezvous was Camp Lowe, in the old fair ground, Xenia, named in honor of Colonel John W. Lowe, who fell at Carnifax Ferry, Virginia, in the early part of the war. The regiment was organized to the extent of seven companies, at Camp Lowe; but on arriving at Camp Chase the following February, three more companies were added, making the complement, and aggregating nine hundred and seventy-eight men.

The regiment was officered as follows: Granville Moody, colonel commanding; Alexander Von Schrœder, lieutenant colonel; A. S. Ballard, major; J. R. Brelsford, surgeon, etc. (See roster at the end of the book.) The duty of the regiment at Camp Chase was, guarding prisoners. Colonel Moody was appointed post-commander.

On arriving at Columbus the regiment was quartered the first night in the state capitol. The next day it marched out to Camp Chase, after being reviewed by Governor Todd. Whatever may be said to the contrary, the prisoners there were well cared for. The writer was detailed several times to help erect tents, etc. They had plenty to eat, and comfortable quarters. The regiment remained at Camp Chase until April 20th, when they were ordered to Nashville, Tennessee, under command of Lieutenant Colonel Von Schrœder — Colonel Moody remaining at Camp Chase.

On arriving at Nashville the regiment marched through the city, and encamped near the river, remaining there only a short time, when they were ordered to move camp. They camped in a beautiful grove, about one mile south of the city, which was called Camp Tod, in honor of Governor Todd. Colonel Von Schrœder was a strict disciplinarian — having been a Prussian officer — he would not allow the men even to spit on dress parade. While in command at Camp Tod his wife visited him. He had issued strict orders that not a man should leave camp after a certain hour in the evening — as some of the boys were in the habit of frequenting the city until a late hour, and then coming into camp in a state of intoxication.

One day he made arrangements with some of the citizens to take tea with them at a certain time. Accordingly he and his wife rode up to the gate, when he was halted by the guard, who told him that he had orders from Colonel Von Schrœder not to let a man pass after a certain hour — it being then after that hour. "Well, but," says he, "I am Colonel Von Schrœder." "I don't know who in the h—l you are," says the guard, "you can't pass here." "Well," says the colonel, "I'll have that order changed in the morning," and turned around and rode back to his quarters. The next morning he sent for the guard who was at the gate at the time he wanted to pass out. The guard approached him with much fear and trembling, no doubt expecting to be severely dealt with, for the colonel looked at him with a stern countenance, and spoke in a very harsh manner, which frightened the poor fellow still worse. "You are the man that wouldn't let me out of camp last evening!" "Well—well—colonel, I—I—had orders not to let any one pass, and—and—I thought I must obey orders." The colonel then changed his voice, and spoke in a very pleasant manner, and said, "You did right. I wish all my men were as good soldiers as you are; we would then have no trouble. I'll promote you to a corporal."

After remaining in camp a short time, a detachment of the regiment was ordered on a scout over the Cumberland Mountains, or at least as far as McMinville. That was the first experience many in the regiment had in the toils, hardships, and fatigues of the march. Part of the regiment was left behind, being detailed on picket duty. Standing picket then was rather a pleasure and a pastime, there being no enemy near; and in the warm season of the year we were plentifully supplied with milk, potatoes, honey, etc., which were generally pretty easy of access — the forest furnishing mulberries, and the orchards cherries, plums, etc. Although the policy then was to guard rebel property, yet it was not always guarded. While on picket we enjoyed many luxuries, of which many times afterward we were deprived. We passed sixteen days thus very pleasantly, until the return of the balance of the regiment.

July 1st the regiment — or four companies of the same — were ordered to march to Lebanon, Tennessee, thirty miles from Nashville. We passed the Hermitage, the former residence of Andrew Jackson, and we saw the monument erected to his memory, underneath which lies the ashes of the hero of Orleans. On the march we gathered blackberries, which grew in immense quantities on each side of the road. The four companies were under the command of Major Ballard. On this march the boys did some foraging, by killing hogs, for which offense they were arrested and confined in jail in Lebanon. The indignation of the boys was very great at this act. They threatened to tear the jail down, and I have no doubt would have done so, had not the prisoners been released promptly.

The regiment was quartered in the spacious college building at Lebanon — the same that John Morgan and his men occupied previous to our arrival. It was a very dirty place, but by hard labor, washing, and scrubbing, we made it fit for soldiers to quarter in. We spent the Fourth of July at Lebanon. It was a very dull day. Our duty while there was light. We performed some picket duty, and had dress parade in the afternoon. The balance of the time was spent in loafing about the building, reading, writing letters home, or going out for blackberries, etc. We also formed a glee club, and used to serenade Union families — when we could find them out. One of our picket-posts was near the residence of ex-Governor Campbell. We went one evening to serenade him. We had just concluded one song — I think it was the "Star Spangled Banner" — when the old governor came out bareheaded, and cordially invited us into the house. "Boys," said he, "it does me good to hear those good old patriotic songs." We sang several more songs. He then had his daughter play for us on the piano. We were about to take our leave, when he told us to wait a few minutes. In a short time his negro man came in with a large tray, or waiter, loaded with nice cake, fruits, cordial, etc. He told us to help ourselves, and we did so. There were some excellent Union families in and around Lebanon, who hailed our approach with joy.

On the 10th of July our camp was thrown into considerable excitement, by the rumor that the rebel cavalry were advancing on us. But as feeble as we were, we commenced making preparations for defense. Our force consisted of four companies of infantry, and part of a regiment of cavalry. On the 11th I was on picket, and was relieved at 9:00 A. M. of the 12th —

no enemy yet. On the 13th we received marching orders for Nashville. It was about eleven o'clock at night when we received the order to march, and by twelve o'clock we were all packed up, armed, and equipped, and in line. While marching out of town all was still as the grave; the quiet of the citizens was not disturbed; no sound of martial music; no colors flying — nought could be heard save the heavy tramp of the soldiers, as they marched out, almost on the double quick; and by the time the gray light appeared in the eastern horizon, we were sixteen miles out on the road to Nashville, when we halted a short time, and got a bite to eat, and by ten o'clock we were in Nashville, having marched thirty miles. That was the time the rebel, Forrest, was expected to make an attack on Nashville. It was a very hot day. Some of the boys came near being exhausted, and one man had a sunstroke. We camped on College Hill, and that night we lay in line of battle for the first time. We were expecting to see the rebel cavalry dash on to us every minute. They came within about three or four miles, and burned a bridge, the light of which we could see. The next day — which was the 16th — Colonel Moody, with the detachment which was sent to Louisville, arrived. An anecdote was told of him here, which I will relate: He came galloping into camp, ordering the men to fall in, inquiring at the same time for the drummer, but the drummer could not be found. Seizing the bass drum he commenced pounding it with his fist. Observing one man without a gun, he inquired of him where his gun was. The man told him he had none. The colonel then told him to get one. The man replied he could not. "Well, then," says the colonel, "get a club; you shall shoot." A strong guard was kept. The city was barricaded with wagons, cotton bales, etc. A cannon was in position on each street, and every precaution taken in case of an attack. In that case the few troops around Nashville would have had warm work, and the rebs would have met with a warm reception. This is the time when it was said the celebrated prayer-meeting was held with Governor Andrew Johnson. A story went the rounds in the papers something like this: It was said that while Colonel Moody was praying, and as he waxed very fervent in his supplications, that the governor kept inching toward him, until at last, putting his arm around him (the colonel), said, "Colonel, I believe in God and the Christian religion; but I'll be d—d if Nashville shall be taken." And it was not taken.

A constant watch was kept for several days. Pickets were thrown out, and guards stationed on the road on which the attack was expected to be made. Several times it rained very hard, and wet the soldiers to the skin. It was very difficult to keep the muskets dry. The rain and mud were disagreeable. We remained at College Hill a short time. During the time we were in camp there we were reviewed by Major General Nelson.

Soon after we changed camp, and camped on the farm of Major Lewis, near town. This we called Camp Lewis. Shortly after we received orders to march to Franklin, Tennessee. I think it was about the 1st of August when we started to Franklin. When within about two miles of Franklin we halted for the night. The following incident occurred at that time, which I will relate:

It is generally known that about that time orders were strict concerning rebel property, which was to be held sacred, the orders coming from one Buell. He was very careful to protect rebels from the assaults of the blue-coats upon hen-roosts, hog-pens, and potato-patches. The hero of this story, George Snyder, was a good soldier. He obeyed orders, as a general rule, but could not see the sin of digging a few potatoes and having an ash-roast once in a while. It was George's fortune to be placed in charge of a pompous southern mansion and surroundings. Vegetables were scarce, and Buell's orders plenty. George concluded to suspend one of the orders touching potatoes. Thereupon his bayonet became a potato-fork, and a few small, scrawny tubers were taken from the sacred soil, carefully roasted, and transferred to George's stomach. For the suspension of this order George was duly arrested, and taken, under guard, to Colonel Moody's head-quarters for examination. The owner accompanied the squad, swearing vengeance on poor Snyder. The pompous son of the South preferred his charges. Moody heard him, spoke of Buell's order, and the necessity of respecting the same, and reprimanded Snyder for presuming to suspend his commanding general's orders. Whereupon the southern nabob waxed wrathy and valiant. He said that such soldiers as Snyder were northern poltroons and cowards; that if it were not for the musket he carried he would have whipped him and kicked him off his premises; and that he could whip half a dozen such fellows. This insulting language aroused Colonel Moody. He listened to the harangue and thought he would give the brave son of the South a chance to clean George out. Thereupon he ordered Snyder as follows: "Lay down that musket, sir." George obeyed. "Take off that haversack." George dropped his sack. "Unfasten that belt, sir." It was done. "Take off your coat." George shed his linen. "Now, sir, I release you from arrest. Step out and whip this brave scion of the South until I tell you to stop." This was the kind of order that George loved to obey, and he sprang back, *a la* Heenan, to the combat. But this the cowardly boaster had not bargained for. His eyes protruded; his knees shook like Belshazzar's; his tongue refused to utter the words he would have said. Moody urged, insisted, and ordered Johnny to make good his boastful words. Snyder, cool, snappy, eager for the fight, was inviting him to "come on." But it was no go. The poor fellow had been trapped and could only back out squarely.

His brother came forward and told the colonel that he (the speaker) was a senator of Tennessee and brother to the palsied victim, and urged Moody to stop the proceedings. The colonel assured Mr. Senator that he was doing all he could to bring the conflict to a close by having George Snyder conquer a peace; and, moreover, that peace he would have, and that neither he nor his doughty brother should insult him or his men by calling them poltroons and cowards. Thus the orders of General Buell were respected and obeyed by George Snyder and his colonel.

We remained at Franklin about a month. The regiment was at that time guarding the Nashville & Columbia Railroad, the different companies being scattered along the road from Nashville to Columbia, Company C occupying Franklin. Colonel Moody's head-quarters were at Franklin. While there we built stockades and did some guard duty. The court-house was occupied by the colonel, he having his head-quarters in it. It was barricaded by taking the large flat stones from off the yard and putting them in the windows, drilling port-holes in them.

Colonel Moody was then acting as chaplain as well as colonel. He would command the regiment during the week and preach on Sunday. The citizens in and about the vicinity of Franklin would come to hear him, although he would denounce them in such terms as only Colonel Moody could.

We lived very well off the products of the country, such as apples, peaches, potatoes, and honey, all of which were plentiful.

About the 1st of September we returned to Nashville. We took a train or two of cars, loaded with corn, to that city. When about half way, the train stopped, and the engineer jumped from his engine and took to the woods, thinking, doubtless, that the train would be captured. But Colonel Moody said the train should go into Nashville if the men had to push it in. However, a man was found who ran the train in.

On arriving in the vicinity of Nashville we went into the

woods and camped. While there a man was cleaning his gun, when it was accidentally discharged, killing a negro. We stayed in camp only one night, when we received orders to change camp. We then camped near the city, on the Franklin pike, where we remained a short time.

A great many negroes were employed at that time, working on the fortifications around the city, especially Fort Negley, near our camp. I used to go to their meetings, which they held out of doors. One evening I attended a social meeting, when one old darkey arose to speak. The substance of his speech was as follows: "My bred'rin', you sees me gwine aroun' drivin' de cart. You do not know whedder I'se got religion or not; but God knows it. By an' by I'll be high up in heaven, an' dese wicked sinners will be low down in hell, where de blue blazes of damnashun will be bilin' out of dar noses." These negroes were very ignorant, making use of some very droll expressions.

We then moved camp south of town, into a field where the weeds were nearly as high as one's head. This camp was called Camp Weeds. We stayed there a few days and then moved a short distance, near the Hillsboro pike, not far from our old Camp Tod. This was about the time of the siege of Nashville, when our communication was cut off. We suffered considerably for want of rations. We could get none from the Government; and I have often thought since that the Government ought to have paid us, as we drew none from its coffers. But about all we could get to eat was what we could get in the county. Foraging parties were sent out every few days, well guarded — often a battery or two of artillery accompanying every expedition. Even then we were not supplied very plentifully. The most we got was corn, which had to go to feed the mules — sometimes a few sweet potatoes or pumpkins. One day I ate nothing else but a small sweet potato. The reason was obvious — I could get nothing else. We named our camp "Starvation;" and in comparison to what we had been used to at home it was really starvation.

After remaining there a while we moved into the Chattanooga Depot. The first day of our arrival was a very busy one, the boys all being engaged in making bunks. It reminded one of a large carpenter-shop, and all hands at work. Some of the boys bunked in old freight-cars. The soldiers suffered much from camp-diarrhea and flux, some of whom died. I will mention a few of them: Thomas Harp and William Frenderburg, of Company C, and Thomas Faulkner, of Company B, with, perhaps, some others.

While here we were all called up before daylight, to drill, every morning, and many were the curses heaped upon the heads of the officers for this order. One morning we were all called up long before daylight and fell into line, and the order was given, "Forward, march," no one knowing where we were going. We marched out about seven miles, and were ordered to halt. A skirmish line was formed, and we were ordered to advance. (It was ascertained beforehand that a band of rebels had been seen, but of course the regiment knew nothing of it.) The regiment advanced a short distance when the advance guard came on a squad of rebels. After a sharp little skirmish they drove them across the river, capturing a few and scattering the rest. The regiment then returned to camp.

Orders were soon received to march toward Lebanon, Tennessee. We marched out some seven miles and halted, where we remained a short time. Then we started back toward Nashville, and camped on Mill Creek. Here the Seventy-fourth commenced building a bridge across that stream, the rebels having burned the old one. This was about the middle of November, 1862.

We were temporarily assigned to the command of Brigadier General Morgan. The general was a very plain-looking man.

He generally wore an old blouse, and did not look much like an officer. One day he visited the regiment to ascertain what progress they were making on the bridge. The men were then about placing a heavy piece of timber in position, when, observing that it was heavy to carry, the general seized hold of it and lifted until he was red in the face. It reminded me somewhat of General Washington and the corporal, although there was no corporal there giving commands. I suppose it is not necessary to repeat the story, as doubtless all my readers are acquainted with it.

While there I saw a revolting sight. A negro having died in one of the out-houses, his body was found, one morning, with his nose and part of his face eaten off by rats.

It was while we were here that I received the sad news of the death of my father, Rev. G. B. Owens. I first heard of his sickness, then of his death. My readers may imagine my feelings — away from home fighting for my country, without the privilege of visiting him in his last hours. Colonel Moody, in his sermon on the next Sabbath, very touchingly referred to his death, which affected me deeply.

About the last of November we again received orders to march before completing the bridge. We were ordered to Camp Hamilton, about seven miles from Nashville, near the Franklin pike. Our camp was on the farm of a Mr. Overton. Here the Army of the Cumberland was encamped, and reviewed by General Rosencranz. When he rode through the camp of the Seventy-fourth he had something to say to each company. To Company C he said: "Boys, when you drill, drill like thunder. It is not the number of bullets you shoot, but the accuracy of the aim, that kills more men in battle." The object of this review was to ascertain what the men needed before going into battle. To an Irishman he said, "Well, Pat, what do you want?" The Irishman replied, "If it's all the same to you, gineral, I want a furlough." The general, turning away, laughing, replied, "Well, Pat, you'll do."

Near the camp was a large canebrake; and the boys used to go at night, with torches, to kill robins, of which there were immense numbers. The light would blind them, and by taking a stick they could be easily killed. Colonel Neibling, of the Twenty-first Ohio Regiment, went into the brake one day and got lost. He had to climb a tree to see which way to get out. We had battalion drill frequently.

On the 26th of December, 1862, General Rosencranz marched from Camp Hamilton, in three columns, toward Murfreesboro; General McCook with the right division, by the Nolensville pike; General Thomas with the center, by the Wilson pike; and General Crittenden with the left on the main Murfreesboro road. The country was hilly and rough, with thickets of cedar, intersected by small streams, with rocky, bluff banks. The road was rough and muddy, and it was only by the utmost efforts that the teams could be got through. General Negley, our division commander, frequently alighting from his horse, pulling off his coat, and rolling up his sleeves, would assist the teamsters in pulling through. Several times Colonel Moody would become impatient, urging us on as we struggled through the mud and rain, telling us that the fight would be over before we got there, as ever and anon we could hear the boom of cannon in advance of us. But I guess the colonel got enough of it.

On the night of the 30th the pickets of both armies could sight each other by the light of burning dwellings. Constant skirmishing had been kept up all day, as General Rosencranz wished to discover the enemy. Occasionally a regiment advanced to clear a thicket; or a battery opened fire for a short time. At one time a cannon-ball took off part of a man's head, who was standing within ten feet of the general, and another fell among his escort. Our losses during the day, in these skirmishes, amounted to three hundred in killed and wounded. I am not speaking now of the Seventy-Fourth, but the whole army. At night the weary soldiers threw themselves upon the cold ground, to snatch a brief repose, conscious that on the morrow they were to be actors in a bloody tragedy. Early on the morning of the 31st, General Rosencranz issued the following address to his army:

"The general commanding desires to say to the soldiers of the Army of the Cumberland, that he was well pleased with their conduct yesterday. It was all that he could have wished for. He neither saw nor heard of any skulking. They behaved with the coolness and gallantry of veterans. He now feels perfectly confident, with God's grace and their help, of striking this day a blow for the country — the most crushing, perhaps, which the rebellion has yet sustained. Soldiers! the eyes of the whole nation are upon you. The very fate of the nation may be said to hang on the issues of this day's battle. Be true, then, to yourselves; true to your own manly character and soldierly reputation; true to the love of your dear ones at home, whose prayers ascend this day to God for your success. Be cool. I need not ask you to be brave. Keep ranks. Do not throw away your fire. Fire slowly, deliberately. Above all, fire low, and always be sure of your aim. Close readily in upon the enemy, and when you get within charging distance, rush upon him with the bayonet. Do this, and victory will certainly be yours. Recollect, that there are hardly any troops in the world that will stand a bayonet charge, and those who make it, therefore, are sure to win."

On the morning of the 31st the army of General Rosencranz was in position on the field in the following order: McCook's command consisted of three divisions — Johnson's on the right, Davis' in the center, and Sheridan's on the left, the latter somewhat withdrawn, and acting as a reserve for the south wing. The two divisions of Thomas, present on the field, held the center of the line — Negley on the right (in which division was the Seventy fourth) and Rousseau on the left. The left wing of the army, under Crittenden, was posted in the following.

order: Palmer's division on the right, Woods' in the center, and Van Cleve's on the extreme left.

The rebel line of battle was formed with the command of Bishop Polk on the right, consisting of two divisions of Preston Smith and Breckenridge; Kirby Smith, with three divisions, held the center; and Hardee, with the three divisions of Cheatham, McCown, and Withers, formed the right wing. This wing was strengthened on the night preceding the battle with the division of Clairborne. In numbers the armies were unequal, as one of the strongest divisions of the Union army, Mitchell's, was left to occupy Nashville. The field of battle was mostly rolling ground, with patches of woodland. The pike and railroad ran near each other, through the lines of battle, and the ground on the right, where McCook was posted, was a dense succession of cedar thickets, open spaces of rocky ground, belts of timber, and small fields. A number of houses were situated in different parts of the field.

Without further describing the relative positions of the army, I will proceed to give a faint description of the battle: At daylight the batteries of Sheridan's division shelled the rebels in a piece of woods in front, and the division advanced. It was immediately assailed with terrible energy by the rebels, who were three times repulsed. They made a fourth attempt, with re-enforcements, and the division was forced back. But the energy of Sill and other gallant officers soon rallied the troops, and the field in front was cleared of the enemy. General Sill had fallen, pierced through the brain by a musket-ball. The whole force of the onset was now brought against McCook's third division, commanded by Sheridan. It fought until one fourth of its members lay bleeding and dying on the field. Then it gave way, and all three of its divisions were hurled back together into the immense series of cedar thickets, which, skirting the turnpike, extended far off to the right.

General Rosencranz, on hearing of the disaster to his right wing, instantly set himself at work to retrieve it. Brigades and batteries from the divisions of Rousseau, Negley, and Palmer, were ordered to the right, to check the progress of the enemy, and rally the fugitives. The infantry were rapidly massed in an array of imposing strength along the turnpike, and facing the woods through which the rebels were advancing. Still the broken divisions of McCook disputed the ground while retreating, and deeds of heroism were performed by officers and men in those dark thickets. But in spite of the desperate struggle which marked every fresh advance of the enemy, in spite of the heroic sacrifice of life on the part of the officers and soldiers of the Union army, the rebels still steadily advanced and came nearer to the turnpike. Nearly two miles and a half had the right wing been driven, and all the re-enforcements that had been hurried into the woods to sustain it, had failed. The roar of cannon, the crashing of shot through the trees, the bursting of shell, and the continuous roll of musketry, all mingled in one tremendous volume of sound, which rolled on nearer and nearer to the turnpike, where the genius and vigor of Rosencranz had massed the forces that were to receive the enemy when he should emerge from the woods, in pursuit of our retreating battalions. At last the long lines of the enemy, rank upon rank, charged from the woods. A sheet of flame burst from the Union ranks, a crash rent the air, and the artillery shook the earth. The foremost lines of the rebel host were literally swept away, and then both armies were enveloped in a vast cloud of smoke. For ten minutes the thunder of battle burst forth from the cloud, and when our battalions advanced they found no rebels between the turnpike and woods, except the wounded, the dying, and the dead. The soil was red with blood, for within a brief space of time the slaughter had been awful, our troops having repulsed the rebel left, pushed into the woods after them, and drove them back over the ground we had first occupied.

It was eleven o'clock when Hardee was repulsed. In the meantime while the battle was raging on the right, an attack was made upon Palmer's division. The rebel's advanced with great impetuosity, but were driven back with terrible loss. There was now a lull in the storm, and scarcely a volley of musketry or boom of cannon was heard for three quarters of an hour. Some hoped that these bloody scenes were ended for the day; but the rebel leaders, disappointed by their failure to penetrate to our camp by way of the right wing, were preparing for a blow at the center. All the reserves were attached to the center of their army, under Polk; and Bragg, in person, placed himself at the head of the columns. And now was presented an imposing spectacle. The nature of the ground in this part of the field was such that every movement of either army could be seen. A fierce cannonading up the turnpike announced the coming onset, and from the very woods out of which the rebel cavalry issued on Monday evening, the first line of battle now sallied forth. It came on in magnificent order, and stretching away diagonally across a great sloping field, its length seemed interminable. At a sufficient interval another line deployed into the open ground parallel with the first, and ere the forward battalions were engaged, a third line of battle came forth from the same woods. It seemed that our feeble lines in that direction must be crushed by the weight of these immense masses of living and moving men. But the ever-watchful eye of Rosencranz had detected the rebel design even before their first line of battle emerged from the trees. The least-exhausted troops of the left and center were hurried forward on the double-quick, to combat this new effort of the enemy; and even from the extreme left, where Van Cleve was posted, a brigade was brought over to take part in the defense.

The same formidable array of batteries and battalions again confronted the foe, as that upon which the violence of Hardee's corps had spent itself, and similar results followed. Almost simultaneously a sheet of fire leaped forth from each of the opposite lines, and for a few minutes both stood like walls of stone, discharging their deadly muskets into each other's bosoms. Then the rebels attempted to charge, but a storm of lead and iron hail burst into their faces and all around them, sweeping them down by the hundreds. If once the Union soldiers wavered, it was only for a moment, and in forty minutes from the time the first rebel line marched forth, all three of them had been dashed to pieces, and the survivors of the conflict, flying in wild confusion over the slope, were disappearing in the depths of the woods.

The battle of the day was over. Until four o'clock the rebels continued to fire a cannon in the direction of Murfreesboro, as though in angry protest against their repulse. But when this ceased there was silence all over the field, so deep by contrast with the tumult of the battle that had raged all day, that it seemed oppressive and supernatural. The battle was over; but who can describe the sufferings which followed! The night air was piercingly cold, and in the midst of these gloomy forests of pine and cedars, where the night winds sighed through the leafless branches, singing, as it were, a requiem to the hundreds of freezing, bleeding, and dying men whom no human hand could ever succor — perhaps even at that very hour their fond wives or loving mothers at home were on their knees offering up their petitions to God for their loved ones on the battle-field. Ah, could they have known their situation then, and had it in their power, how they would have gone, with rapid speed, to administer to their wants. Oh, how often on that long and dreary night of the 31st of December, 1862, as I lay wounded on the ground, at the field hospital, with no covering but part of an old blanket — which Sergeant A. B. Cosler kindly procured for me — did I think of my loving wife and dear mother at home. You, my dear friends, who never participated in the toils, sufferings, and hardships of a soldier's life, know but little about it, only as you have read or heard soldiers tell of it. Yet I am sorry to say that there are some who are unwilling to give the soldier a small pension. If every soldier that fought and bled for his country was to receive a pension, he never could be paid for what he has suffered. Shame on the narrow, contracted soul — if he has a soul — that begrudges pensioning the soldiers.

The rebel pickets advanced at night to the edge of the woods skirting the open ground which was the scene of Hardee's terrible repulse. The hostile lines of battle were probably a thousand yards apart. The intervening space was covered with wounded, who could not be carried off. He who chose to risk it could crawl carefully up to the edge of the wood, and hear shrieks, cries, and groans of the wounded men who were lying by hundreds among the trees. The men in our advance-line lay down, as well as they could, upon ground over which the storm of battle had swept. It was difficult to distinguish the bodies of the sleepers from the corpses. Living and dead were slumbering peacefully together, with this difference: the one was to rise again to renew the conflict, the other had fought his last battle on earth. There were places that night where sleep came not to steep the senses in gentle forgetfulness. The poor soldier, whom the bullets had not reached, could gather a few sticks or cornstalks for a bed, clasp his faithful musket in his arms, with his blanket around him — if he were so fortunate as to have one — and sleep; but not that deep, profound slumber had he been at home in his warm bed. Ever and anon he would awake, his frame shivering with the bitter cold. He could build no fires, for that would reveal our position to the enemy. But the mangled hero, lying on the field or in the hospital, knew no repose; and to those who felt themselves maimed for life the keen mental anguish must have been even more intolerable than physical pain.

On Thursday morning the sun arose without clouds, but along the eastern horizon was a broad zone of mist and fog through which the great luminary looked red and bloody, as if in sympathy with the horrors of the battle-field. It was just eight o'clock when the roar of cannon re-commenced, with a terrible significance unknown a few days before. A skirmish had begun between the pickets in front of Palmer's lines and those of the enemy. Our batteries immediately commenced shelling the woods from which the rebel fire proceeded. Two dozen pieces of the enemy's artillery opened in reply, and having by this time accurately obtained the range of the elevated ground between the pike and railroad upon which so many of our troops were massed, their guns were worked with greater effect than ever before. Every form of shell, shrapnell, round shot, spherical case and oblong shot were hurled in most unpleasant confusion over the field. Our infantry, unable to take any part in this terrible duel, lay close upon the ground, the fiery missiles continually whizzing and bursting over their heads, and tearing up the earth among them and around them. It is wonderful that so few were injured by this iron tempest; yet there was scarcely a regiment all along the center that did not have some of its members killed or wounded. The Seventy-fourth was not the only regiment that lost members. Several Greene County boys in other regiments were killed and wounded. I have reference here to Greene County soldiers. I wish I had a list of all soldiers that were killed or wounded. But as Major Peters said at the reunion of the Seventy-fourth at Xenia, September 20, 1883, we never will know to a certainty. Some never could be found.

The Eighth Indiana Battery, Lieutenant Estepp commanding, was moved nearest the rebel lines, and did great service in finally silencing the enemy's guns. Several of its brave men were wounded, one third of the horses were disabled, and some of the pieces were drawn to the rear by hand. This day, like the preceding Tuesday, passed off in a series of skirmishes. Late in the afternoon a body of rebel cavalry appeared on a rising ground in front, but Colonel Loomis turned a couple of his Parrott guns in that direction, and a stampede quickly followed. The army passed another uncomfortable and cheerless night upon the battle-field; but General Rosencranz was not idle. During the night he sent the division of Van Cleve across the river on the left, where it got into position.

Early on Friday morning the thunder of rebel artillery called the troops to arms. Our batteries soon replied to theirs, and the fierce cannonading was kept up for half an hour, and then ceased on both sides. During this time one rebel gun was dismounted, and the battery to which it belonged, silenced. Hour after hour passed by and no earnest attempt was made by the rebels to renew the battle. At last, about four o'clock in the afternoon, a heavy cannonade, that had opened on the left, was followed by a deafening crash of musketry, and the whole army at once comprehended that the battle was renewed by an attack on Van Cleve's division, on the other side of Stone River. Bragg had massed three of his divisions, the whole under the command of Breckenridge, and hurled them against the division of Van Cleve. Our brigades struggled for a time with great bravery against the tremendous odds; but being literally overwhelmed by superior numbers, two of them gave way. The third held its ground for awhile, but the prospect of being surrounded brought on a panic. Then it broke with the others and fell back to and across the river. The rebels made preparations to follow, but by this time Negley, who had been hurried over from the center to re-enforce Van Cleve, suddenly confronted them with his compact lines of battle. The divisions of Wood and Davis, and the Pioneer Brigade of Morton, were placed in position by General Rosencranz, to support Negley, and open with all their batteries upon the host of Breckenridge. The rebel batteries were also in commanding position. The rebels soon recoiled under the terrific fire poured into them by Negley's division, and fell back from the river, followed, however, by our brave troops, who forded the stream and made a lodgment on the opposite side in a narrow strip of timber, destitute of underbrush and bounded by a rail fence. At this fence the rebels rallied, and as our men ascended the bank they were greeted by a storm of bullets, which, for a moment, checked their advance. By the exertions of Stanley and Miller the division was formed rapidly upon the bank, and with a tremendous shout they charged the rebel lines. The latter wavered and then broke. The ground over which they retreated was a low, wooded one. Our troops followed closely in the pursuit. The Seventy-eighth Pennsylvania captured the flag of the Twenty-sixth Tennessee. The divisions of Wood and Davis followed that of Negley. The flying regiments of Breckenridge debouched from the woods upon open cornfields, in the edge of which their batteries of fourteen guns were in position. A charge was made upon these, and the Nineteenth Illinois captured three guns Colonel Miller's command took a battery, the Seventy-fourth Ohio capturing it. The rebels again fled, followed by a tempest of bullets, which covered the ground with wounded and dead. Beyond was a dense forest, reaching to the town of Murfreesboro. It was now night, and Negley deemed it expedient to enter the woods at that time. From the cornfields to the river the distance was about one mile, and within that space the evidences of the terrible carnage were everywhere visible. Nearly one thousand rebels were killed outright in this attack, and the woods resounded with the shrieks and groans of the wounded and dying.

At twelve o'clock that night it commenced raining, and the unsheltered soldiers had a hard time of it. When Saturday morning came it was still raining, and the men had barely time to prepare their rations before they were called to arms by the roar of artillery on the center. An onset had been made on the Forty-second Indiana, which was out on picket-duty. The men behaved well, but met with considerable loss. All day the rain poured down; but General Rosencranz was busy guarding every point with hastily-constructed works. A slow advance toward the enemy was made by a series of rifle-pits. A brick house, the inside of which had been burned out, sheltered the enemy's sharp-shooters. General Rosencranz soon removed the annoyance by the aid of Loomis' and Guenther's batteries. In ten minutes the walls were leveled to the ground. Near this house the enemy had constructed rifle-pits, from which they fired upon our pickets. It was determined to drive them out, and Colonel John Beatty was selected to lead the storming party. Taking with him the Third Ohio, his own regiment, and the Eighty-eighth Indiana — Colonel Humphreys — he advanced with the utmost intrepidity, drove out the enemy at the point of the bayonet, and triumphantly held the works. Another night was passed on the battle-field, and the soldiers awoke on Sunday morning to find the ground covered with snow. As the day advanced the snow melted, and the mud became very disagreeable. It was a glad moment when the announcement was made to the army that Bragg had retreated, with all his force, from Murfreesboro, and that the Union army would march forward into the town.

On Sunday, January 4th, General Rosencranz entered Murfreesboro. The day will be a memorable one in our country's annals.

Our losses in the battle of Stone River were as follows: Officers killed, 88; officers wounded, 367; men killed, 1,386;

men wounded, 646. Total, 8,287. Loss in Pioneer Brigade, 48; loss in cavalry, 150—making a total loss of 8,485. In addition to these losses, the number set down as missing amounted to 2,800.

The rebel loss was estimated at over 14,000 in killed and wounded. Some four thousand of our wounded men were removed to Nashville, and two thousand were placed in hospitals at Murfreesboro. About fifteen hundred of the rebel wounded were left at the latter place when Bragg retreated.

Large numbers of surgeons proceeded immediately from the North to these two points, to attend to the sufferers, accompanied by agents of state and general government sanitary commissions. The following extract from a letter written by one of these gentlemen, Mr. Sessions, who accompanied the corps of surgeons, and directed the work of the sanitary commission from Columbus, Ohio, gives us an idea of the condition of our own and also of the rebel hospitals after this sanguinary battle. The women of the North can also see a small portion of the beneficent results of this association, flowing from their noble efforts in establishing and sustaining societies to aid the suffering soldiers. Mr. Sessions writes from Murfreesboro, eight days after the battle, as follows: "We arrived here last Saturday, after a pleasant ride in an ambulance, from Nashville—thirty miles. We saw, everywhere, the effects of war, and that two large armies had skirmished and fought most of the way. For fifteen miles nearly every house was burned, and all looked devastation and ruin. One village—Lavergne—was burned; and near by were the ruins of our large army train, burned by the rebels on the first day of the battle. Horses and mules burned to death gave one a horrid picture of war. For the remaining fifteen miles, every house was occupied as a hospital, where our poor soldiers are suffering from wounds, and the loss of limbs, and the groans of the dying are heard as you pass."

At Murfreesboro, Mr. Sessions visited the rebel hospitals, which he found in charge of a former acquaintance of his from the North. He says: "I visited, with him, the rebel hospitals under his charge, and found them wanting many things — indeed almost everything to make them comfortable. Men badly wounded were lying upon the hard floor, without straw, because it could not be obtained from us; and the poor men were calling out for something to eat. I asked him why this was so. He replied, 'Because we have not got it to give them.' He was kind and attentive to the men, and was doing all in his power to make them comfortable. The other rebel hospitals were in a wretched condition — filthy, and not half cared for by their surgeons. Gangrene was making its appearance from the wounds. There are about fifteen hundred wounded rebels here. In a large church, with upper and lower rooms occupied by them, they had only one candle to see to attending several hundred men during the night; and one of our party took some over to them. I understand they took away or burned all their hospital stores when they evacuated the city; and the first thing, on our entrance, they made a requisition for everything on our medical director." Another instance of their unscrupulousness in throwing the whole burden of providing for them on us.

In reference to our own hospitals he says: "We have about two thousand wounded here and in the vicinity, and all are well cared for — a better supply of hospital stores and medical supplies than there were either at Fort Donaldson, Shiloh, or Antietam. The government supplies were good, and the United States Sanitary Commission, under the direction of Dr. J. S. Newberry, western secretary, at Louisville, had forwarded sixty or seventy tons of all kinds of clothing, dried and canned fruit, concentrated beef and chickens, etc., necessary for the comfort of the sick and wounded. Dr. Read, their inspector, with his assistants, was busy night and day distributing articles to the surgeons and hospitals, arranging and controlling the operations, removing our own wounded from rebel hospitals, etc. Eight wagon-loads of supplies were sent on Monday, and seven on Wednesday, from Nashville, and a large amount distributed among our four thousand wounded in Nashville. It was an exceedingly gratifying sight to see boxes of sanitary goods, at the different hospitals, with the imprint of 'Soldiers' Aid Society, Cleveland,' boxes marked with contents from 'Soldiers' Aid Society, Columbus,' and other places. Our soldiers think, as one said, they come from God's country."

As evidence that the benevolent labors of the United States Sanitary Commission were properly appreciated by the army, we quote the following letter from the Rev. Granville Moody, then colonel of the Seventy-fourth Ohio Regiment. It was addressed to Dr. Read, the inspector of the commission:

SIR:— I desire to express to you, and through you to the generous and patriotic donors sustaining the Sanitary Commission, my high regard and appreciation of the works of love in which they are engaged. As I have visited the various hospitals in this place and looked upon the pale faces of the sufferers, and marked the failing strength of many a manly form, I have rejoiced in spirit as I have seen your benevolence embodied in substantial food, delicacies, and clothing, judiciously and systematically distributed by those who are officially connected with the army. If the donors could only know how much good their gifts have done, and could hear the blessings invoked upon their unknown friends by the suffering ones, they would more fully realize the divine proverb, "It is more blessed to give than to receive." We would advise all who wish to extend the hand of charity so as to reach the suffering officers and soldiers who have stood "between their loved homes and foul war's desolation," to commit their offerings to the custody of "the United States Sanitary Commission," an organization authorized by the secretary of war and the surgeon general, having the confidence of the army, and affording a direct and expeditious medium of communication with the several divisions of the army free of expense to the donors, and entirely reliable in its character. It is also worthy of special note that the goods intrusted to the commission are distributed to those who are actually sick or convalescent; and this is under the scrutiny of the most responsible persons in its employ, and through regularly established official agencies in the army. If the patriotic donors of the several states would direct their contributions into this channel, it would save much expense of agencies, blend the sympathies of Union men of the several states, and prevent unpatriotic distinctions in the patients in the hospitals, who are from every regiment, from every state. Side by side they fought and were wounded, and side by side they suffer in hospitals; and the commission, through appropiate agencies, extends its aid alike to the sons of Virginia and Pennsylvania, Ohio and Kentucky, Indiana and Tennessee, Michigan and Missouri, thus giving prominence to our cherished national motto, "We are many in one." As an illustration, the other day an agent of a Wisconsin society came to a hospital with sanitary goods for Wisconsin soldiers, and went along the wards, making careful discrimination in behalf of Wisconsin soldiers, but soon saw it was an ungracious task, and handed over his goods to the United States Sanitary Commission. Learning this, one of the Wisconsin soldiers said, "I'm glad of that; for it made me feel so bad when my friends gave me those good things the other day and passed by that Illinois boy on the next bed there, who needed them just as much as I did. But I made it square with him, for I divided what I got with him." Brave, noble fellow! His was the true spirit of a soldier of the United States. We have a common country, language, religion, interest, and destiny; and we should closely weave the web of our unity, so that the genius of liberty may, like Him "who went about doing good," wear a "seamless garment." We believe in the constitutional rights of states, but most emphatically believe in our glorious nationality, which, like the sun amidst the stars, has a surpassing glory and is of infinitely greater importance, and should be cherished in every appropriate form of development.

           GRANVILLE MOODY,
        Colonel Commanding Seventy-fourth Regiment.

OFFICIAL REPORT OF GENERAL ROSENCRANZ.

HEAD-QUARTERS DEPARTMENT OF THE CUMBERLAND,
MURFREESBORO, TENNESSEE, February 12, 1863.

GENERAL:—As the sub-reports are now nearly all in, I have the honor to submit, for the information of the general-in-chief, the subjoined report, with accompanying sub-reports, maps, and statistical table of the battle of Stone River.

To a proper understanding of this battle it will be necessary to state the preliminary movements and preparations. Assuming command of the army at Louisville, on the 27th day of October, it was found concentrated at Bowling Green and Glasgow, distant about one hundred and thirteen miles from Louisville, whence, after replenishing with ammunition, supplies, and clothing, they moved on to Nashville, the advance corps reaching that place on the morning of the 7th of November—a distance of one hundred and eighty-three miles from Louisville.

At this distance from my base of supplies, the first thing to be done was to provide for the subsistence of the troops and open the Louisville & Nashville Railroad. The cars commenced running through on the 26th of November, previous to which time our supplies had been brought by rail to Mitchelville, thirty-five miles north of Nashville, and thence, by constant labor, we had been able to haul enough to replenish the exhausted stores for the garrison at Nashville and subsist the troops of the moving army.

From the 26th of November to the 26th of December every effort was bent to complete the clothing of the army, to provide it with ammunition, and replenish the depot at Nashville with needful supplies to insure us against want from the largest possible detention likely to occur by breaking of the Louisville & Nashville Railroad; and to insure this work, the road was guarded by a heavy force posted at Gallatin.

The enormous superiority of numbers of the rebel cavalry kept our little cavalry force almost within the infantry lines, and gave the enemy control of the entire country around us.

It was obvious, from the beginning, that we should be confronted by Bragg's army, recruited by an inexorable conscription, and aided by clouds of mounted men, formed into guerrilla-like cavalry, to avoid the hardships of conscription and infantry service.

The evident difficulties and labors of an advance into this country, and against such a force, and at such distance from our base of operations — with which we were connected by a single precarious thread — made it manifest that our policy was to induce the enemy to travel over as much as possible of the space that separated us, thus avoiding for us the wear and tear and diminution of our forces, and subjecting the enemy to all these inconveniences, besides increasing for him, and diminishing from us, the dangerous consequences of a defeat. The means taken to obtain this end were eminently successful. The enemy, expecting us to go into winter-quarters at Nashville, had prepared his own winter-quarters at Murfreesboro, with the hope of possibly making them at Nashville, and had sent a large cavalry force into West Tennessee to annoy Grant, and another large force into Kentucky to break up the railroad. In the absence of these forces, and with adequate supplies in Nashville, the moment was judged opportune for an advance on the rebels. Polk's and Kirby Smith's forces were at Murfreesboro, and Hardee's corps on the Shelbyville and Nolensville pike, between Triune and Eaglesville, with an advance guard at Nolensville, while our troops lay in front of Nashville, on the Franklin, Nolensville, and Murfreesboro turnpike.

The plan of the movement was as follows: [But as the plan has already been given it is not necessary to repeat it here.—AUTHOR.]

General Rosencranz addressed General McCook as follows: "You know the ground — you have fought over its difficulties — can you hold your present position for three hours?" To which General McCook replied, "Yes, I think I can." The general commanding then said: "I don't like the facing so much to the east, but I must confide that to you, who know the ground. If you don't think your present the best position, change it." And the officers then retired to their commands.

At daylight on the morning of the 31st the troops breakfasted [some of them, not all.—AUTHOR.] and stood to their arms, and by seven o'clock were preparing for the battle.

The movement began on the left by General Van Cleve, who crossed at the lower fords. Wood prepared to sustain and follow him. The enemy, meanwhile, had prepared to attack General McCook, and by half past six o'clock advanced in heavy columns, regimental front, his left attacking Willich's and Kirk's brigades of Johnson's division, which, being disposed as shown in the map, thin and light, without support, were, after a sharp but fruitless contest, crumbled to pieces and driven back, leaving Edgarton's and part of Goodspeed's battery in the hands of the enemy. The enemy following up, attacked Davis' division and speedily dislodged Post's brigade. Carlin's brigade was compelled to follow, as Woodruff's brigade, from the weight of testimony, had previously left its position on his left. Johnson's brigade, on retiring, inclined too far to the west, and were too much scattered to make a combined resistance, though they fought bravely at one or two points before reaching Wilkinson's pike. The reserve brigade of Johnson's division, advancing from its bivouac near Wilkinson's pike, towards the right, took a good position, and made a gallant but ineffectual stand, as the whole rebel left was moving up on the ground abandoned by our troops.

Within an hour from the time of the opening of the battle a staff officer from General McCook arrived, announcing to me that the right wing was heavily pressed and needed assistance; but I was not advised of the rout of Willich's and Kirby's brigades, nor of the rapid withdrawal of Davis' division, necessitated thereby. Moreover, having supposed his wing posted more compactly and his right more refused than it really was, the direction of the noise of battle did not indicate to me the true state of affairs. I consequently directed him to return and direct General McCook to dispose his troops to the best advantage, and to hold his ground obstinately.

Soon after a second officer from General McCook arrived, and stated, that the right wing was being driven—a fact that was but too manifest by the rapid movement of the noise of battle toward the north. General Thomas was immediately dispatched to order Rousseau—then in reserve—into the cedar brakes to the right and rear of Sheridan. General Crittenden was ordered to suspend Van Cleve's movement across the river, on the left, and to cover the crossing with one brigade, and move the other two brigades westward across the fields, towards the railroad, for a reserve. Wood was also directed to suspend his preparations for crossing, and to hold Hascall in reserve. At this moment fugitives and stragglers from McCook's corps began to make their appearance through the cedar brakes in such numbers that I became satisfied, that McCook's corps was routed. I therefore directed General Crittenden to send Van Cleve in to the right of Rousseau, Wood to send Colonel Harker's brigade further down the Murfreesboro pike, to go in and attack the enemy on the right of Van Cleve, the Pioneer brigade, meanwhile, occupying the knoll of ground west of the Murfreesboro pike and about four or five hundred yards in the rear of Palmer's center, supporting Stockton's battery.

Sheridan, after sustaining four successive attacks, gradually swung his right from a south-easterly to a north-westerly direction, repulsing the enemy four times, losing the gallant General Sill of his right and Colonel Roberts of his left brigade, when, having exhausted his ammunition — Negley's division being in the same predicament, and heavily pressed — after desperate fighting, they fell back from the position held at the commencement, through the cedar woods, in which Rousseau's division, with a portion of Negley's and Sheridan's, met the advancing enemy and checked his movements.

The ammunition train of the right wing, endangered by its sudden discomfiture, was taken charge of by Captain Thurston, of the First Ohio, a regular ordnance officer, who, by his energy and gallantry, aided by a charge of cavalry and such troops as he could pick up, carried it through the woods to the Murfreesboro pike, around to the rear of the left wing, thus enabling the troops of Sheridan's division to replenish their empty cartridge-boxes. During all this time Palmer's front had likewise been in action, the enemy having made several attempts to advance upon it.

At this stage it became necessary to re-adjust the line of battle to the new state of affairs. Rousseau and Van Cleve's advance having relieved Sheridan's division, withdrew from their original position in front of the cedars and crossed the open field to the east of the Murfreesboro pike, about four hundred yards in the rear of our front line, where Negley was ordered to replenish his ammunition and form in close column in reserve

The right and center of our line now extended from Hazen to the Murfreesboro pike, in a north-westerly direction, Hascall supporting Hazen, Rousseau filling the interval to the Pioneer brigade, Negley in reserve, Van Cleve west of the Pioneer brigade, McCook's corps refused on his right and slightly to the rear on the Murfreesboro pike, the cavalry being still further to the rear, on the Murfreesboro pike, and beyond

Overall's Creek. The enemy's infantry and cavalry attack on our extreme right was repulsed by Van Cleve's division, with Harker's brigade and the cavalry.

After several attempts of the enemy to advance on this new line — which were thoroughly repulsed, as also their attempts on the left — the day closed, leaving us masters of the original ground on our left, and our new line advantageously posted, with open ground in front, swept at all points by our artillery.

We had lost heavily in killed and wounded, and a considerable number in stragglers and prisoners; also, twenty-eight pieces of artillery, the horses having been slain, and our troops being unable to withdraw them by hand over the rough ground. But the enemy had been thoroughly handled and badly damaged at all points, having had no success where we had open ground and our troops were properly posted — none which did not depend on the original crushing on our right and the superior masses which were, in consequence, brought to bear upon the narrow front of Sheridan's and Negley's divisions and a part of Palmer's, coupled with the scarcity of ammunition, caused by the circuitous road which the train had taken and the inconvenience of getting it from a remote distance through the cedars.

Orders were given for the issue of all the spare ammunition, and we found that we had enough for another battle, the only question being where that battle was to be fought.

It was decided, in order to complete our present lines, that the left should be retired some two hundred and fifty yards, to a more advantageous ground, the extreme left resting on Stone River above the lower ford and extending to Stokes' battery. Starkweather's and Walker's brigades arriving near the close of the evening, the former bivouacked in close column, in reserve, in rear of McCook's left, and the latter was posted on the left of Sheridan, near the Murfreesboro pike, and next morning relieved Van Cleve, who returned to his position on the left wing.

After careful examination and free consultation with corps commanders, followed by a personal examination of the ground in the rear as far as Overall's Creek, it was determined to await the enemy's attack in that position, to send for the provision train, and order up fresh supplies of ammunition, on the arrival of which, should the enemy not attack, offensive operations should be resumed.

No demonstration being made on the morning of the 1st of January, Crittenden was ordered to occupy the points opposite the ford on his left with a brigade. About two o'clock in the afternoon the enemy, who had shown signs of movement and massing on our right, appeared at the extremity of a field a mile and a half from the Murfreesboro pike, but the presence of Gibson's brigade, with a battery, occupying the woods near Overall's Creek, and Negley's division and a portion of Rousseau's on the Murfreesboro pike opposite the field, put an end to this demonstration; and the day closed with another demonstration by the enemy on Walker's brigade, which ended in the same manner.

On Friday morning the enemy opened four heavy batteries on our center, and made a strong demonstration of attack a little further to the right; but a well-directed fire of artillery soon silenced his batteries, while the guns of Walker and Sheridan put an end to his effort there.

About three o'clock P. M., while the commanding general was examining the position of Crittenden's left, across the river, which was now held by Van Cleve's division, supported by a brigade from Palmer's, a double line of skirmishers was seen to emerge from the woods in a southeasterly direction, advancing across the fields; and they were soon followed by heavy columns of infantry, battalion front, with three batteries of artillery. Our only battery on that side of the river had been withdrawn from an eligible point; but the most available spot was pointed out, and it soon opened fire upon the enemy. The line, however, advanced steadily to within one hundred yards of the front of Van Cleve's division, when a short and fierce contest ensued. Van Cleve's division gave way and retired in considerable confusion across the river, followed closely by the enemy. General Crittenden immediately directed his chief of artillery to dispose the batteries on the hill on the west side of the river so as to open on them, while two brigades of Negley's division, from the reserve, and the Pioneer brigade were brought up to meet their onset. The firing was terrific, and the havoc terrible. The enemy retreated more rapidly than they had advanced. In forty minutes they lost two thousand men. General Davis, seeing some stragglers from Van Cleve's division, took one of his brigades and crossed at a ford below, to attack the enemy on his left flank, and by General McCook's order the rest of his division was permitted to follow; but when he arrived two brigades of Negley's division and Hazen's brigade of Palmer's division had pursued the flying enemy well across the field, capturing four pieces of artillery and a stand of colors. It was now after dark, and raining, or we should have pursued the enemy into Murfreesboro. As it was, Crittenden's corps passed over, and with Davis occupied the crest which was intrenched in a few hours. Deeming it possible that the enemy might again attack our right and center thus weakened, I thought it advisable to make a demonstration on our right by a heavy division of camp-fires, and by laying out a line of battle with torches, which answered the purpose.

On Saturday, January 3d, it rained heavily from three o'clock in the morning. The plowed ground, over which our left would be obliged to advance, was impassable for artillery. The ammunition-train did not arrive until ten o'clock, it was therefore deemed unadvisable to advance, but batteries were put in position on the left, by which the ground could be swept, and even Murfreesboro reached by the Parrott guns. A heavy and constant picket firing had been kept up on our right and center, and extending to our left, which at last became so annoying that in the afternoon I directed the corps commanders to clear the fronts. Occupying the woods to the left of Murfreesboro pike with sharpshooters, the enemy had annoyed Rousseau all day, and General Thomas and himself requested permission to dislodge them and their supports which covered a ford. This was granted, and a sharp fire from four batteries was opened for ten or fifteen minutes, when Rousseau sent two of his regiments, which, with Speer's Tennesseeans, and the Eighty-fifth Illinois Volunteers, that had come out with the wagon trains, charged upon the enemy, and, after a sharp contest, cleared the woods and drove the enemy from his trenches, capturing from seventy to eighty prisoners.

Sunday morning, January 4th, it was not deemed advisable to commence offensive movements; and news soon reached us that the enemy had fled from Murfreesboro. Burial parties were sent out to bury the dead, and the cavalry was sent to reconnoiter.

Early on Monday morning General Thomas advanced, driving the rear guard of rebel cavalry before him six or seven miles, toward Manchester. McCook and Crittenden's corps following, took position in front of the town of Murfreesboro. We learned that the enemy's infantry had reached Shelbyville by 12 M. on Sunday; but owing to the impracticability of bringing up supplies and the loss of 557 artillery horses, further pursuit was deemed unadvisable.

It may be of use to give the following general summary of the operations and results of the series of skirmishes, closing with the battle of Stone River and occupation of Murfreesboro. We moved on the enemy with the following forces: Infantry, 41,421; artillery, 2,223; cavalry, 3,296. Total, 46,940. We fought the battle with the following forces: Infantry, 37,977; artillery, 2,223; cavalry, 3,200. Total, 43,400. We lost in killed: Officers, 92; enlisted men, 1,441. Total, 1,533. We lost in wounded: Officers, 384; enlisted men, 6,881. Total, 7,245. Total killed and wounded, 8,778. Our loss in prisoners is not fully made out, but the provost marshal general says, from present information they will fall short of 2,800.

If there are many bloodier battles on record, considering the newness and inexperience of the troops, both officers and men, or if there has been more true fighting qualities displayed by any people, I should be pleased to know it. On the whole, it is evident that we fought superior numbers on unknown ground, inflicting much more injury than we suffered. We were always superior on equal ground, with equal numbers, and failed of a most crushing victory on Wednesday by the extension and direction of our right wing.

This closes the narrative of the movements and seven days' fighting, which terminated with the occupation of Murfreesboro. Beside the mention which has been already made of the service of our artillery by the brigade, division, and corps commanders, I deem it a duty to say that such a marked evidence of skill in handling the batteries, and in firing with effect, appears, in this battle, to deserve special commendation. Among the lesser commands which deserve special mention for distinguished service in the battle is the Pioneer Corps, a body of 1,700 men, composed of details from the companies of each infantry regiment, organized and instructed by Captain James St. Clair Morton, corps of engineers, chief engineer of this army, which marched as an infantry brigade to the left wing, making bridges at Stewart's Creek; prepared and guarded the ford at Stone River on the nights of the 29th and 30th; supported Stokes' battery, and fought with valor and determination on the 31st, holding its position until relieved on the morning of the 2d; advancing with the greatest promptitude and gallantry to support Van Cleve's division against the attack on our left, on the evening of the same day; constructing a bridge and batteries between that time and Saturday evening; and the efficiency and *esprit du corps* suddenly developed in this command, its gallant behavior in action, the eminent service it is continually rendering the army, entitle both the officers and men to special public notice and thanks, while they reflect the highest credit on the distinguished ability and capacity of Captain Morton, who will do honor to his promotion to a brigadier general, which the President has promised him.

The Eighteenth Regiment of Ohio Volunteers, at Stewart's Creek, Lieutenant Colonel Bark commanding, deserves especial praise for the ability and spirit with which they held their post, defended our trains, succored their cars, chased away Wheeler's rebel cavalry, saving a large wagon-train, and arrested and returned in service some two thousand stragglers from the battle-field.

The First Regiment of Michigan, engineers and mechanics, at Lavergne, under the command of Colonel Innis, fighting behind a slight protection of wagons and brush, gallantly repulsed a charge from more than ten times their numbers of Wheeler's cavalry.

For distinguished acts of individual zeal, heroism, and gallantry, and good conduct, I refer to the accompanying list of special mentions and commendations for promotion, wherein are named some of the many noble men who have distinguished themselves and done honor to their country and the starry symbol of its unity. But those names there are by no means all whose names will be inscribed on the rolls of honor we are preparing, and hope to be held in grateful remembrance by our countrymen. To such men as Major General George H. Thomas, true and prudent, distinguished in counsel and on many battle-fields for his courage; or Major General McCook, a tried, faithful, and loyal soldier, who bravely breasted battle at Shiloh, and at Perrysville, and as bravely on the bloody field of Stone River; and Major General Thomas L. Crittenden, whose heart is that of a true soldier and patriot: I doubly thank them, as well as the gallant, ever-ready Major General Rousseau, for their support in this battle. Brigadier General D. S. Stanley, already distinguished for four successful battles—Island No. 10, May 27th, before Corinth, Iuka, and the battle of Corinth—at this time in command of our ten regiments of cavalry, fought the enemy's forty regiments of cavalry, and held them at bay, and beat them whenever he could meet them. In such brigadiers as Negley, Jefferson C. Davis, Johnson, Palmer, Hascall, Van Cleve, Wood, Mitchell, Cruft, and Sheridan, and such brigade commanders as Colonels Carlin, Miller, Hazen, Samuel Beatty of the Nineteenth Ohio, Gibson, Gross, Wagner, John Beatty

of the Third Ohio, Harker, Starkweather, Stanley, and others whose
names are mentioned in the accompanying report, the government may
well confide. To these I offer my most heart-felt thanks and good wishes.
Words of my own can not add to the renown of our brave and patriotic
officers and soldiers who fell on the field of honor, nor increase respect
for their memory in the hearts of our countrymen. The names of such
men as Lieutenant Colonel J. P. Garesche, the pure and noble Christian
gentleman and chivalric officer, who gave his life an early offering on the
altar of his country's freedom; the gentle, true, and accomplished
General Sill; the heroic and ingenious Colonels Roberts, Milliken,
Shaeffer, McKee, Reed, Foreman, Fred. Jones, Hawkins, Knell, and the
gallant and faithful Major Carpenter, of the Nineteenth Regulars, and
many other field officers, will live in our country's history, as well as many
others of inferior rank, whose soldierly deeds on this memorable battle-
field won for them the admiration of their companions, and will dwell in
our memories in long-future years, after God, in his mercy, shall have
given us peace, and restored us to the bosoms of our homes and families.
Simple justice to the gallant officers of my staff — the noble and lamented
Lieutenant Colonel Garesche, chief of staff; Lieutenant Colonel Taylor,
chief quartermaster; Lieutenant Colonel Simmons, chief commissary;
Major C. Goddard, senior aid-de-camp; Major Ralston Skinner, judge
advocate general; Lieutenant Frank S. Bomb, aid-de-camp of General
Tyler; Captain Charles Thompson, my aid-de-camp; Lieutenant Byron
Kirby, Sixth United States Infantry, aid-de-camp, who was wounded on
the 31st; R. S. Thorn, Esq., a member of the Cincinnati bar, who acted
as volunteer aid-de-camp, behaving with distinguished gallantry; Colonel
Barnett, chief of artillery and ordnance; Captain G. H. Gilman, Nine-
teenth United States Infantry, inspector of artillery; Captain James
Curtis, Fifteenth United States Infantry, assistant inspector general;
Captain Wiles, Twenty-second Indiana, provost marshal general; Captain
Michler, topographical engineer; Captain Jesse Merrill, of the signal
corps, whose corps behaved well; Captain Elmer Otis, Fourth Regular
Cavalry, who commanded the second courier line, connecting the various
head-quarters, most successfully, and who made a most opportune and
brilliant charge on Wheeler's cavalry, routing the brigade, and recaptur-
ing three hundred of our prisoners; Lieutenant Edson, United States
ordnance officer, who, during the battle of Wednesday, distributed
ammunition under the fire of the enemy's batteries, and behaved bravely;

Captain Hubbard and Lieutenant Newberry, who joined my staff on the field, acting as aids, rendered valuable services in carrying orders on the field; Lieutenant Byse, Fourth United States Cavalry, commanding the escort of the head-quarters train, and distinguished himself with gallantry and efficiency, who not only performed these appropriate duties to my entire satisfaction, but accompanied me everywhere, carrying orders through the thickest of the fight, watched while others slept, never weary when duty called — deserve my public thanks, and the respect and gratitude of the army.

With all these facts of the battle fully before me, the relative numbers and positions of our troops and those of the rebels, the gallantry and obstinacy of the contest, and the final result, I say, from conviction, and as a public acknowledgment due to Almighty God, in closing this report, "*non nobis, Domine, non nobis; sed nomine tuo da gloriam!*"

    WM. S. ROSENCRANS, Major General Commanding.
BRIGADIER GENERAL L. THOMAS, Adjutant General, U. S. A.

I was slightly wounded in the battle of Stone River, and taken to the field hospital, five miles toward Nashville. It was impossible to supply all the wounded with tents. Rails were hauled and fires built, and they were laid on the ground before the fires. Men were wounded in every conceivable way — some with their arms and legs shot off, some in the head, and some in the body. It was heart-rending to hear their cries and groans. One poor fellow, who was near me, was wounded in the head. He grew delirious during the night, and would frequently call for his mother. He would say, "Mother, O mother, come and help me!" The poor fellow died before morning, with no mother near to soothe him in his dying moments or wipe the cold sweat from his brow. I saw the surgeons amputate limbs, then throw the quivering flesh into a pile. Every once in a while a man would stretch himself out and die. Next morning rows of men were laid out side by side, ready for the soldiers' burial. No weeping friends stood around; no coffin and hearse to bear them away to the grave; no funeral orations delivered;

but there, away from home and kindred, they were wrapped in the soldiers' blanket, a trench dug, their bodies placed side by side, like they fought, a few shovelfuls of earth thrown upon them, and they were left alone.

Among those who were wounded were Charles M. Wolf, James Seldomridge, A. B. Cosler, and perhaps some others from Company C, Seventy-fourth Ohio Regiment.

Through the kindness of Sergeant Cosler, I fared pretty well. He procured an old blanket for me, and I lay by the fire all night, much more comfortable than the night before, on the battle-field. I said "comfortable." It may be imagined that there was not much comfort anywhere. I was wounded just above the left knee, by a musket-ball or a piece of shell, I am unable to tell which. Although my leg pained me considerably, so that I slept very little during the night, still I did not complain, as there were others who were hurt a great deal worse than I was. Soon after I arrived at the hospital a surgeon proposed to dress my wound; but I told him to attend to others around me, who needed attention first.

The next day it rained; and, having no shelter-tent, it was very disagreeable. It was on Wednesday I was taken to the hospital, and on Saturday, being able to hobble around with the aid of a stick, I resolved to get back to the regiment. I accordingly started to the front. Being lame, I made slow progress.

I had not gone far before I came up to a squad of men guarding muskets which had been picked up on the battle field. I had lost my gun during the battle, or, rather, I gave it to a soldier to carry for me as I was going to the rear, and he set it up against a tree and left it. I approached the officer who was in command of the squad, and told him I had lost my gun. He told me to go to the stack and select one for myself. I selected a nice Enfield rifle, nearly new, and took it, and went on toward Murfreesboro.

On arriving at the front, which was in the after part of the day, I was puzzled to find the Seventy-fourth, as I had been told they had moved their position; but after passing several regiments and brigades, I inquired of some soldiers of an Indiana regiment if they knew where the Eighth Division (General Negley's) was. They informed me that the division was only a few yards ahead of me, the left resting on the river. They were preparing supper when I came up. I spoke to them, and asked them if they could give a wounded soldier something to eat, as I had eaten nothing since leaving the hospital in the morning. They replied that they did not have much, but would divide with me, and give me something. I wish I knew the name of that regiment. Such generosity is not always found, and especially among soldiers who are living on quarter rations. I ate a hard-tack and a small piece of meat, thanked them, and then set forward again.

After the battle of Stone River the soldiers had a hard time to get something to eat. As much as twenty-five cents was offered for a single hard-tack. Money could not buy rations. They could not be had.

I found the Seventy-fourth near the river. The boys appeared glad to see me; and it is certain I was glad to see them. Soon after I arrived they were called out, but soon returned. It was expected that the rebels would make an attack; but they did not. No doubt they had enough of the Yankees, as they called the Union troops. That night it rained, and I slept but little. It was a very quiet day compared to what it had been for a few days past. We remained close to the river until near evening. That night some one stole my Enfield.

We received orders to march, as we supposed, into Murfreesboro, late on Saturday afternoon. We went over the field so hotly contested, and no one, only those who have been over a battle-field after a hard fight, can form an idea of the spectacle it presents. Numbers of dead men and horses were strewn over the ground like old logs in a clearing or deadening. Guns, knapsacks, pistols, cartridge-boxes, etc., and squads of burying parties gathering up the dead, were to be seen on every side. We moved up to the rebel breastworks, near the river. The battery sent over a few shells, to ascertain whether the rebels had gone or not. We spent the night among the dead, who were lying all around us.

I will here subjoin a letter written soon after the battle:

THE KILLED, WOUNDED, AND MISSING OF THE SEVENTY-FOURTH REGIMENT.

HEAD-QUARTERS SEVENTY-FOURTH REGIMENT, O. V. I.,
MURFREESBORO, TENNESSEE, January 10, 1863.

MESSRS. EDITORS:—We copy from a report from the commanding officer the following names of men killed, wounded, and missing in the two late engagements before Murfreesboro. The battle was one of the hardest and most terrible of the war. Our men suffered severely, both before and after the fight, having to march through mud and rain, and being obliged to lie out in the cold and wet, without tents or blankets.

On the morning of the 28th we took up our line of march to the scene of the conflict, skirmishing through the day, and at eleven o'clock at night we were ordered out to support a battery; and there we lay on the cold ground, without fire, until sunrise. I suffered more that night than in any night during the war.

At sunrise we were relieved; but, after swallowing a hasty breakfast —in fact, some not eating anything—we were ordered out again, and in a short time we were engaged in deadly conflict with the enemy. Our position was on the left center, in a dense growth of cedars, hiding, to some extent, the enemy from our view. We, however, soon had the privilege of giving them the contents of our guns, and with our trusty and brave Colonel Moody, and gallant Major Bell, and Adjutant Armstrong, the Seventy-fourth went in with a will.

Colonel Moody's horse was shot from under him, and he narrowly escaped with his life, his clothes being cut in several places. A ball struck his pistol, which no doubt saved his life. But at all times he was cool, not appearing the least excited, and giving his orders with great firmness. The men also stood up to the work without flinching. I think the Seventy-fourth deserves great praise for the manner in which it acted during the fight.

Some of our brave boys who went into that fight fell as martyrs to their country. But their blood has not been shed in vain. Every drop that they have shed is a lasting memorial of their undying love for their country, and their memories will be held sacred for generations to come. General Rosencranz, General Negley, and General Miller passed the highest encomiums on the Seventy-fourth. General Rosencranz said he believed the Seventy-fourth was a "fighting regiment." And if every brigade and every division had done as well as General Negley's and Colonel Miller's we would have whipped them out the first day.

Several of our officers lost their horses. Major Bell and Adjutant Armstrong lost theirs. There were a great many horses, as well as men, killed.

As you no doubt will get a statement of the losses on both sides before this reaches you, I will close.

Yours respectfully. IRA S. OWENS,
Private Company C, Seventy-fourth O. V. I.

The following are the names of the killed, wounded, and missing in the battle of December 31st:

KILLED.

Company A.—Corporal Isaac I. Smith. Privates Wyatt H. Jones and Jacob Bushert. Total, 3.

Company F.—Sergeant William H. Smith. Private B. G. Hughes. Total, 2.

Company I.—Private John Hawkins.

Company K.—Corporal John D. Halson.

WOUNDED.

Colonel Granville Moody, slightly.

Company A.—Sergeant A. C. Mahan, slightly. Corporals Samuel Schooley and James R. Hayslet. Privates Daniel S. Wilson Barney Walters, Michael McMarrah, Jesse Curry, Jacob Shields. Total, 8.

Company B.—Sergeant James McCann, slightly. Privates John A. Seiss, seriously; William H. Pratt, Ephraim Dickenson, Jacob Wildermott, and Jesse Stevens, slightly; Henry C. Edwards and James Bone, badly (wounded accidentally). Total, 8.

Company C.—Privates Henry G. Forbes, William T. McDaniel, Philip Tracy, and Ira S. Owens, slightly; Alfred Harold, badly; James H. Seldomridge, wounded badly in the back; Charles M. Wolf, in the arm; Chauncey White, in the leg; Samuel T. Miller, accidentally in the foot. Total, 9.

Company D.—Privates Philip Minehart, mortally; John Q. Collins and Richard Galloway, slightly; J. Coppie, leg (since amputated); P. Castello, J. McCune, William McAfee, F. Hunter, and A. Ames. Total, 10.

Company E.—Corporal John Cox. Privates Ed. C. Snyder and Wesley Snyder. Total, 3.

Company F.—Captain Walter Crook. Lieutenant M. H. Peters. Sergeants Enos H. Walters and Cyrus Phillips. Orderly Sergeant Charles C. Dodson. Corporals David Bansman and Edon Schumer. Privates John Elder, George W. Beck, and Patrick McConor. Total, 10.

Company G.—Orderly Sergeant M. K. McFadden. Corporal L. Baker. Privates. Hiram Cox, John Handy, William Chambers, and J. C. Mansfield. Total, 6.

Company H.—Captain Joseph Ballard. First Lieutenant David Snodgrass. First Sergeant Raper A. Spahr (since died). Corporals Philip Stumm and Albert F. Johnson. Privates Calvin Curl (since died), Dudley Day, Joseph Wyburn, John A. Donald, and Augustus Houmard. Total, 10.

Company I.—First Lieutenant Robert Cullen, severely. Sergeant John Toole. Privates Michael Connell, Terrence McLaughlin, and James McCarty. Total, 5.

Company K.—Corporal William Carter. Private David Steith. Total, 2.

MISSING.

Company A.—Privates Alex. Walthal and Charles Hummer. Total, 2.

Company B.—Privates Patrick McNary, Edward Persinger, George C. McClellan, and Charles Lucas. Total, 4.

Company D.—Corporals J. H. McClung and J. Hamilton. Privates S. G. Stewart, Henry Frock, and William Drummonds. Total, 5.

Company E.—Private Isaac M. Keiser.

Company F.—Privates Jonathan Townsend, John O'Brien, and Jacob Candell. Total, 3.

Company G.—Private Charles Weaver.

Company H.—Corporal Fred Shull. Privates Christopher Cline, Morris Haley, and Urs Yagge. Total, 4.

Total number of killed, 7; wounded, 78; missing, 22.

I regret that I have lost the list of those killed on the 2d of January, 1863.

The following letter was also written while at Murfreesboro, to the Xenia *Torchlight:*

A VISIT TO THE GENERAL FIELD HOSPITAL, NEAR MURFREESBORO.

CAMP NEAR MURFREESBORO, TENNESSEE, }
May 20, 1863. }

MESSRS. EDITORS:—Yesterday morning I left camp, and visited the general field hospital, situated one mile west of Murfreesboro, Tennessee, on Stone River. The river runs nearly around it, forming almost an island, the ground being in the shape of a horseshoe. Here I found several of the Seventy-fourth boys who are detailed—among them, John F. Reed, formerly of Cedarville, Greene County, who is clerking and partly assisting in the washing and laundry department. Through him I was enabled to gain considerable information pertaining to the hospital; and it may be interesting to your many readers to give a description of the same.

In company with Mr. Reed I visited, first, the washing and laundry department. Here they employ thirty-two females (colored), and they wash and iron about five thousand articles of clothing per week. Captain Frink's lady, of the United States regular army, superintends this department.

I next visited the garden. It contains about forty acres. Here I found different kinds of vegetables growing — onions, potatoes, etc. The ground is neatly laid out in squares, with streets running each way for vehicles. In the center, where the streets cross, I understand it is the intention to plant the Stars and Stripes.

George Sargent, of Company C, Seventy-fourth Regiment O. V. I., is ward-master of the hospital, which is divided into eight wards, the streets being about fifty feet wide, with an avenue between each ward, where the cooking is done. In each ward there is a frame house to cook and eat in. There are two tables in a room, sufficient to accommodate about eighty men at a time. I partook of their hospitality, and ate with them. They have plenty to eat, and it is gotten up in good style.

There are about twenty ladies here from the northern states, who are administering to the wants of the patients. And here let me say that if I were to be sick in the army, I would rather be here than anywhere else, with these angels of mercy to attend me while away from home.

M. Woodruff, formerly of the Seventy-fourth Illinois Volunteers, is steward; George Davis, druggist; J. Wilkerson, of Company A, Seventy-fourth O. V. I., postmaster; and Rev. Mr. Stuff, chaplain.

I also visited the clerk's office. The clerk showed me the books, and the manner in which they are kept. There were about five thousand in the hospital. They are sending away an average of seventy-five men a day. The average rate of deaths is thirty per week. There are fifteen hundred men in the hospital at present. The hospital is under the command of Dr. J. T. Findley.

The Seventy-fourth regiment is now commanded by Major Thomas C. Bell, Colonel Moody having resigned. The health of the regiment is good. The weather continues fine, and all is quiet here at present.

Yours truly,   IRA S. OWENS.

On the 10th we started back to Murfreesboro, and marched eight miles and halted in the woods. That night it rained, and we spent a disagreeable night. The next day we marched as far as Lavergne, and halted and spent the night. It rained quite hard that day and it was very disagreeable marching.

On the 14th we went foraging for corn. On our return to camp it rained quite hard, and we got very wet.

On the 16th I was taken sick — had an attack of neuralgia, caused from exposure. The next day I was sent to No. 8 Hospital, Murfreesboro. I was very sick, and remained in the hospital until the 7th of March, when I returned to the regiment.

On the 27th we moved camp west of town, to the fortifications, where we were engaged working until the 21st of April, when we moved camp and joined the brigade, near where we camped first.

On the 25th I was detailed as clerk in the mustering office at General Negley's head-quarters. Captain William Taylor was the mustering officer. He is a grandson of President William H. Harrison. I remained in the mustering office until the 12th of May, when I reported to the regiment.

May 16th Colonel Moody appointed me ordnance-master of the regiment. Colonel Moody resigned this day. I continued to act as ordnance-master as long as we remained at Murfreesboro.

Colonel Josiah Given, of the Eighteenth Ohio Volunteer Infantry, was appointed colonel of the Seventy-fourth, and took command after Colonel Moody's resignation.

June 24th we received marching orders. Tore up camp and started, it raining, as usual, when we started on a march. We marched eight miles toward Manchester, it raining all the time. We carried our knapsacks, and at night halted and slept in the woods, being wet all through with the rain, which continued all night; yet so wearied were we that we enjoyed a good rest notwithstanding the rain.

Next day we started again, and marched some two or three miles, halting on the side of a hill, where we remained all night. Fighting in front. Several ambulances, with wounded men, went to the rear. The fighting was at Hoover's Gap. On the 26th we started again toward Manchester, and passed through Hoover's Gap.

In December, 1862, the Seventy-fourth was placed in the Seventh Brigade (Miller's), Eighth Division (Negley's), formerly part of the center (Thomas') Fourteenth Army Corps, Department of the Cumberland. The Seventy-fourth went into the battle of Stone River with three hundred and eighty effective men, of whom it lost, in killed and wounded, one hundred and nine, and forty-six prisoners.

On the re-organization of the army at Murfreesboro, Tennessee, in February, 1863, the Seventy-fourth was assigned to the Third Brigade (Miller's), Second Division (Negley's), Fourteenth Army Corps (Thomas').

Several changes took place among the officers. Colonel Moody, Major Bell, and Captains Owens, McDowell, and Ballard resigned, which made necessary the following promotions: To colonelcy, Josiah Given, late lieutenant colonel of the Eighteenth Ohio; to captaincies, Mills, Armstrong, McGinnis, Tedford, and McElravy; to first lieutenantcies, McMillen, Hunter, Hutchinson, Weaver, and Bricker; to second lieutenantcies, Adams, Scott, Drummond, and McGreavey.

After passing through the gap, the regiment had a toilsome march through mud and rain. The enemy had been driven back. We waded one creek thirteen times, and marched on until after night. Most of the boys gave out before reaching Manchester, and halted and lay beside the road until morning. I, with several of the boys of Company C, lay all night at the foot of a tree, with no covering, using our cartridge-boxes for pillows. The next day, which was the 27th, we marched into

Manchester, and I was taken sick. The regiment was sent back to Murfreesboro to guard a wagon-train, but I remained at Manchester quite sick.

On the 28th the regiment was ordered forward. I, with several others, was sent to a house that was formerly used for a rebel hospital, where we remained one week, and then were sent to Tullahoma. While at Manchester, we heard of the fall of Vicksburg.

On arriving at Tullahoma we were placed in the hospital which they were just starting. The accommodations were poor, but better than at Manchester. I remained at the hospital four weeks. The First Ohio Regiment was camped near, and some of the boys would come to see me every day. Meanwhile, the regiment was in camp at Deckherd Station, on the Nashville & Chattanooga Railroad.

From Tullahoma I was sent to Nashville, to No. 1 Hospital. We arrived at Nashville at midnight, and were conveyed in ambulances to the hospital. I was very much fatigued on arriving at Nashville, having had to sit up all the way from Tullahoma. I was consigned to Ward 3, in the third story. The ward-master and nurses were very kind to me. As soon as convenient I was shown my cot, and lay down, very tired and sleepy, and had just got into a refreshing sleep when the nurse aroused me, announcing something to eat. Hungry as I was, I would rather have slept than eat. I remained in the hospital about five weeks; then was sent to the convalescent camp, about a mile south of the city. Several of the Seventy-fourth boys were sick at different hospitals at the same time, and were also sent to the convalescent camp.

After remaining in the camp a short time I was detailed by General Granger — who was commanding the post at Nashville — as nurse in Hospital No. 8. Here I found it a very arduous duty — much more so than camp duty — attending upon the sick and wounded who were brought in from the Chickamauga battlefield, which required all my time. I got but little rest. Here I formed the acquaintance of several comrades in arms whom I shall never forget. Hard as was the duty to be performed, I spent some very pleasant hours while there. We had preaching every Sabbath. There was also quite a revival of religion. Several professed to have been converted.

After having been there several weeks the duty was not quite so hard. I was promoted to ward-master in Ward No. 3, which duty was not quite so hard as nursing. I had more leisure time.

We formed a lyceum in the hospital, and had some very interesting meetings. Once in a while we would give public entertainments in the large hall, or lecture room, which was fitted up with a fine stage, curtains, etc. At first our fare was poor, rations being scarce.

There was not a man in the hospital who liked the surgeon. He was proud, aristocratic, domineering, and mean. He could hardly speak a kind word to any of the nurses. I do not suppose he ever smelled powder or was in a battle. We had a good many just such men in the army. They were remembered afterward. Those who used a little brief authority while they could, fared worse afterward. Many a soldier who was abused by such aristocrats swore vengeance on them, and got even with them. But an officer who was kind, and spoke pleasantly to his men, ever had their respect; and even now, in speaking of certain officers, the remark is often made, "He was a good fellow."

I will mention one incident which transpired in the army. On one of the hard and toilsome marches, when the soldiers — to use a homely expression — were nearly "fagged out," a certain colonel, observing one of his men nearly exhausted, dismounted from his horse and bade the soldier mount, while he (the colonel) walked along beside and carried the soldier's gun. The lieutenant colonel observing this, remarked, "Why, colonel, that is not military!" "I don't care," said the colonel, "it is human." That colonel lives in Greene County at present, and has the respect of every one who knows him.

I remained at No. 8 Hospital until the Seventy-fourth returned from Chattanooga on its way home, they having re-enlisted, and were going home on furlough. I was making out my evening report when some of my comrades came to the hospital and told me that the regiment was at the landing, on its way home, on veteran furlough. I threw down my pen without finishing my report, and told them I was going, too. I immediately went to the baggage-room, got my knapsack, and commenced packing it. While so engaged, the surgeon came along (not the one, however, who was there when I first went there — he was quite a different man), and asked me where I was going. I told him I was going home. He remarked, "I can not spare you." I told him the reason. He said, "I am sorry; but I suppose I can not hinder you." I was then released from the hospital, and, after bidding them an affectionate farewell, I started down stairs. On the way I met Miss Chase, the matron. I bade her good-bye. She gave me both her hands, and said, "Ira, good-bye. You have been a faithful servant here. God bless you."

In a short time I was at the landing, and found the regiment on board the boat, ready to start. I re-enlisted; and in an hour afterward we were steaming down the Cumberland, bound for home — yes, home, sweet home. Oh, how glad we felt to think that we were on our way home, to see our friends and loved ones once more! It seemed that the boat could not go fast enough.

It was on the 26th day of January, 1864, when we left Nashville. We arrived at Xenia about the last of January.

The regiment was received with great honors and demonstrations of joy by the good citizens of Xenia and vicinity, who assembled at the depot to welcome them back, and by whom a bountiful repast was set before us, which we ate as only hungry soldiers can eat. Oh! what a joyful time it was! Fathers and mothers here met their sons, sisters their brothers, and wives their husbands, in loving embrace. But in some respects it was sorrowful as well as joyful; for some had been left behind. Some had fallen in battle; some had sickened and died; and others, who still survived, had not re-enlisted. The regiment was granted a furlough of thirty days, to visit their friends, re-assembling at Xenia on the 17th of March.

Before leaving for the field the regiment passed resolutions returning their hearty thanks for the kindness with which they had been treated. The soldiers of the Seventy-fourth will never forget the good people of Xenia.

The regiment being re-organized numbered, with the addition of one hundred new recruits, six hundred and nineteen men.

The Seventy-fourth, once more ready for the field, started for the front on the 23d of March, 1864. And now came another trying time. Friends bade each other adieu — many for the last time. It was much harder to leave home than at first.

I will now quote from my journal, kept on the march:

Thursday, 24th. Left Cincinnati on steamer. Rained at night. Slept on top of the boat.

Friday, 25th. Landed at Louisville about six o'clock this morning. Marched from the boat to the Soldiers' Home. An amusing little incident occurred while marching through the streets of Louisville An Irishman, a few paces in advance of me, was indulging in a smoke. Having, as he thought, extinguished the fire in his pipe, he put it in his pocket; but pretty soon a strong smell of something burning was experienced. The

Irishman, however, kept marching on. After a while he remarked that he smelled burnt rags; and, clapping his hands behind him, he drew his coat tail around, exclaiming, at the same time, "Be jabbers, and it's meself that's burning!"

Saturday, 26th. Left Louisville about three o'clock P. M. for Nashville, Tennessee. Rode all night. Arrived at Nashville next morning about daylight.

Sunday, 27th. Marched through the city to the south side, and camped near our old camp-ground. Drew shelter-tents. Went back to town and visited No. 8 Hospital. Here I met several of my former acquaintances. They received me very kindly, and introduced me to the ward-master as their old wardmaster. I stayed all night with them, and enjoyed a good night's rest on a nice, clean cot, which was very refreshing after being up all the night before.

The next morning I ate a good breakfast, and then started back to camp. We drew rations that day, preparatory to starting on the march to Chattanooga. Rained at night.

Tuesday, 29th. Started on the march to Chattanooga, by way of Murfreesboro; from thence to Shelbyville, Tennessee. Not being used to heavy marching, the first day or two our feet became very sore and painful. At Shelbyville we heard Governor Andrew Johnson make his celebrated Union speech.

Monday, April 4th. Arrived at Tullahoma.

Thursday, 7th. Crossed the Cumberland Mountains. From the top of the mountains a fine view of the valley below is had, stretching for miles, as far as the eye can reach — plantation after plantation, verdant fields, and small streams of water which resemble threads of silver. We camped at night in Crow Creek valley.

Friday, 8th. Arrived at Stevenson, Alabama, and remained all night. Here I ascended the mountain about half way up, and had a splendid view of the country.

Saturday, 9th. Embarked on cars for Chattanooga, having marched from Nashville. There is splendid scenery along the route from Stevenson, Alabama, to Chattanooga, Tennessee. We passed Shell Mound, the mouth of Nicajack Cave, and the famous Lookout Mountain. We arrived at Chattanooga after night. It was dark, and rainy, and cold, and as we had no place to go we had to remain near the railroad, in the mud and rain, without shelter, while, doubtless, generals and high officials, who were getting big pay, were quietly snoozing in their tents. In the morning we went to the Soldiers' Home for breakfast. Question — Why could they not have taken us there the night before?

On the 12th of April, 1864, we started again on the march, and marched out to Graysville, Georgia, where we went into camp, remaining there until the 3d of May, 1864, when we broke up camp and started to Ringgold, Georgia.

On the night of the 6th there was a splendid illumination of the Fourteenth Army Corps. A candle was placed in front of every tent — some on poles and trees; also, large fires were built in every street in the vast encampment. It was a grand and imposing sight.

On the 7th of May, 1864, the great Atlanta campaign was commenced. I will refer to my journal from time to time, in order to give the particulars of that march.

Saturday, May 7th. Marched this morning, at daylight, for the front. Formed line of battle at Tunnel Hill. Fighting in front. On picket at night

Sunday, 8th. Marched again, and halted in the woods near "Buzzard's Roost."

Monday, 9th. Advanced, again, about two miles. Commenced an attack on the rebels. Heavy skirmishing. The Seventy-fourth under fire. Severely shelled by a rebel battery on the mountain. One man killed and several wounded. Among the wounded was Adjutant M. H. Peters.

Tuesday, 9th. Still fighting. Rebels strongly fortified. Went back to the rear, in the afternoon, for rations. Returned to the front. Regiment in line of battle.

Here let me remark, one has a peculiar feeling, standing in line of battle, expecting every moment to be ordered forward, it may be to certain death. It is no use to run back, for in a battle it is about as dangerous in the rear as in the front. I have known instances where men were killed in the rear, while the front would escape unhurt.

We had left our knapsacks at the foot of the mountain before being ordered forward. We halted on the side of the mountain, and remained in line all night. Our lodging that night was not the best. The accommodations were very poor. We had orders to sleep on our arms, and not to take off our cartridge-boxes. The side of the mountain was steep, and covered with little, sharp stones. I threw my gum-blanket on the ground, unbuckled my belt, slipped my cartridge-box around for a pillow, and, with my gun at my side, slept soundly. When I awoke in the morning I had slipped about two feet down the hill, and the regiment was anything but in line. We soon, however, straightened up and got in line again, ready for action.

Wednesday, May 11th. Went out on skirmish-line at daylight. Very steep climbing. Remained on skirmish-line all day. Heavy firing in the afternoon. Rebel shells fell very near us. Marched to the rear at midnight, and remained until morning.

Sherman, leaving one corps in front of Buzzard's Roost, marched the rest of his army to Snake Creek Gap, about sixteen miles, thus flanking the enemy. The rebels, as soon as they found it out, left, and fell back to Resaca.

At Buzzard's Roost the Seventy-fourth lost sixteen men

killed and wounded. At Resaca we had another battle, in which the Seventy-fourth lost nine men killed and wounded.

On the 15th the rebels left Resaca, leaving many of their dead on the field. Here we captured a large amount of cornmeal.

The morning of the 17th of May we left, in pursuit of the rebels. Crossed the Coosa River. Passed through the town of Calhoun. Halted, and remained all night on the side of a hill, in the woods.

Marched next day, and halted at night and built fortifications. Weather very warm.

On the 23d of May we arrived at the Etawah River. The march, that day, was a hard one, it being very dry and dusty, so much so that we could not see from one end of the regiment to the other.

Before coming to the river we got word that we would have to wade it, the rebels having burned the bridge. When we arrived at the bank of the river we found it even so. I suppose the Etawah is something near the size of the Great Miami River. Some of the boys prepared to wade, by taking off their shoes and pantaloons. Others went right in, without taking off anything. I did so myself. When about half way across, where the water was nearly breast deep and running very swift, I thought I would go ahead of some who were ahead of me, when I stumbled and fell, losing my gun, and getting a complete wetting, filling my haversack with water and soaking my hardtack. I recovered my gun, which would not have been of much use, should we have had occasion to use it.

It was a ludicrous sight to see the Seventy-fourth wading the river. If some artist had been present and sketched the scene, it would have made a laughable picture for some of our pictorials.

One man of our regiment thought he would not wade the

river, but mounted on behind one of the boys, who was riding a mule. When about half way across, the mule stumbled and fell, throwing them both over his head, completely ducking them. When we got over to the other side the dust was all washed off.

We stayed an hour or so, and by the time we started again we were dry, it being very hot. After all, it was an advantage to us, for we were relieved of the dust; and the bathing caused us to feel very much refreshed.

On the 26th we arrived at the Altoona Mountains, where we were again under fire, shells bursting very near. We were ordered across a field directly in front of the enemy, and, although much exposed to shells and bullets, not a man was hit. We proceeded a few rods, and were ordered to lie down. We remained in line all night, when we went back to the rear.

Colonel Neibling, of the Twenty-first Ohio, was wounded by a cannon-ball. His arm had to be amputated.

After retreating to the rear, we built what we called double breastworks; that is, we fortified on both sides of us, as we were on an elevation, and exposed to rebel fire on both sides.

In the engagement of the 27th of May, 1864, the conduct of the Seventy-fourth, and other regiments of the Third Brigade, elicited from the division commander the following commendatory notice:

HEAD-QUARTERS FIRST DIVISION, FOURTEENTH ARMY CORPS,
NEAR DALLAS, GEORGIA, May 28, 1864.

COLONEL:— General Johnson desires to express to you his high appreciation of the gallantry exhibited by the noble troops of your brigade in the night engagement of the 27th instant. The admirable spirit displayed by them on that occasion is, above all things, desirable and commendable. Soldiers animated by such courage and fortitude are capable of the very highest achievements.

(Signed) E. F. WELLS, A. A. G.

On the 2d of June we were ordered to the front again. Soon after we were in line a terrible storm arose, and the rain fell in torrents. It seemed that the artillery of the skies and that of earth vied with each other. At last the batteries were silent; but the awful roar of the thunder, the forked lightning, and the dashing rain still continued. Some three or four men were killed by the lightning, in a brigade not far from us.

I will now refer to my journal again.

Friday, June 3d. Relieved this morning by the left wing of the regiment. Went back into breastworks and got breakfast. Stayed until night. Went on skirmish-line.

Saturday, 4th. Shot several rounds. Rained considerable. Very muddy in the rifle-pit. Although it was very disagreeable, still we had our fun. Some of the boys concluded to play a trick on the rebels; so they would take off their blouses and caps, put them on their ramrods, and elevate them just above the top of the works, when the Johnnies would send a volley at them. They would then drop them as though they had been shot. We imagined we could hear the rebs saying, "'There goes another d—d Yank." This was continued some time, until they found out the trick. Fighting on our left. On reserve at night.

Sunday, 5th. Rebels left this morning. Some sharp shooting. Milton Bennett, of Company E, was killed this morning while cleaning his gun. Although not in front, still a shot would come over us once in a while, and the sharp "ping" of the Minnie-ball, as well as the coarser sound of the cannon-ball, could be heard. Went over to the rebel lines, or, rather, what had been their lines. Notwithstanding they had been driven back, and retreated from place to place, defeated at every point, still they told the most extravagant stories and published the most arrogant lies in order to deceive the people of the South and keep them in good spirits. Yet the rank and file of the rebel army were discouraged, and would have given up long before the war ended, had it not been for their leaders. A southern gentleman, not a great while ago, who had been a soldier in the rebel army, while taking on this subject, remarked that they hated Jeff Davis probably as bad as we did, and would have shot him had they the chance. Notwithstanding they were enemies, and on the field we shot at them, still there were some good fellows among them; and when not engaged in battle we would often trade with them, while on picket, meeting each other half way. We gave them coffee, and they would give us tobacco or cornmeal. Sometimes we would trade papers, when we had them.

I will give a little incident that transpired once, although not in our regiment. I got it for truth: One morning, while our boys were preparing breakfast, I suppose the aroma of the coffee — something scarce with the rebs — greeted the olfactory organs of some of them who were on duty not far from the Union lines. A Johnnie got up on the works and shouted over, "Hello, Yanks! what are you doing over thar?" "Getting breakfast," was the reply. "Got any coffee?" "Yes." "Will you give a feller some if he will come over?" "Yes; leave your gun." "Honor bright?" "Yes." And over he came. "Why," said he, "you fellers live pretty well, don't you? Always got this much to eat?" "Yes," was the reply. [I guess they stretched the blanket a little here.—AUTHOR.] They invited him to stay and get breakfast. He did so. After breakfast he said, "I believe you live better than we do. I believe, if you will let me stay, I'll not go back." He did stay, and made a good Union soldier, and was finally mustered out as such.

June 6th. Marched after the rebels. Marched on till about ten o'clock, and halted and remained in the woods all day and night.

June 7th. Moved about two hundred yards up in the woods, and put up tents. Some rain in the evening.

June 8th. In camp. Drew rations. Received mail.

June 9th. In camp. Inspection of arms.

June 10th. Started on the march again. Marched out of camp and rested. Resumed the march. Thunder shower. Rained quite hard.

June 11th. Rained this morning. Captain Armstrong joined us this morning. Marched in line of battle through the woods. Halted and commenced fortifying, but quit and marched on about a mile. Maneuvered around considerable during the night, but finally got into position and built breastworks; then camped for the night.

Sunday, 12th. A very wet and disagreeable day, consequently the chaplain did not preach.

Monday, 13th. By request of the regiment, the chaplain preached a thanksgiving sermon, which was afterward printed and published.

Tuesday, 14th. Went out on picket at six o'clock A. M., and then advanced the line. After standing picket two hours, we were thrown forward as skirmishers, and came near being shot. As we neared the rebel lines we were marching in column down a road, with trees and bushes on either side. Although there was no firing in front, yet we could hear the skirmishers on our right and left. We were going to fill up a gap, and had advanced farther than we supposed, when suddenly there came a whistling of bullets about our ears. We did not wait for the command to deploy as skirmishers, but every man hunted a tree and went to work, and, strange to say, although the balls whistled very close to us, not a man in our squad was touched. But the same bullets that were fired at us went on to the regiment, killing one man and wounding another. This corroborates the statement made elsewhere, that it is as dangerous in the rear as in front.

That was the day, I think, the rebel General Polk was killed. He was killed by the Sixth Indiana Battery, I think, though I may possibly be mistaken. It is said that General Sherman, seeing a group of rebel generals on Pine Mountain, rode up to the lines and inquired for a battery. He was told that one was close at hand. He ordered it brought up, placed in position, loaded, and discharged. He then ordered it loaded a second time and discharged. Then he said, "That will do;" and he immediately rode off. That battery was immediately in our rear, and the balls went over our heads.

That afternoon I stood up behind a tree, scarcely large enough to protect my body, from two o'clock until after dark, loading and firing, discharging sixty-three rounds of cartridges. The tree was skinned in several places by rebel bullets. Had I ventured to look around I might have had my napper taken. We loaded and fired at will, no officers being there to give orders. It was when the privates were on picket that they were their own men. They were not often troubled with officers then.

An incident transpired that afternoon which I will relate: Not far from the tree where I stood, a soldier was squatting down behind a tree, when a bullet from a rebel gun penetrated the ground immediately under him, without touching him. As may readily be supposed, he immediately arose to his feet and got on the other side of the tree. An old, gray-headed man belonging to another regiment — I can not say what one — some rods in the rear, seeing the man jump up so quickly and change his position, without any orders, came down to where our picket was standing, and, on learning the cause of the sudden movement — the soldier telling him he thought the bullet came from a rebel sharp-shooter in a tree — the old man proceeded forthwith, as he said, to see if he could find out where that fellow was. It seemed that he had no fear, as he advanced beyond the line and peered up among the trees as though he were hunting a squirrel. He was gone but a few minutes, when he returned and told the man he might sit down again, as he did not think the fellow would shoot any more — intimating as much as that he had fixed him.

On the 15th of June we again advanced, driving the rebels before us. We then halted and fortified.

June 16th. Moved to the right, and drew rations. Pretty sharp shooting on the right. Heavy cannonading, supposed to be shelling the rebel train.

June 17th. Advanced about half a mile. Built works. Heavy fighting. Took fourteen prisoners to day. Drew rations. Heavy skirmishing at night.

June 18th. Advanced again. Got under fire of rebel shells and bullets. Built works under fire. Three of the boys wounded to-day, among them Sergeant T. C. Hook, of Company A. Rained very hard while lying on our faces in line of battle.

June 19th. I was on picket, and went out to the rebel works; but they were gone. Our pickets followed them about two miles, when we returned to the regiment. We were then approaching Kennesaw Mountain, the Seventy-fourth in the rear. It was a grand sight as we approached the mountain, the shells from our batteries exploding on the side of the mountain, and the rebel shells from the top.

June 20th. The Seventy-fourth in the rear. Drew rations. Moved a short distance and put up tents, with orders for inspection at four o'clock. Cleaned guns. Were ready for inspection, when we received orders to move right away. We moved in front, to Leatherbreeches' or Buckskin's battery. This Leatherbreeches' right name was Captain Dilger. He was the most skillful and plucky officer in the Union service. When the war broke out Captain Dilger was an artillery officer in the Prussian service. A short time after the battle of Bull Run, an uncle of Dilger's — a merchant in New York — wrote that the present was an opportune time to visit America, etc. Dilger was desirous of studying war as carried on in the western world, and to this end procured leave of absence for a year. As soon as he arrived he joined the Army of the Potomac as an artillerist, and commanded a battery. As his year drew to a close he managed to get his leave indefinitely extended. The term of his battery — the First Ohio Artillery — having expired, he was ordered to Cincinnati, to be mustered out of the service. His next appearance with his battery was under General Hooker; and by the name of Leatherbreeches, or Buckskin, he became known to every officer and soldier in the Army of the Cumberland. In all the battles which occurred, from Lookout Mountain to Peach Tree Creek, Captain Dilger was on hand. He was the first to open fire on the eve of a battle, taking his guns nearly up to the skirmish-line. On the eventful day of the Hooker and Johnson contest, Captain Dilger took his guns up to the skirmish-line, and for half an hour poured a raking fire of grape and canister into the enemy. So conspicuous and marked were his movements that he became at one time the target for three rebel batteries, and lost seven men during the day. He fired by volley when he got a good thing, and the acclamations of the infantry drowned the reverberations of the cannon's roar. On all such occasions Captain Dilger impressed every one by his fine appearance. He always wore close buckskin breeches — which gave him the name — with top boots, and stood by his gun in his shirt sleeves during battle, eliciting the admiration of the whole army by his coolness and intrepidity in action. I have seen him sitting in a port-hole of the works, with his glass, watching the effect of his shots on the enemy. The Seventy-fourth was ordered to support this battery, the men being in the works on each side of a large twelve-pound Napoleon gun. For two days and nights we were in this position, and, although the roar of artillery was almost deafening, still we could sleep.

On the 22d of June the rebels shelled us from the mountain, and the air was filled with bursting shells. I believe this was the day when Colonel Findley had erected his shelter-tent a little way from the works, and had gone to the woods for some leaves and twigs to sleep upon. When he returned, his tent was perfectly riddled. I suppose it was struck by grape-shot. Had he remained in his tent he would most undoubtedly have been killed. The Colonel removed his quarters after that.

On the 23d we moved to the right, after dark, where we remained until the 3d of July.

While lying before Kennesaw Mountain we had some heavy fighting. One day a solid twelve-pound shot struck our works, burying itself in the earth, and almost cutting a log in two six inches through.

July 1st. I was on the skirmish-line. Samuel Mulford, of Company B, was wounded in the arm. Stood up behind a small tree and shot forty-five rounds of cartridges that afternoon. Some of the rebel shots came very close to me. The tree, doubtless, saved my life.

July 2d. Went on fatigue duty to the left, to build works, and worked all night. During the night the rebels left the mountain, and the next day we started in pursuit of them. They left some of their dead on the field. We passed through the town of Marietta, and on the Fourth of July we halted in an oat-field. Cut bushes and made a shade, it being very hot. We then fell into line and marched about a mile. Halted, stacked arms, and remained an hour, and then returned to camp.

July 5th. Advanced about three miles, and went on the skirmish-line. Remained all the afternoon and night. Sergeant Stipe, of Company B, was wounded.

July 6th. Relieved from picket. Went to the rear and drew rations. Had a view of Atlanta from the hill-top, where they were planting a battery.

July 7th. Resting behind the hill in the wood. Very hot. Went up to Buckskin's battery and took a view of Atlanta, through a glass, distant from that point eight miles. We were then approaching the Chattahoochie River. We went into camp, and remained until the 17th of July.

On the 9th we went out to the front line, which was advanced. Sergeant James, of Company E, was here wounded.

On the 10th the rebels retreated beyond the Chattahoochie, we following them to the river, skirmishing through the woods.

July 17th. Received orders to march at seven o'clock. Accordingly we packed up, ready, but did not march until the afternoon. Crossed the Chattahoochie on pontoons, skirmishing through the woods. Advanced about a mile and fortified.

July 18th. In advance. Drove the rebels to-day. Halted and fortified.

On the 20th we advanced about a mile, and halted in an old field, where we remained until about three o'clock in the morning; then marched on and crossed Peach Tree Creek at a mill. Went on a little further, and halted in the woods and remained till morning. Advanced again in skirmish-line. We were not long on the skirmish-line when we were relieved by the Twentieth Corps. We moved to the right, and got under cover of the hill, and remained all night.

On the next day the regiment advanced, and several of the Seventy-fourth boys were wounded, among whom was Captain McElravy, of Company G.

July 22d. Advanced toward Atlanta. This day we lost three of our boys: John Forbes, John Hennessy, and Addison Tolbert. Several others made narrow escapes. George Kempher, of Company C, had a hole shot through his knapsack while lying on his face toward the enemy. General McPherson was killed to-day. We were on the second line of fortifications. Immediately in the rear was the Twenty-first Ohio Volunteer Infantry. A man was killed, to-day, by a shell. The shell passed through the top of the tree where I was sitting, and a fragment of the same struck the man on the head, completely taking off the upper portion of the same, and scattering his brains all around. I saw it strike him. He never knew what hurt him. Such a sight now would seem terrible; but we had become accustomed to it then.

July 24th. Not much fighting to-day. A demonstration was made at night, in order to find, if possible, the enemy's batteries. It was done in this wise: At a given signal, every man along the line was to fire his gun and yell at the top of his voice, which was done; but it did not serve to draw the enemy out.

July 26th. We moved to the rear about a quarter of a mile.

July 28th. Fell into line and moved to the right about four miles. Very hot. Some of the boys came near giving out. Hard fighting on the right. Rebels charged our lines seven times, and were repulsed every time with heavy loss. We marched to the extreme right flank and built works after night, and remained until morning. Next day we returned to our old camp, had a meeting of Company C, and appointed a committee to draft resolutions in regard to the death of the boys who were killed on the 22d.

July 30th. Wrote resolutions, which were approved by the company, and sent to friends and papers.

August 2d. We moved to the right again, and relieved the Forty-second Indiana Regiment. The next day we were relieved by the Twenty-third Corps. Drew rations, and moved to the right and put up tents.

August 4th. This was a day of fasting and prayer, appointed by the President. Chaplain preached in the morning. Moved, in the afternoon, to the right. We had a hot, fatiguing march of several miles, and directly back again.

August 5th. Lying back of works. Rebels threw several shells at us. Moved back into works that we left. Bands of music playing at night.

August 6th. In front line. Skirmish advanced. Building works.

August 8th. Was detailed to work on works in front. Worked a while, when the regiment came and worked likewise. Rained in afternoon.

August 9th. In front line. Skirmish-line advanced to-day. Building works in front.

August 10th. Went out at twelve o'clock at night to work on breastworks in front. Worked until daylight. Relieved by the Twenty-first Ohio. Came back to camp.

August 11th. Went on picket at night, it being dangerous to relieve pickets in the daytime, the picket-line being within a few rods of the rebel line. Stayed in reserve until four o'clock in the morning. It was very disagreeable that night, raining a good portion of the time, so as to render sleep impossible. When we got into the pit, it was nearly filled with mud and water; and after daylight it was very risky standing up. We could not stand up, lie, or sit down, but had to remain in a crouching position, which was very tiresome. The pits were about a rod apart, and there were about six men in a pit. Sergeant Slasher, Charley Newman, Faber, of Company K, and myself were in the same pit. While Sergeant Slasher was going from one pit to another, he was just in the act of jumping down into our pit when a rebel shot at him, grazing his back. He said it smarted like fire, and got me to examine it; and right across the small of his back was a red streak, but no blood. The sergeant was talking, before that, of going to the regiment for some rations; but he concluded to stay in the pit until after night, and do without his dinner. I had my bayonet shot from my gun in the same pit, the rebs and our men keeping up a constant fire day and night.

August 13th. Moved over to the front line and relieved the Sixty-ninth Ohio.

August 14th. John Quinn, of Company A, was wounded, this morning, while cooking his breakfast; and Pat. Doyle, of Company I, was wounded while going out on skirmish-line.

August 15th. Very hot. John Seldomridge, James, and myself put up a tent, and then cut some bushes for a shade.

August 18th. There was some heavy fighting. Although not actively engaged, we fell into line behind the works and took arms, expecting every moment to be called out.

August 19th. The regiment moved to the rear line. It rained very hard at night. I secured a board, and laid it on a couple of logs, to keep off the ground. I then took my government blanket and spread it on the board to lie on, then took my gum blanket and stretched it over me; and, although the rain fell in torrents, in the morning I was dry and comfortable.

August 20th. Went on skirmish-line. Very disagreeable from the rain. Came near being shot. I had become very tired in the pit, and in the afternoon, the firing having slacked up, I thought I would get out on the bank and rest a while, the rebel works being in plain view only a few rods away, although I could see no rebs. They had logs on top of their works, and a crack underneath to shoot through, without being exposed themselves. The thought struck me that perhaps I was too much exposed, and that I had better get back into the pit, when I put that thought into immediate execution. I had hardly got down —my head being just below the works— when zip! a bullet came, and went into the ground just behind me. Had I remained in that position a second longer, I would have been shot through the body.

August 25th. We left the front of Atlanta at night, marched about five miles, and halted till morning.

August 26th. Moved over to the edge of the woods, to the shade. Rained to-day. Moved out a short distance, and then back again in the same place. Remained there a while, then marched to the right. Halted at the works, and remained all night.

August 27th. Put up tents at daylight; then moved about the length of two battalions. Cut tent-poles. Fortified and remained all night.

August 28th. Ordered to march at six o'clock. Passed the Fourth Army Corps, and marched on to the Atlanta & Montgomery Railroad. Halted in a cornfield, and had green corn for supper.

August 29th. Arose early, and had another mess of green corn for breakfast. The method of cooking roasting-ears, as adopted by some of the boys, was as follows: They would take an ear of corn, stick it on the end of a ramrod, and hold it over the fire until roasted. Another way was to throw the ear into the fire with the husk on, and by the time the husk was burned off the ear would be done. We marched down the railroad a mile and a half, tore up the track, burned the ties, and twisted the rails. We could see the smoke for miles.

August 30th. . Started on the march to the Macon Railroad. Marched a few miles and halted on a hillside. Went on picket at night.

August 31st. Started on the march again. Moved a piece to the right, and halted in the woods. Marched on farther, to a farm-house. Saw some wounded men, who had been in a fight on the railroad.

September 1st. Marched on the rebels, the Seventy-fourth

in front. Charged on the rebel skirmishers, across an open field. The rebels had a field-piece on their skirmish line, and a shot from it wounded a man in Company B. We advanced a short distance, and were ordered to lie down. In a short time we were ordered to arise, and forward march. There was a fence about two hundred yards ahead of us, and Colonel Given said, "Boys, if we can gain that fence the day is ours." So on we went, on the double quick, raising the yell. We reached the fence in safety, the rebel bullets, most of them, falling short of us, though some struck near. When a bullet struck the ground it would raise the dust. After reaching the fence we rested a while. Meanwhile the rebels had made a precipitate retreat. We followed them up, wading a stream of water, but never stopping till we got to the top of the hill, when we sent a volley after them; then loaded and gave them a second volley as they were retreating through the woods. I presume, however, that they were too far off by the time we reached the top of the hill for our balls to reach them, as they were cavalry. We were then ordered to build breastworks, and commenced work, but did not complete them before we were ordered forward again. We marched on until we came in sight of the railroad; then formed line of battle and marched through the woods until our skirmishers again encountered the rebels and drove them into their works. We then advanced across another field, the line of battle on our right steadily advancing, and keeping up a steady fire of musketry, not much artillery being used. We advanced to the woods; and, while marching on the right flank, Melville Davis, of Company C, was shot and mortally wounded. As he fell, he brushed me as he went down. I immediately called for a stretcher, and we placed him on it and carried him a short distance, out of range of the bullets, and laid him down on the grass. I knelt down beside him and asked him if he was hurt much. He looked up in my face—and, oh! such a look, a look which only a dying man could give—and said, "O Ira, I am mortally wounded!" These were the last words he ever spoke to me, as I had to immediately join the regiment, which was now passing forward in the thickest of the fight.

Melville Davis was my schoolmate, and my nearest neighbor. I had known him from a child, being a little older than he. He had been married, but his wife had preceded him to the better land a short time before he enlisted. His time was nearly out, lacking only a few days. He had never been home since he left. He was fondly anticipating the near approach of his discharge, when he should be allowed to go home to see his widowed mother, brothers, and friends. He and I often conversed about them; and that very morning, before we entered the field, expecting a battle, he talked of home and friends, and said to me if he should be killed that day he hoped he would be better off. He spoke of his darling wife, whom, he said, was free from all the anxieties and cares of this world. He was taken to the hospital, where he died in a day or two. A short time before he died, I have been informed, he called for his knapsack, and requested his wife's picture. On its being handed him, he looked at it, then kissed it, saying, "I will soon be with you." Melville was a good boy, and I have no doubt that he has joined his companion in a world where there is no more war or parting of friends.

But to return to the regiment. On we went, through a thick growth of pine, amid a perfect shower of grape and canister—for we were fronting a rebel battery—and minnie-balls, literally cutting shrubs, bushes, and branches of trees, at which time eleven of the Seventy-fourth were killed and thirty-three wounded, a number of whom afterwards died. William H. Hollenberry, another near neighbor, was also killed. He, and Davis, and I lived in sight of each other. He was the son of a widow, also, Mrs. Hannah Hollenberry. I did not see him fall, for we fought until after dark, and I got lost from the regiment. They had retreated to the rear, and I did not know it. I suppose, however, in groping my way back, I stumbled over his dead body, as we found it next morning where I suppose I felt it. I helped to carry him across a field and bury him where we buried the others. Before we put him in the ground I took my knife and cut off a lock of his hair, and sent it to his mother and sisters. He did not re enlist, and his time was nearly out. But, poor fellow, he received his final discharge. Henry was a good boy, and a good, faithful soldier. James H. Moore, of Company C, was also killed in that engagement.

The Seventy fourth was repulsed, the first time, and fell back to the edge of the woods, but immediately rallied, driving the enemy out of their works. We then fell back in good order, and remained all night, leaving our dead on the field, the rebels keeping up an artillery fire until after dark, and leaving their dead and wounded.

General Sherman, leaving the Twentieth Corps, withdrew the rest of his army from before Atlanta, and the rebels began to rejoice over his supposed retreat, when he suddenly re-appeared to their astonished vision, fifteen miles south of Atlanta, attacking them at Jonesboro, and capturing their works, ten guns, and two hundred prisoners, and inflicting upon them a loss of three thousand killed and wounded. The rebel General Hood, being completely "hoodwinked," in the words of General Sherman, blew up his magazines at Atlanta, and left in the night-time. We could hear the noise very distinctly, from Jonesboro, and supposed it was a battle between the Twentieth Corps and Hood. But General Slocum, with the Twentieth Corps, took quiet possession of the city. The next day we buried our dead in an old orchard. It was a sad time. We carried them about a half mile, laid them down on the ground until we dug their graves, and then committed them to the ground, putting, sometimes, two in one grave. Considering the chances we had, they were interred very decently. We rolled them carefully in their blankets, and then procured boards and put around them, to keep the dirt from their bodies. Thus we left our comrades who, only the day before, were as full of life and bid fair to live as long as any of us. We left them alone, in an enemy's land, and on the 6th started for Atlanta, and marched a short distance the next day. We marched within three miles of Atlanta and went into camp, remaining at that place until the 10th, when we moved about a mile and again went into camp. Our marching and fighting was now over, at least for a while.

In order to show how we passed the time while in camp near Atlanta, I will again refer to my journal.

September 11th. Regiment on picket.

September 12th. On fatigue.

September 13th. Regiment went to bury Lieutenant Bricker, who died at the divison hospital, in consequence of wounds received at Jonesboro.

September 14th. In camp. Fine weather. Chaplain preached at night.

September 16th. In camp. Meeting of Company C. Drew up resolutions in regard to the death of Melville Davis, W. H. Hollenberry, and James H. Moore.

September 18th. Meeting at night. A committee appointed to draft resolutions in regard to soldiers who had died in battle. Meeting adjourned until next day.

September 19th. Meeting of the Seventy-fourth. Chaplain McFarland made a few remarks. Resolutions adopted.

September 20th. John Norwood, James Johnson, and Basel Lucas came to the regiment to-day.

September 23d. Corps inspection.

September 24th. Went to Atlanta.

September 25th. Inspection at eight o'clock in the morning.

September 26th. Regiment on picket.

September 28th. Came into camp.

September 30th. Battalion drill.

October 1st. Colonel Given had dress parade for the last time, this evening, at which time he made a farewell address to the regiment, and presented his sword to the officers.

October 3d. Started on the march after Hood. Colonel Given beat the drum out of camp, and then left us. We marched on to the Chattahoochie River, and crossed after night. Hard marching, and very tired. Rained at night. The next day we resumed the march, and continued on the tramp all day, halting in an open field where there was plenty of grass.

October 4th. Drew rations at one o'clock at night, with orders to march at four o'clock, but did not start until noon.

October 5th. Again on the march, along a very crooked road, toward Kennesaw Mountain. Marched on until after night. Dark and muddy. Halted, and got a cup of coffee; then marched on again about a mile and a half, and halted on the side of a stony hill and camped. Rained at night. The next morning it was still raining, and very disagreeable. Started on the march, in the rain. Passed Kennesaw Mountain. The roads were quite muddy. Went about five miles and halted, camping near the Big Shanty.

October 7th. Resting and cleaning up. Some fighting to-day. A wounded rebel general was brought in.

October 8th. Started on the march again at three o'clock, and marched until we reached Lost Mountain, and then turned to the north. Met some rebel prisoners. Weather much cooler.

October 9th. Cool to-day. Went on picket, where we experienced the cold quite severely. Continued marching the next day, passing through the Altoona pass.

October 11th. The regiment halted on the roadside and held the election. Marched to Kingston, and halted in the thick woods and camped. I was quite sick, here, with the chills.

October 12th. Received mail just as we were starting on the march. Rode in ambulance to-day.

October 13th. Went into camp not far from Rome, and stayed until nearly night, when we started again. Rode in the ambulance until midnight, then joined the regiment.

October 14th. Marched hard all day, passing through Calhoun, and on to Resaca, where we again camped, near the railroad. Saw where the rebels had torn up the road. Fighting in front.

October 15th. Again on the march. Marched on until after night, to the foot of the mountain, when we encamped.

October 16th. Began to climb the mountain, which was very hard, laborious work, indeed, there being merely a bridle-path. Part of the way the path was so narrow that we had to march Indian file. We descended the mountain into Snake Gap, through which we passed, taking a southern course until night, when we camped again, in sight of Lookout Mountain.

October 17th. Started again on the march, in the Chatooga valley. Fine country. Taylor's Ridge on our left. Passed through some rebel camps, which had been occupied only a short time previous.

October 20th. We passed into Alabama, to-day, through some fine country, camping at night near Galesville, where we remained for several days, foraging around, principally for potatoes, which were a scarce luxury.

October 24th. Drew rations, and started on a scouting expedition with the Third Brigade—Colonel Hambright—among the Chatooga Mountains, in search of the rebel Gatewood and his band, who were supposed to be secreted in the mountains. We marched about eight miles, crossed the Chatooga River, and then camped. The regiment were very indignant at this marching of the men so far for nothing. It proved nothing but a wild-goose chase. The men had a hard, toilsome march; yet those in authority were not satisfied with that, but must make the men march some fifty or sixty miles for nothing, while they were taking their ease, smoking their cigars, lounging around their head-quarters, and getting big pay, while the poor private soldiers, who got the least pay, did all the work. On that scout I thought of the rich man and Lazarus. The rich man was clothed with purple and fine linen, and fared sumptuously every day, while Lazarus lay at his gate and begged the crumbs that fell from the rich man's table. But Lazarus died, and the rich man also died. He had his good things in this world. But I need not follow the subject. All Bible readers are acquainted with the sequel.

October 28th. We started on the march toward Rome, passing through Galesville, and crossing the Chatooga River. We marched about two miles, and camped.

October 29th. Marched to Rome, twenty-two miles, and camped near the Coosa River.

November 2d. Marched to Kingston. It rained, which made it very muddy and disagreeable. Marched eighteen miles, and camped near Kingston. While in Kingston we voted, it being the presidential election.

November 8th. We remained at Kingston until the 12th, when we left, and marched to Cartersville, eighteen miles. Left Cartersville next day and crossed the Etawah River, passing over the Altoona Mountains. Marched on to Big Shanty. Tore up the railroad at night. Marched on to the Chattahoochie River and camped. Passed Kennesaw Mountain and Marietta.

November 15th. Marched to Atlanta and received new colors. Camped near the city and drew clothing, and prepared for the grand march to the sea. The city of Atlanta was burned at night, making a grand and magnificent sight.

November 16th. We started on what is known as "Sherman's March to the Sea." Marched twenty-five miles toward Augusta, and camped at a little town called Lithonia.

November 17th. Marched on to Yellow River and camped.

November 18th. Again on the march. Passed through Covington, the Seventy-fourth in advance. It was amusing to see the negroes running to see "de Yankees," and hear their remarks. "Why," they said, "dey looks just like our people; dey ain't got no horns." An old woman caught sight of our new colors, and said, "Law sakes! Did you eber see such a pretty thing?" We passed one house where there were a lot of girls standing in the door. I overheard one remark to another, "Why that is not half as pretty a flag as ours." Another soldier heard the remark, and asked her if she would not like a piece of his shirt for a flag. We halted about noon on the plantation of a Mr. John Harris, and remained there during the day and night. Drew rations at night. General Sherman's head-quarters were on the same plantation. I was at his head-quarters in the afternoon. He had his tent pitched in the yard, and was sitting in the porch of the mansion watching some soldiers, who had found a barrel of molasses in an out-house. The boys had got one head out, and were going for the molasses, dipping in and strewing it all around. The general sat there laughing at them. When he saw that a few were appropriating it all to themselves, he ordered the barrel taken to the commissary's and issued out, so that it might be equally distributed.

On the march we passed through a place called Shady Dale, which consisted of a large plantation and a small town of negro quarters, or cabins. The brigade band played a quickstep tune as we went through, and the negroes flocked out to see us and hear the music, particularly the women, some of  whom followed us for over a mile, or, rather, kept up with the band, dancing and keeping time to the music, and cutting up all kinds of didoes.

We passed through the village of Sand Town on the morning of the 21st, in the rain, without breakfast; but after marching some miles we halted and got something to eat.

November 22d. On the march again. The Seventy fourth detailed as train-guard. Camped at Mud Creek, at night, in a pine grove.

November 23d. Again on the march, the morning being cold and the ground slightly frozen. Arrived at Milledgeville, the capital of Georgia, which we left the next day at seven o'clock, marching until about three o'clock. We then camped and went on picket duty, and also drew rations.

November 25th. The regiment went foraging, and caught an old bushwhacker and brought him into camp, together with plenty of forage.

November 26th. Started and marched a few miles, to a swamp, and camped.

November 27th. Marched through the swamp, it having previously been corduroyed, or, in other words, made passable by poles being cut and laid crosswise. After passing the swamp we marched over a good road until we came to the Georgia Central Railroad, about four miles from Davisboro, where we camped during the remainder of the day, having passed through the town of Sandersville.

November 28th. On the march. Passed through the town of Davisboro. Here the boys found a lot of peanuts, up stairs, in an untenanted building, the floor being about a foot thick with the same. Some went, with sacks, and loaded themselves, and, as a consequence, the road was soon strewn for a long distance with the hulls. Crossed the Ogeechee River at night, on pontoons. Here we saw the palm-leaf growing.

November 29th. Marched a short distance, passing through the town of Louisville, Jefferson County, Georgia.

November 30th. Marched to Sebastopol Station.

December 1st. Marched a short distance to the crossroads and went on picket, remaining all night, the Twentieth Corps passing in the night.

December 2d. Started again, and marched to another crossroads; then turned to the right and marched until noon, halting for dinner in a cotton-field. Marched six miles farther and camped, making about fifteen miles that day.

December 3d. Marched around and across fields. Crossed Buckhead Creek on pontoons. Marched on to the Augusta Railroad and camped.

December 4th. Tore up the Augusta & Savannah Railroad; then started again on the march, camping a few miles farther on. Rebels in our rear, firing at us.

December 5th. Marched nearly all day through pine woods, and camped at night in a sandy cornfield.

December 6th. Again on the march. Warm weather. Camped in the woods. On picket.

December 7th. On the march. Rain. Very warm

weather. Hard marching. Boys went foraging and brought in some fresh meat. Had to carry it until after night, when we halted twenty-seven miles from Savannah.

December 8th. Started again. Marched about three miles; then halted, and remained until about ten o'clock. Marched again, crossing Ebenezer Creek. Went about two miles and camped near a grave-yard, in the woods. Heard cannonading in the direction of Savannah. Skirmishing in the rear.

December 9th. We crossed the great swamp, and halted in a field for dinner. Camped in the woods at night. Skirmishing in front.

December 10th. Passed a rebel fort on the road. Went a few miles and camped. Rained at night.

On the 11th of December we arrived at, or in front of, Savannah, or as near the city as we could get, the rebels having fortified it. There is a canal leading from the Savannah River to the Ogeeche, for the purpose of supplying water to the rice plantations, as rice grows under water. A short distance apart there are flood-gates, and when they wish to overflow the land they hoist these gates. The rebels made use of these gates to overflow the country, so that Sherman's army could not approach the city. We, however, camped along the canal and threw out a picket-line, and prepared to stay until communications by water should be opened around Savannah. There is a long moss that grows on the trees, hanging in festoons from them, sometimes four or five feet long. The boys used to get this moss, and cut the palm leaves, and, by spreading the palm-leaves on the ground and the moss on them, it made a very comfortable bed.

There was a battery almost directly in front of our regiment that used to fire every day; but the balls would always go over our heads. This they kept up for several days, until, one day, it was noticed that they did not fire any. Toward night, or after night, the battery spiked all their guns and came over on the Union side. They said they had been watching for an opportunity to desert the rebels ever since the Union troops arrived, but were watched by their officers. By making a feint, however, of keeping up a cannonading at the Union lines, they so deceived their officers that they thought they might trust them alone; but as soon as the rebel officers left they came over.

December 13th. Fort McAllister was taken to-day, which caused great rejoicing along our lines. As soon as the news came, they commenced at one end, and the cry went from one brigade to another, "Fort McAllister is taken, and the cracker line is open!"

On the 16th we went to the Ogeeche River for rations, the Savannah River not yet being open to the city. We arrived at the river and camped near it, waiting our turn to load, the next day. We remained at the Ogeeche River until the 23d. During the time we were there, it being very warm weather, we had to live principally on rice, which we gathered from the fields. Near our camp were some negro cabins, and in them we found mortars, with which we would make the negroes hull our rice, which was done by putting the unhulled rice into the mortars and pounding it. Then we took it out, and, putting it in our blankets, blew the chaff out. We loaded our wagons and started back to Savannah. Meanwhile the rebels had left, and our troops were in peaceable possession of the city.

December 25th. Went to Savannah, and went to the Baptist church. Heard a sermon delivered by the Rev. Mr. Landrum. After church I started around the city, and, passing along the street, I saw an old negro woman standing in a door. I spoke to her, and asked if she could give a soldier something to eat. She replied, "Yes, massa, I do dat; come in." I went in; and the old woman had what is called an ash-cake in the fireplace. An old Virginian would know what an ash cake is. It is made by taking corn dough and covering it up in the ashes, and putting fire on it, like roasting potatoes. Taking her ash-cake from the fire and putting it on the table, she procured part of a turkey the white folks had given her, and some buttermilk. She invited me to sit up and help myself. I did so, being very hungry. I thought I never ate a better meal.

December 27th. There was a grand review of the Fourteenth Corps by General Sherman. Several high officials from Washington were in Savannah that day; among the rest, Secretary Stanton.

December 30th. Laid out and moved to a new camp, and put up a tent. Several of the boys joined together and put up tents. We cut poles and built open about ten feet square, then joined our shelter-tents together and made a roof in these tents. We remained until the 20th of January. Although there was a great deal of snow in the North that winter, yet there was none where we were. In fact it looked like summer-time. There the trees were evergreen all winter, especially in the city of Savannah. The streets were lined on each side with the tree known as the "Pride of India," or live-oak, whose leaves are evergreen. During the time we were in Savannah we worked on the fortifications around the city.

January 20th. Received orders to march, and started out of camp in the rain. Marched eight miles through the mud and rain, until the army got mudbound, and could go no farther. We then turned out into a pine woods and halted. There was not a dry stick to be found anywhere — nothing but green pine. The boys cut a tree and tried to make a fire, but it was no go. The rain put it out as fast as they could kindle it. We had marched in the rain nearly all day, and I had neglected to put on my gum blanket; consequently I was wet through. The ground was also covered with water. By taking a spade and ditching, and throwing up the earth, we made a place to stretch our tents; then taking our gum blankets and spreading them down, and our government blankets on them, we made our beds and retired without supper. I lay all night in my wet clothes, and the next morning there was the print of my body on the blanket; yet, strange to say, I took no cold. The next day we managed to get a fire and something to eat, and about ten o'clock we went on picket, it raining nearly all day.

January 25th. We left camp at seven o'clock in the morning, and marched fifteen miles and camped.

January 26th. Started again at seven o'clock. Marched hard, through swamps and woods, all day.

January 27th. Regiment detailed as train guard. Marched all day.

January 28th. Started again at noon, and marched through swamps and woods. Weather clear and cool. Camped two miles from Sister's Ferry.

January 29th. Marched to Sister's Ferry.

We remained at Sister's Ferry, on the Savannah River, until the 5th of February. While at the ferry we spent the time in writing letters, skiff-riding, etc. One evening as four or five of us were out on the river, coming down to camp, we espied a flatboat, or barge, floating down the river, and which finally lodged against some trees or boughs on the opposite side of the river. We immediately headed our skiff for the boat, and, on coming alongside, discovered that no one was on board. We made our skiff fast alongside, and immediately boarded her. It proved to be a boat loaded with salt beef, which had broken loose from her moorings at the landing, about a mile above, and had drifted down. We found a barrel that had the head out, and soon had some meat in the skiff, and then pulled for camp. When we landed it was getting dark; so we conveyed our property — for we considered it ours then — to camp, under cover of the darkness. It leaked out, however, some way, that we had found meat, and how we got it; and several boat-loads were brought into camp early next morning. So much was missing that the men who came after the boat suspected the boys taking it; and on coming to camp some of the meat was found. An order was immediately issued that all the stolen meat should be brought to head-quarters. We had been very careful to secrete ours securely; and when the officers came around hunting and searching for the meat, none could be found in our quarters. Consequently we had plenty of meat for several days.

Here our regimental band made fine progress. They would serenade the head quarters of the different departments. At one place — I do not now remember which one — there was a little negro boy who used to dance. Of all the droll antics and manners, he beat them all. He would sometimes stand on his head and keep time to the music, with his heels in the air. The boys played well, and made very good music.

February 5th. Started at daylight and went two miles up the river and camped. Then loaded teams with rations, and drew clothing.

February 6th. Started again on the march. Went some seven miles and camped. We were now on the soil of South Carolina, and the buildings along the road were all burned. No restrictions were laid here; and it seems that the soldiers, if possible, would have burned up the state — the hot-bed of secession. Whenever they came to a fine, palatial mansion — especially if it was ascertained that the owner was in the rebel army — the torch was soon applied. Houses, fences, trees — in fact, everything that it was possible to burn — were burned. A large amount of cotton and cotton-gins were burned to the ground and laid in ashes. There was a track made of about sixty miles wide, inside of which everything was destroyed —

some think very unjustly, but I think just to the contrary; for Sherman's raid, I think, broke the backbone of the rebellion. I will not, however, discuss that question. It has already been done by abler men and abler writers than I am.

February 7th. Again on the march. Boys went foraging, and brought in fresh pork and sweet-potatoes. Marched twelve miles, and then camped.

February 8th. Marched about a mile; then camped and drew rations. Foragers came in well loaded with pork and potatoes.

February 9th. Continued on the march. Cool and cloudy weather, with some snow.

February 10th. Marched about fifteen miles to-day; then camped and went on guard.

February 11th. Left camp early, and marched to Barnwell and halted for dinner. We found the town burned. Camped that night two miles north of Barnwell.

February 12th. Marched at seven o'clock. Crossed the Charleston & Augusta Railroad at Williston Station.

February 13th. Stayed in camp all day, and started on the march at dark. Marched two miles, when we went into camp and drew rations.

February 14th. Left camp at eight o'clock. It rained and sleeted all day. Marched twelve miles, and camped at dark.

February 15th. Left camp at eight o'clock and marched until four. Got dinner; then marched until ten o'clock at night. Marched twenty miles that day. Went on guard at night. Rain.

February 16th. Left camp at nine o'clock and marched till noon. Halted for dinner at Lexington. Marched till dark.

February 17th. Started again at seven o'clock. Marched

through a good country. Forage plenty. Crossed the Saluda River, and camped five miles north of Columbia.

February 18th. Left camp at ten o'clock. Went out on the road, and halted and stayed till three o'clock. Marched three miles and camped. Forage plenty. Got flour, meal, bacon, and molasses.

February 19th. Sunday, and in camp. Chaplain preached. Left camp at dark. Marched until two o'clock in the morning. Crossed Broad River; then marched eight miles and camped.

February 20th. Left camp at eight o'clock. Marched five miles and went into camp. Drew rations of coffee and sugar.

February 21st. Left camp at eleven o'clock. Most of the buildings burned. Country hilly, and very thickly settled. Weather good.

February 22d. Left camp at nine o'clock this morning. Marched two miles, and halted at the Catawba River. Got dinner, and crossed the river. Very muddy. Teams could scarcely get along. Had to help push wagons up hill. Went as far as we could, and then halted in the road. Rained all night.

February 25th. Cut and carried poles, and laid them in the road. Mud nearly knee deep. Helped wagons up the hill. Country very hilly. Got into camp about two o'clock P. M. Rained all day and night.

February 26th. In camp. Chaplain preached, it being Sunday. On guard.

February 27th. In camp. Got some corn ground. Rations scarce.

February 28th. In camp. Rained in the morning. Fighting in the rear.

March 1st. Started again on the march. Went about fourteen miles. Very hilly. Roads bad.

March 2d. On the march. Went about fifteen miles. Country very broken. Marched until night. On guard.

March 3d. Again on the march. Most of the road very bad. Went ahead as pioneers. Worked hard, and very tired at night. Camped in the edge of the woods. A rebel came into our lines this morning. Raining.

March 4th. Started again on the march. Halted and waited until the train passed. Rebels said to be in our rear, capturing some of our men. Got into North Carolina at night. Saw a man, Mr. Junius W. Whiting, who had escaped from Wheeler's cavalry.

March 5th. Again on the march. Went about fifteen miles and camped, about two o'clock, near the Great Pedee River. Foragers came in with meat, meal, etc.

March 6th. Started again and marched to the river, and waited all day and all night to cross. Mules harnessed all day and night.

March 7th. Started again, and went down to the river and got breakfast. Crossed over about ten o'clock, and marched about eighteen miles.

March 8th. Again on the march. Marched about nineteen miles, it raining nearly all day.

March 9th. Stayed in camp until noon; then marched ten miles. Made some corduroy road. Rained.

March 10th. Marched about ten miles. Kilpatrick's camp surprised this morning. Cannon heard on our left. Camped before night.

March 11th. Marched to within about two miles of Fayetteville and camped. On guard.

March 12th. In camp. Chaplain preached in the afternoon.

March 13th. Marched, this morning, into the town of Fayetteville. Crossed the Cape Fear River on pontoons. The town of Fayetteville is quite a nice place, of five or six thousand inhabitants, most of the citizens remaining at home. Marched about a mile and a half and camped.

March 14th. In camp. Went foraging. Got a few sweet-potatoes and a gourdful of soft soap.

March 15th. Rained quite hard. Packed up in the rain, and moved a short distance. Marched in the night, some five or six miles, and camped. Bad roads, and raining. On guard at night.

March 16th. Moved a short distance, and camped at a church. Cut up the benches for wood. Raining. Fighting in front.

March 17th. Marched about seven miles. Bad roads. Got some corn meal to-day. Had corn-cakes for supper.

March 18th. Marched about eight miles, and crossed Black River. Camped on an old rebel camp-ground. Heard cannon at night.

March 19th. Marched some twelve miles, over corduroy roads, mostly. Fighting in front, at Bentonville. Our brigade lost heavily.

March 20th. Marched six miles and camped. Some of our foragers captured, and three teamsters killed. Eight wagons captured out of ten.

March 21st. Marched about five miles toward Kingston, when we marched back again, having been ordered to issue rations to the troops. We turned to the right. Very bad roads. Teams sticking in the mud. Raining. Halted in the woods and camped after night.

March 22d. Started again at sunrise. Caught up with the division. Rebel army retreated toward Raleigh. Passed through the battle-ground. Marched twelve miles. Roads swampy and bad.

March 23d. Started again for Goldsboro, passing through General Terry's command. Crossed the Neuse River on pontoons. Several colored troops were there, belonging to the Twenty-fourth and Twenty fifth corps. Arrived at Goldsboro about five o'clock, the Twenty-third Corps on parade to receive General Sherman. The general rode along the lines, and was hailed with demonstrations of joy.

The next day we received orders to march to Kingston for rations, and the morning of the 25th we started and rode in the wagons some twenty-five or thirty miles. We arrived at Kingston at about five o'clock P. M.

March 26th. At Kingston, waiting for rations. We remained at Kingston until the 28th, when the wagons were loaded and ordered to start at six o'clock, when we received a dispatch to move into breastworks and wait a while, as rebel cavalry were seen on the flank. We moved back and waited an hour or two, then started back to Goldsboro. Went about half way, and halted for the night.

March 29th. Started again. Arrived at Goldsboro about twelve o'clock. The next day we drew some clothing, and on the 31st we moved to town, about two miles distant, to guard commissary stores. We were assigned quarters in a building— that is, three companies of the Seventy-fourth, namely, Companies A, D, and C. For the first two nights I preferred sleeping out of doors; but the third night there were indications of rain, when I moved my quarters into the house, and Columbus McDonald and I occupied a bunk.

We remained in town until the 9th of April, when we moved back to the regiment. During our stay in town we attended church, as there was quite a revival of religion in town at that time. On the 6th we got the news of the fall of Richmond, which caused much excitement, shooting cannon, and fireworks at night.

On the 10th we started again on the march. Skirmishing in front. Marched eleven miles and camped.

April 11th. Again on the march. Detailed again as train-guard. Marched about eight miles.

April 12th. Pioneers to-day. Went in front of the train. Bad roads, and had to work hard. Heard the news of Lee's surrender. Marched about twelve miles, passing through the town of Smithfield, on the Neuse River.

April 13th. Started again on the march. Passed through a little village on the railroad. Marched along the railroad. Cars came inside, to-day, with the governor of North Carolina. Marched about sixteen miles, to the capital of North Carolina. Raleigh is handsomely decorated with fine gardens, and the air is heavily laden with the perfume of sweet flowers. The ladies are quite handsome. A large majority of the inhabitants are loyal, so I have been told. Joe Johnson's army retreated at the approach of General Sherman's invincible army. Raining. On guard.

April 14th. Left Raleigh. Marched about fifteen miles, a western course, along the railroad, and then camped.

April 15th. Raining this morning. Went foraging. Had to wade a creek which was swollen out of its banks. Got wet. Came to Holly Springs in the evening, and stopped by the side of the road. Rain. So muddy that the regiment did not get up.

April 16th Train and regiment came up about nine o'clock. Went a few miles and camped.

April 18th. We received the news of the assassination of President Lincoln. The order was read to the regiment, which caused a sudden change of feeling, from that of joy to that of sorrow. We were both glad and sorrowful. Glad that we soon expected to return home, and sorrowful because our beloved President was no more.

It will be remembered that the Seventy-fourth was guarding train. Consequently we were not with the division all the time, but on the 20th we started to the division, which was about six miles away. Upon arriving at the place we unloaded rations, and started to Raleigh for more. We went back to where we left camp, and halted for the night. The order from General Sherman was read to us to-day in regard to the suspension of hostilities and looking to peace, when we gave three rousing cheers. The next day we went to Raleigh and loaded the wagons. Remained at Raleigh until Monday.

On Sunday I attended church five times during the day, and once at night.

We started back again to the division, and camped three miles from the division.

The order came for consolidating the Seventy-fourth with the Sixty-ninth Ohio. Colonel Findley rode back to Raleigh to see General Sherman about it. Regiment very much depressed in spirits. Strong talk of stacking arms and refusing to be consolidated. They said they went into the field as the Seventy-fourth, fought as the Seventy-fourth, and they were going home as the Seventy-fourth.

On the 25th we were ordered to report to the Second Brigade, First Division, General Buell (not Carlos Buell, but a general by that name, commanding the Second Brigade). The regiment was slow falling into line, supposing they were going to be consolidated. We went to General Buell's head-quarters, when he ordered us into camp, not consolidated. Went into camp not far from head-quarters. Two companies were detailed by Captain Deton, of the commissary department.

On the 26th of April we moved a short distance and camped in the woods, remaining there until the 28th, when we received orders to march northward and homeward—the most welcome order that we had ever heard. About ten o'clock in the morning we were ordered to the regimental head quarters, and the order read. The division commander General C. C. Walcutt, said, "Boys, you have done it all. You may make as much noise as you please from this until you start home." There was no more sleep that night. The boys commenced shooting; the artillery, which had been parked, was at once in position, and the noise commenced, louder, if possible, than if we had been in a regular engagement. General Beard, who commanded the Second Division, was stationed several miles toward Raleigh, who, hearing the noise, supposed that we had got into an engagement with Joe Johnson, and, it is said, double-quicked his men nearly five miles to support, or, rather, re-inforce us, before he found out what was the cause of the hubbub.

Started next morning at six o'clock, midst cheering and great rejoicing. We had now set our faces toward home. Left camp, band playing, "The Girl I Left Behind Me," and "Yankee Doodle." Marched about twenty-two miles, and camped in the woods.

April 29th. Started again, about seven o'clock, and went a few miles and halted about four hours; then started again, and went about four miles farther. Colonel Findley informed us that we were still the old Seventy-fourth; and we gave three cheers.

April 30th. At Morrisville Station. Chaplain preached. Started for Richmond at one o'clock. Marched about twenty miles, to Neuse River, and camped.

May 1st. Started at five o'clock. Marched about twenty-five miles, going as far as Tar River, to dinner. Crossed Tar

River, and marched on through Oxford, and camped about a mile beyond.

May 2d. Again on the march. Passed through a little town called Williamsburg, to the Roanoke River. Crossed the line into old Virginia, Mecklenburg County, about six o'clock P. M. Camped near the river. Went boat-riding on the Roanoke. The next day we crossed the river on pontoons, and passed through Boydton. Marched seventeen miles.

May 4th. The Seventy fourth again on the march. Hard marching. Marched thirty-one miles to-day.

May 5th. Started again. Raining some. Crossed Notaway Creek at the falls. Passed Notaway Court house. Very tired at night. Marched thirty miles.

May 6th. Started about six o'clock. Crossed the Appomattox River. Marched on to within nine miles of Richmond. Very warm. Marched twenty-four miles.

May 7th. Started at daylight for Richmond. Marched to James River, and halted on the bank opposite Belle Isle, in full view of the city. Saw where the Union prisoners were kept, and also the dead line, a ditch where, if a prisoner stepped beyond, he was shot. Many a poor fellow stepped over the line purposely, choosing rather to be shot than to be starved to death. We remained at that place till about two o'clock, when we received orders to march five miles and go into camp. We marched out on the Danville Railroad, and camped in the woods. We remained in camp, resting, cleaning up arms, etc., until the 11th of May.

When we started again, as we passed through Manchester we had a reception by the troops of the Twenty-fourth Corps. We crossed the James River on pontoons, passing by Castle Thunder and Libby Prison, and marched through several streets. Here the negroes seemed to be our only friends. They had water at every corner along the streets, and waited on the boys, supplying them with water; and many a "God bless you, massa," was uttered by them. We marched out toward Alexandria, crossed the Chickahominy River, and toward night, though a thunder-storm was rising, still we marched on, the clouds threatening to overtake us, until at last, just at dusk, we filed out to the right, and were ordered to halt and stack arms. We had no sooner obeyed the order when it became very dark, and the rain came down in torrents. There we were in the darkness, without tent or shelter, having marched nearly all day, tired and hungry. We procured our gum blankets and sat down on our knapsacks. As soon as the rain ceased coming down so hard, I procured a hatchet, and, groping my way along in the darkness, seeing a little when there was a flash of lightning, found some brushes, cut some poles, and went back and tried to erect a tent; but in the darkness it was slow work. We managed, however, to get our tent up, and had spread our blankets on the wet ground and just laid down when there came a gust of wind, upsetting our tent and exposing us and our blankets to the storm and rain; for it had not ceased raining. We arose and adjusted our tent as best we could, and, going to the stack of arms, procured guns, and, with the bayonets, staked our tent down.

The next morning we moved a short distance and halted beside the road, our blankets wet and heavy. When we halted, the sun came out warm and pleasant, and we soon had our blankets hung out to dry. We did not start again until about four o'clock, by which time our blankets were dry as well as the roads, and everything appeared more pleasant and comfortable. Marched some nine miles, passing Hanover Court house. Went as far as Pamunky River. The river was high, and we had to wait until bridges were made and the troops ahead had crossed over. We had to halt several times before we reached the river. Night coming on, we spread our blankets and laid down three times that night. We finally crossed the river and camped at four o'clock next morning.

May 13th. Started again on the march, crossing the river and taking a westerly course, toward the Blue Ridge Mountains. Marched about twenty miles.

May 14th. Again on the march. Went about twenty miles.

May 15th. Started again. In sight of mountains. Marched about twenty miles.

May 16th. Started again. Turned northward, crossing the Rapidan at Raccoon Ford. Passed the battle-ground of Cedar Bluff.

May 17th. Crossed the Rappahannock River at Kelly's Ford. Camped at Cedar Creek and drew rations.

May 18th. Started again at five o'clock. Very warm. Marched over part of Bull Run battle-ground. Saw the fortifications, and the ground strewn with old knapsacks, haversacks, and other relics of a battle-field. Halted at Bull Run. Crossed it and got dinner. Went into the creek, swimming. Marched about three miles farther, making eighteen miles on that day. Rained at night.

May 19th. Started at five o'clock. Passed Fairfax Courthouse. Arrived in sight of Alexandria and Washington City, and camped about five miles from the capital.

May 20th. In camp. Raining. Several of the boys came to the regiment to day, among whom were George Kempher, L. Wright, S. Mullen, Clinton Randolph, C. Holsman, B. Crossy, John Norwood, and S. Kildow, of Company C. While encamped at this place the grand review came off— the review of the Army of the Potomac on the 22d, and the next day the review of the Army of the West, General Sherman's. It was a grand affair. Never before was there anything like it, and, I presume, never will be again. Among the many mottoes and devices were such as these: Liberty and Freedom; Patriots, Welcome Home; Western Heroes; Shiloh; Vicksburg; Atlanta; Stone River; Savannah; Raleigh; Mission Ridge; Lookout Mountain, etc. We marched up Maryland Avenue, around the Capitol, down Pennsylvania Avenue to the treasury building and president's house, where we were reviewed by Generals U. S. Grant, Sherman, and Mead, President Johnson, Secretary Stanton, and others. We then marched out by the Aqueduct bridge, and back to camp.

On the 26th we broke up camp and moved across the river on the long bridge, marched through the city, and went into camp about a mile west of the city, near the Baltimore pike. While marching through the city part of the regiment represented Sherman's bummers and foragers, some on mules, with tin pans, kettles, corn-fodder, chickens, bacon, tobacco, etc., etc., just as they used to be seen going through Georgia and the Carolinas. The day was rainy and disagreeable, but we had become accustomed to that.

We remained in camp until the 9th of June, nothing of importance transpiring during the time. We did some guard duty. The rest of the time was spent in resting in camp or visiting the city and the most public places, such as the Capitol buildings and grounds, the Patent Office, Smithsonian Institute, etc.

On the 9th we took the cars for Parkersburg, West Virginia, by way of Harper's Ferry.

We arrived at Parkersburg on the 11th, without accident, notwithstanding the greater part of the regiment rode on top of the cars, day and night, through several tunnels. While at Cumberland City the regiment was furnished with coffee.

On the 12th we embarked on board the steamer Elenora, and arrived at Louisville on the 14th, camping about four miles from the city.

On the Fourth of July General Sherman made us a farewell speech. We formed line in the morning, and marched out into a field about a mile from camp. The field was grown up in weeds about as high as a man's head. It was an exceedingly hot day. We remained in line about two hours, waiting for the general; but he did not come. We returned to camp, and in the afternoon the general made his speech, on horseback, in the camp, we being drawn up in line to receive him.

On the 11th we broke up camp and marched to Louisville, and went on board the steamer General Buell.

We arrived at Cincinnati on the 12th, and took the cars for Camp Dennison.

On the 14th the regiment took the cars for Xenia, at which place it had a reception. Here we remained until the 17th, when we again went to Camp Dennison, and on the 18th of July, 1865, we were paid off, received our discharge papers, and became citizens once more, having served the country nearly four years. The same day we took the cars for Xenia, and the Seventy-fourth was no more.

RECAPITULATION.

The aggregate loss of the Seventy-fourth in the Atlanta campaign, ending with the battle of Jonesboro, was eighteen killed and eighty-eight wounded. At that time several officers resigned and were mustered out, namely, Colonel Given, Captains McMillan, Armstrong, and Baldwin, and Lieutenants Adams and Baldwin.

The Seventy fourth was the last to leave Kingston, Georgia, in the new campaign through that state, severing the link that connected it with the North on the 12th of November, 1864 We arrived at Savannah, December 21st, and left that place for the South Carolina campaign January 25, 1865. Owing to the bad condition of the roads, which had to be corduroyed before they could be passed, the corps made slow progress.

The Seventy-fourth was, about this time, detailed as train-guard — a post of danger and responsibility, as the enemy were watching eagerly for a chance to capture the supply-train. The Seventy-fourth was with the supply-train through the Carolinas, and on May 7th arrived at Richmond, having averaged thirty-two miles a day, being the third regiment to arrive at the river, where we stacked arms with but one man missing from the ranks.

On the arrival of all the troops, on the 11th of May, the march to Washington began.

The muster-out rolls of the Seventy-fourth were made out bearing date July 10, 1865, and signed by the mustering officer of the First Division; and on the 11th of July the regiment, having received the farewell addresses and thanks of their corps, division, and brigade commanders, started for Camp Dennison, Ohio.

The reception at Xenia, on the 16th of July, will not soon be forgotten. An immense crowd was gathered in the city. Congratulatory addresses were delivered, and tables, loaded with all the choicest delicacies, were spread by the fair daughters of Xenia. Bouquets and wreaths of flowers were showered through the ranks, and everything was done that could in any way express the unbounded joy and gratitude of fathers, mothers, wives, sisters, and friends.

On the 17th of July the regiment returned to Camp Dennison, and on the 18th received pay and final discharge papers.

After starting on the Atlanta campaign the regiment was under an almost continuous fire of rebel musketry and artillery for over one hundred days. At Buzzard's Roost we were especially engaged in the attempt to storm that stronghold, at which place, on the 9th of May, we lost sixteen men killed and wounded, and at Resaca, May 15th, nine men were killed and wounded. In the engagement of the 27th of May, the conduct of the Seventy-fourth and other regiments of the Third Brigade elicited the highest encomiums from the division commander.

COLONEL MOODY.

The following anecdote of the Seventy-fourth and Colonel Moody has been in print before, but I will give it to my readers :

Colonel Granville Moody, commanding the Seventy-fourth Ohio Volunteers, is a famous Methodist preacher. He relinquished the altar for the sword. Malicious people insinuated that the gospel had lost the services of a good advocate, and that the army was not promoted by its accession from the pulpit. But the colonel proved that he was a tremendous fighter as well as a good preacher. He is fifty or more, perhaps, but well preserved, with magnificent front, and six feet two or three inches of stature. He has a fine, genial face, fiery dark eyes, and vocal range that would have excited the envy of roaring Ralph Stackpole. He carried into battle a spirit of enthusiasm which inflamed his boys to the highest pitch of daring, and won for him the admiration of thousands.

Lieutenant Colonel Von Schrœder, inspector general on the staff of General Thomas, than whom a braver or better soldier never resisted the storm of battle, had not been on friendly terms with Moody for some months, but admiring his splendid gallantry, he approached him in the heat of desperate conflict, extended his hand, expressed his earnest approbation of the colonel's heroism, and begged that peace ever after might exist between them. A little later Moody's "boys" — as he paternally called them — were obliged to withstand a terrific fire, without enjoying an opportunity to return it. Moody galloped to General Negley and protested, "This fire, general, is perfectly murderous; it will kill all my boys." But there was no help for it. His martial flock, imposing upon his benevolent nature, sometimes indulged a little sly humor at his expense. In the midst of a battle an Irishman in the regiment shouted, "His riverence, the colonel, has been fightin' Satan all his life. I reckon he thinks hell's broke loose now."

Not long after the battle General Negley merrily accused him of having used heterodox expletives in the ardor of engagement. "Is it a fact, colonel," inquired the general, "that you told the boys to give 'em hell?"

"Now," replied the colonel, reproachfully, "there's some more of the boys' mischief. I told the boys to give the rebels Hail Columbia, and they wickedly perverted my language."

This was true. The colonel said, "Now, boys, say your prayers, and give them Hail"— he had just got the word hail out, when the rebels let loose a volley at us, and drowned the Columbia.

But there was no doubt that one of his injunctions to his regiment sounded marvelously like a fervent ejaculation swelling up from the depths of the "amen chorus" in an old-fashioned Methodist church. This fact must be imagined that the anecdote may be appreciated. The colonel's mind was saturated with piety and pugnacity. He praised God and pitched into the rebels alternately. He had been struck by bullets four times already. He had given the rebels Hail Columbia once, and they reeled back to cover. Now they are swarming back to renew the contest. Moody's regiment were lying on their bodies, waiting for them to come up. He had a moment to spare, and he thought he would exhort them. The rebels were advancing sharply, and probably cut him short; but as they approached he said, quietly, "Now, boys, fight for your country and your God." "And," said one of his boys, "we all thought he was going to say, 'Amen!' but at that instant the rebels let fly, and the old hero roared with the voice of a Stentor, 'Aim low!'" Weeks after, when the colonel passed through the camp, the mischievous boys would shout behind him, "Fight for your country and your God — Aim low!"

INCIDENTS.

Mr. James A. Lynch, of Company C, related to me the following incidents:

"When the Seventy-fourth was on picket near Nashville, in 1862, while at my post, a proud Johnnie drove up in a buggy. I halted him, and demanded his pass. He remarked that he lived in sight, and that he had shown it a few days ago, and was about to drive on, when I drew my gun up close to his breadbasket. He then succumbed to a Yankee mudsill, and ever after that, when I saw him coming, I would exchange posts with the boys, so as to demand his pass. I understood he had been cashier of a bank at Nashville.

"When near Franklin," continues Mr. Lynch, "I went into a sweet-potato patch, and got a good supply of potatoes, when the old lady came out and begged me to give them up. The sack was on my shoulder, and I told her not to be troubled; that I would see the colonel, and have him issue an order to the effect that the boys should not molest her sweet-potato patch. I returned to camp, untied my sack, and poured out my sweet-potatoes. When young Clark asked me where I got them, I directed him to the place, and told him that the old lady was clever, and invited the Seventy-fourth boys to come and get potatoes. Clark took the sack, and was gone a short time, but returned with only a few potatoes, and evidently disappointed. The old lady told him a man had promised her that he would see the colonel, and have him prohibit the boys getting any more potatoes. At the same place," says Lynch, "a Mr. Irvine took a notion to forage a little, but as General Buell had issued an order prohibiting foraging, we thought we would forage on our own hook. Accordingly we started and went a long way from camp, taking only our revolvers with us. Pretty soon we came across a nice lot of hogs, near the river. They were very wild, but we fired at one, slightly wounding it. It took to the water, and Irvine on one side and I on the other, began pelting it with rocks, etc., when it soon submitted to have its hide taken off. We saw at a distance some men, whom we supposed to be rebels, so we started back to camp on the double quick."

Mr. Lynch was detailed into the pioneer corps. He says: "At one time, when near Kenesaw Mountain, the rebels shelled us. My comrade and I laid a rail down on a rock to build a fire and get dinner, but as we stood on one side a cannon-ball struck the rail and knocked it into splinters. We then gathered up the pieces, made our coffee, and laughed at the Johnnies for making us fire-wood.

"In the same corps," says Mr. Lynch, "our squad captured a negro man, to cook for them. He was dissatisfied, and wanted to leave. The boys wanted to have some fun, so they formed a ring around the darkey, and called to me to come and swear him in. I ordered him to take off his hat. He stood up like a man, and I swore him in as follows: 'You do positively swear in the presence of these Yankees, the searchers of all meat-houses, that you will faithfully perform your duty, as you shall answer to Abraham Lincoln?' He replied, 'Yes, sah.' He shortly after left in the night.

"As I was returning to my regiment — the Seventy-fourth," — Mr. Lynch says again, "I was placed on guard-duty, to guard a train loaded with ammunition, going to Chattanooga, from Stevenson, Alabama. Our force consisted of one hundred and fourteen men. Twelve hundred rebels attacked us at the foot of a mountain. Samuel Smith, of Company H, and I pledged ourselves to stand by each other, and take care of the other should either be wounded. We had a hard fight, and the enemy whipped us. They broke Smith's arm, but I stood by him, and we waded the river and made our escape. I took him back to the hospital at Stevenson, and there left him."

THE LUCKY REB.

While cut off from rations at Nashville, it was our rule to go out into the country to forage, and invariably we had with us the advance-guard, or cavalry. They generally got the best forage, and if any sport was on hand they fared the best. One day I borrowed the quartermaster's horse, and armed with a good carbine, concluded to accompany the cavalry squad, which numbered about twenty or thirty men. I fell in with a young man who belonged to the Second Kentucky Cavalry. We took our course down the river. About sixteen miles from the city we discovered a squad of rebs, and accordingly "went for them." "Kaintuck" and I singled out a reb mounted on a fine sorrel mare, and began a vigorous race, both of us firing, but to no effect. Finally, by taking short cuts, we came up to him, while nearing a brook. He suddenly dismounted and jumped into the water, and sat down, so that his head was above the water. As we rode up he begged us not to shoot, and we ordered him out. He came out and surrendered his horse and shot-gun, and said he had just enlisted in his company only the day before. "Kaintuck" remarked, "You are a darned sight luckier than I was — to enlist one day in the service and get out the next."

THE MAN WHOSE WIFE WOULD BE UNEASY.

During the time the Seventy-fourth regiment was at Nashville, and when the Louisville & Nashville Railroad was cut, we not unfrequently were called out in line of battle to meet Morgan, or Forrest, or some other band of guerrillas. One evening while lying in line on College Hill, awaiting what we then thought an attack, a man on a small white pony was seen outside the lines riding leisurely around, as though in search of something. Colonel Moody sent out for him, and on being interrogated as to his business, he said he was looking for his hogs. The colonel told him he must stay with us that night, at which he became very restive, and said he lived only a few miles away, had a nice home, and his wife would be uneasy if he did not return that night. The colonel said to him, "There are lots of fellows here who have nice homes, and the flowers bloom just as fresh in their yard as in yours, and their wives will be uneasy, too, because they are not there; so tie up and try soldiering one night. Here is a blanket to lie on." He refused to tie up, but sat down on the ground, holding his pony's bridle-rein in his hand until morning. I don't think he moved from his first position during the night. In the morning the colonel told him he could go home. I judge he had a poor opinion of soldier-life.

CAMPAIGN SONG.

BY IRA S. OWENS,
COMPANY C., SEVENTY-FOURTH REGIMENT, O. V. V. I.

TUNE—" HAPPY LAND OF CANAAN."

On the third day of May we started on our way,
   The boys then were not complainin'
That they then had to go to meet the rebel foe;
   So we started for the happy land of Canaan.

CHORUS.

Ho, boys, ho, we'll for the rebels go,
   And whip them, too, we are aimin';
And we'll never give them rest,
   But we'll drive them from their nest;
For we're bound for the happy land of Canaan.

At Buzzard's Roost they made a stand;
   But the Yankees were on hand;
And to whip the rebels they were aimin';
   But we went around Snake Gap to catch them in a trap;
For we're bound for the happy land of Canaan.

Chorus—Ho, boys, ho, etc.

At Resaca we pressed so tight that we had another fight,
   For we were so fast on them gainin';
Till at last they left the place, then we had another race;
   For we're bound for the happy land of Canaan.

Chorus—Ho, boys, ho, etc.

At Dallas they made a stop, to give us another pop—
   The rebels that still were remainin';
But the Yankees were so tough that the Johnnies got enough;
   For we're bound for the happy land of Canaan.

Chorus—Ho, boys, ho, etc.

The Yankees now in force, then took another course,
    Although it was muddy and a rainin';
But we didn't stop for rain, but went for them again;
    For we're bound for the happy land of Canaan.

        Chorus—Ho, boys, ho, etc.

At Kenesaw we had to halt, but that was Johnny's fault;
    For every nerve we were strainin';
But we'll whip the rebs so bad, 'twill make them very sad;
    For we're bound for the happy land of Canaan.

        Chorus—Ho, boys, ho, etc.

The twenty-second day of June, late in the afternoon,
    The rebels' shells were a rainin';
But they couldn't shell us out, and we gave them turn about;
    For we're bound for the happy land of Canaan.

        Chorus—Ho, boys, ho, etc.

Then on the second of July the rebels had to fly,
    For Kenesaw mound we were gainin';
It was getting rather hot, so they had to leave the spot;
    For we're bound for the happy land of Canaan.

        Chorus—Ho, boys, ho, etc.

The next place of renown was Marietta town,
    In it were people yet remainin';
But Sherman traveled on, for the rebels they were gone;
    For we're bound for the happy land of Canaan.

        Chorus—Ho, boys, ho, etc.

At Chattahoochee's banks he thought to stop the Yanks —
    General Johnson, with his army, to sustain him,
For his works were very strong, but he couldn't hold them long;
    For we're bound for the happy land of Canaan.

        Chorus—Ho, boys, ho, etc.

And now we will determine, with our leader, General Sherman,
   And the balance of the army to sustain him,
To crush the rebel band, and to redeem the land;
   For we're bound for the happy land of Canaan.

   Chorus—Ho, boys, ho, etc.

Now the rebels thought they would, by getting General Hood,
   Whip the Yankees that were then on them gainin';
So they charged with might and main, but we drove them back again;
   For we're bound for the happy land of Canaan.

   Chorus—Ho, boys, ho, etc.

Now, to get the rebs to fight, we marched unto the right,
   And to draw the rebels out we were aimin';
But when Hood found out the trick, he left Atlanta quick,
   For we're bound for the happy land of Canaan.

   Chorus—Ho, boys, ho, etc.

The railroad track we tore a dozen miles or more,
   To cut off the reb's supplies we were aimin';
For Sherman is the man to flank the rebel clan,
   For we're bound for the happy land of Canaan.

   Chorus—Ho, boys, ho, etc.

Atlanta now is ours, and by all the southern powers,
   With Jeff Davis and his minions to sustain him;
Our flag shall proudly wave o'er many a traitor's grave;
   For we're bound for the happy land of Canaan.

   Chorus—Ho, boys, ho, etc.

At last when we are through, and have whipped the rebel crew,
   Although it is very hard campaignin';
We will not regret the past, but all go home at last;
   For we're bound for the happy land of Canaan.

   Chorus—Ho, boys, ho, etc.

THE VOLUNTEERS.

BY IRA S. OWENS.

We left our homes and friends so dear,
    To fight for freedom's cause;
Yes, for our country's sake we're here,
    And to protect its laws.

The Union we will still preserve,
    Although we have to fight;
From duty we will never swerve,
    But stand up for the right.

In days of yore our fathers fought,
    And bled, and died, that we
Might share the glories so dearly bought,
    And that we might be free.

Those patriot sires, that noble band,
    We'll not forget them, no;
They fought and saved our native land,
    And conquered many a foe.

Then by our country's flag we'll stand,
    The Union we will save;
O'er North and South, o'er all the land
    Our flag shall proudly wave.

Since we obeyed our country's call,
    And flew to its relief,
It's caused the tears of friends to fall,
    And filled their hearts with grief.

God speed the time when war shall cease,
    When rebels shall succumb;
When we shall once again have peace,
    And traitors hear their doom.

For then shall war be heard no more;
    Then friends shall meet again;
And fighting then shall all be o'er,
    And peace triumphant reign.

ON THE DEATH OF R. S. DILWORTH.

The soldier sleeps his last long sleep,
His friends in anguish o'er him weep;
For his country's flag his life he gave,
He is sleeping now in an honored grave.

No more at the bugle's call he'll come,
Or march to the music of the drum;
His voice is hushed, his spirit fled,
Ah! yes, he's numbered with the dead.

Rest, soldier, rest; thy warfare's o'er,
No more you'll hear the cannon's roar;
No night alarms disturb your breast,
Then sweetly slumber, sweetly rest.

Ah! how sad the thought to those
Fond friends at home; ah! yes, who knows
The depths of sorrow hearts must feel;
But God alone the wound can heal.

The noble hero patriot fell;
His work is done, he did it well;
His sword is sheathed; let it remain,
He ne'er shall take it up again.

Although we feel his loss is great,
Heaven has thus decreed his fate;
His friends and comrades speak his fame,
Forever honored be his name.

There is one fond heart now left to mourn,
From whose embrace so lately torn,
On whom will fall the hardest blow,
Will be the deepest grief, we know.

The loving wife so soon must part
With the idol of her loving heart;
But trust in God, grace will be given,
And meet your dearest one in heaven.

Friends will drop affection's tears,
The lapse of months or lapse of years
Shall not banish from the mind
Thy many acts of love so kind.

When war is o'er and victory won,
We'll think of thee, the absent one —
In years to come when once again
Sweet peace shall universal reign.

Lieutenant Dilworth's work is done,
He rests in peace, his race is run;
Whilst many hearts with grief o'erflow,
Naught can disturb his sweet repose.

Farewell, soldier, noble friend,
And when this toilsome life shall end,
When all earth's sorrows shall be past,
We hope to meet in heaven at last.

THE FOUR DAYS' SCOUT.

I will now write a song, and I think I am right,
About the trip that we took with Hambright;
Of the farms that we passed, and the nice little villas,
The time we went hunting the rebel guerillas.

The time that we started was the month of October,
The twenty-fourth day, we being all sober;
We traveled eight miles, and then we encamped,
And for that day this was as far as we tramped.

We marched the next day as far as Dirt Town,
Where, off in the woods, some saddles were found.
Sometime in the day, when we came to a halt,
We saw an old man who was loaded with salt.

He had five or six barrels in his wagon he had bought,
All the way from Blue Mountain his salt he had brought;
He said that the rebels to Blue Mountain had gone,
So onward we went and left him alone.

That night we encamped right close to a mill,
(If the mill isn't gone I guess it's there still);
The way that we went, and the road that we took,
We followed our leader, whose name was Cap. Crook.

Of potatoes and molasses we had plenty to eat,
Besides, we had pork, the best of fresh meat;
So we had plenty of forage, of the very best kind,
Though sometimes the brigade would leave us behind.

Now Crook, as a leader, we very well knew
Was gallant and brave, and so was he true;
And should we have chanced to have heard a big noise,
Captain Crook is the man who would have staid with his boys.

In battle the captain has often been tried,
No one his courage has ever denied;
And if you should happen on the captain to call,
You will find he is kind and courteous to all.

Since the captain is going to leave his command,
And return once again to his own native land,
To lay down his sword, and cease fighting his foes,
May joy go with him wherever he goes.

The next day we marched, and at night there was rain,
And the next day we marched to our division again;
Four days and three nights we were out on the scout,
And I guess no one knew what we were about.

Twelfth Regiment, O. V. I.

Under the call for seventy-five thousand three months' troops, the Twelfth Ohio Infantry was organized at Camp Jackson, Ohio, May 3, 1861. It moved to Camp Dennison May 6th, there re-enlisted, and was re organized and mustered into the service for three years on the 28th of June, 1861. The Twelfth left Camp Dennison for the Kanawha Valley, July 6th, arrived at Point Pleasant on the 9th, and on the 14th reached Pocotaligo River.

On the 17th of July the regiment fought the battle of Scary Creek, the enemy being strongly fortified beyond a ravine. The regiment fought three hours, and after exhausting its ammunition, fell back in good order to its camp at the mouth of the Pocataligo, with a loss of five killed, thirty wounded, and four missing. The regiment entered Charleston, West Virginia, on the 25th, and reached Gauley Bridge on the 29th, where it captured a large quantity of arms and ammunition. Eight companies marched down the Kanawha to Camp Piatt, August 13th, and from there moved to Clarksburg, West Virginia, and were there assigned to General Benham's brigade.

Marching south through Weston, Sutton, and Summerfield, they arrived at Carnifex Ferry, September 10th, and engaged in the battle of that place, losing two killed and ten wounded. It was here that the brave Colonel John W. Lowe fell. Two days after this they were engaged in a slight skirmish on the Gauley with guerillas, then marched to Camp Lookout, and from there, on October 10th, moved to Hawk's Nest, on New River.

In the meantime the two companies left at Gauley Bridge surprised and routed two hundred rebel cavalry under Jenkins, on the 25th of August. They were engaged in several skirmishes and reconnoissances, and finally joined the other eight companies at Hawk's Nest, on the 16th of October.

On the 1st of November the Twelfth marched to the mouth of Loop Creek, and attempted to flank Floyd, who was threatening Gauley. It soon after engaged in the pursuit of Floyd's forces, and having followed him until near Raleigh C. H., gave up the chase and returned to Loop Creek. The regiment was transferred to General Cox's brigade, December 10th, and moved to Charleston, and went into winter quarters.

On the 3d of May, 1862, the regiment left Charleston and joined Scammon's brigade at the mouth of East River. It skirmished at the narrows of New River, fell back to Princeton, then to Blue Stone River, then to the Summit of Flat Top Mountain, and fortified. From the 20th of May until the 14th of August, the regiment scouted the country in every direction, made some heavy marches in the mountains, and captured many bushwhackers. It was ordered to the Army of the Potomac August 15th, and arrived at Alexandria on the 24th.

The Twelfth regiment met the enemy at Bull Run bridge, August 26th, was severely engaged for six hours against a greatly superior force, and was compelled to fall back to Fairfax Station, with a loss of nine killed, sixty-eight wounded — six mortally — and twelve missing. The regiment returned to Alexandria, rejoined Cox's brigade, and marched to Upton Hill. On the 7th of September it advanced into Maryland, and after a sharp skirmish at Monocacy Bridge, on the 12th, entered Frederick City. On the 14th of September it engaged in the battle of South Mountain, participating in three bayonet charges and capturing three battle-flags, a large number of small arms, and over two hundred prisoners, and sustaining a loss of sixteen killed, ninety-one wounded, and eight missing. On the 17th the regiment was engaged at Antietam, and lost six killed and twenty-nine wounded. After the battle it marched for West Virginia via Hagerstown and Hancock, Maryland; but on arriving at Hancock it moved into Pennsylvania to operate against Stewart's cavalry. Stewart having retreated, the Twelfth returned to Hancock, and arrived at Clarksburg, West Virginia, October 16th. The regiment marched from Clarksburg October 25th, in Crook's division, through Weston, Sutton, and Summerville, endeavoring to gain the rear of the rebel forces in the Kanawha Valley, and arrived at Gauley Bridge November 14th, the rebels having retreated before the division arrived.

On the 4th of December the regiment marched to Fayette C. H., West Virginia, and went into winter quarters. Here it was assigned to the second brigade, third division, and eighth army corps. The brigade, under Colonel White, repulsed the enemy's attack on Fayette C. H., May 9th, 1863, the regiment losing two killed, nine wounded, and eight missing. It pursued the retreating rebels to Raleigh C. H., and then returned to Fayette. C. H. On July 13th the Twelfth marched against the enemy at Piney Creek, but the rebels retreated, and the regiment returned to Fayette C. H.

The brigade was ordered to Ohio July 17th, to assist in capturing John Morgan, and after proceeding up the Ohio River as far as Blennerhassett's Island, and guarding fords for several days, it returned to Fayette C. H. During the months of August and September the regiment was employed in constructing fortifications. On the 4th of November it marched against Lewisburg, but the enemy fled, and the regiment again returned to Fayette C. H. On the 9th of December it made another move on Lewisburg, as a diversion for General Averill. Bushwhackers were very troublesome on this march, and the regiment lost two killed, two slightly, and two mortally wounded, and two missing. The Twelfth went into quarters at Fayette C. H., and was engaged in holding outposts and in watching the enemy.

On the 3d of May, 1864, the regiment left Fayette C H., marched to Cloyd's Mountain, and there engaged the enemy on the 9th. The fight lasted over an hour, and the regiment lost eleven killed and sixty-eight wounded. In addition to these Surgeon Graham and nineteen men, left on the field in charge of the wounded, fell into the enemy's hands. The regiment pursued the fleeing rebels to New River Bridge, where a heavy artillery fight ensued, in which the enemy was driven back. The regiment crossed New River at Pepper's Ferry, and destroyed a number of bridges and a large amount of property belonging to the Virginia and Tennessee Railroad.

The Twelfth Regiment marched northward, and on the 19th reached Blue Sulphur Springs, where it remained until the 31st, when it moved on Staunton. Arriving at Staunton June 8th, it joined the forces under Hunter, marched southward, flanked Lexington, and on the 12th assisted in destroying large quantities of ammunition, and in burning the Virginia Military Institute. On the 16th it destroyed the railroad between Liberty and Lynchburg, and burned several large bridges. The next day it marched on Lynchburg, and met the enemy at Quaker Church, three miles from the city. The Twelfth and Ninety-first Ohio regiments charged the enemy in fine style, and drove them back in disorder. The Twelfth captured a number of prisoners, and lost eight killed, and eleven wounded. The next day the regiment was engaged before the enemy's works, but withdrew after dark, and on the 19th marched to Liberty. It moved along the Virginia and Tennessee Railroad to Salem, and from there proceeded northward, via Catawba Valley, New Castle, Sweet Springs, White Sulphur, Lewisburg, and Gauley, to Camp Piatt, on the Kanawha, where it arrived June 29th. On this march both men and horses suffered considerably from hunger and thirst.

The Twelfth regiment was finally ordered to Columbus, Ohio, July 2d, and mustered out of the service at that city on the 11th of July, 1864. During its term of service the regiment moved, on foot, by rail and water, a distance of four thousand and forty-nine miles, and sustained a loss in killed, and wounded, and missing, of four hundred and fifty-five men.

TWELFTH O. V. I. REUNION.

From Xenia Torchlight, October 10, 1883.

The members of the Twelfth O. V. I., from Cedarville, were escorted from the depot early this morning to the St. George Hotel. The early music aroused the citizens from their short naps after the election returns, and everybody imagined the successful candidate had been announced, but a moment's thought rectified the mistake, for this is the day of the Twelfth O. V. I. reunion.

At about ten o'clock the band went to the depot to meet a delegation which, in company with all the members of the regiment, was escorted to the Opera House. The stage to day is very elaborately and tastefully decorated by our city florist— Lambert. In the decorations the battle flags of the regiment hold conspicuous places.

ADDRESS OF WELCOME, BY THOMAS E. SCROGGY, ESQ.

I have been introduced as Comrade Scroggy. It was not my privilege to have been a member of your regiment, excepting a short time in the beginning of the war, when I served as a member of Company B, on the bloody field of Camp Jackson, although I contributed liberally of my relatives — a brother and brother-in-law, who were members of Company D, and whom many of you remember.

Soldiers of the Twelfth Ohio Regiment: — On behalf of the resident members of your regiment, and the citizens of Xenia, I have the honor and pleasure of extending to you, each and all, a most cordial welcome. Next to my own — the Thirty-ninth Ohio — there was no regiment to which I have been more warmly attached than to the Twelfth; and I can assure you that the people of Xenia cherish with fond remembrance your magnificent achievements. Of the two hundred regiments which Ohio sent to the field, none performed their duty better, nor are entitled to greater renown, than yours. During those years of war, when Ohio proved her loyalty to the Union and to her soldiers in the field; when her loyal people were giving us aid, comfort, and consolation; when her sons on other theaters of the war were performing their part in the awful tragedy, the soldiers of the Twelfth Ohio were following that battle-torn old banner wherever it was waving, in triumph, or were sleeping their last sleep on the fields which their valor has contributed to win. The battle-fields of Scarrey Creek, Carnifax Ferry, Gauley, Bull Run Bridge, South Mountain — and who of you will ever forget that terrible conflict, when you made three charges — the Twelfth Ohio charging the Twelfth North Carolina — when you captured three battle-flags and two hundred prisoners, the battle-field of Antietam, Fayette Court House, Cloyd Mountain, New River Bridge, Quaker Church, Lynchburg, and others which I do not recall, over which your flag has floated in triumph, are enough to render your name and fame of this grand old Twelfth immortal.

Well then might Ohio be proud of the record you were making for her. On whatever battle-field you stood, a new luster was added to her name; and as one of her sons, my heart used to swell with joy and pride, as time after time tidings came from your far-distant camp-fires in Virginia, that the brave old Twelfth, whose ranks had been torn by shot and thinned by shell, still stood at her post of duty. Nobly did you fulfill your arduous trust during those stirring years of war. Soldiers of the Twelfth Ohio, let come what may, the record you have made is beyond reproach. So long as patriotism, constancy, and valor are esteemed, so long will your immortal deeds be cherished and revered by brave men and noble women. The historian will look in vain to find a grander example of true patriotism than yours. Many of your bravest, truest, and best boys who went out with you did not return. You left them on the fields of battle, and on the mountains, and by the streams of Virginia, where no voice of mother, wife or sister, will ever wake them; where no kind hand will ever strew flowers upon their graves. They died for liberty — they died for us, and by us they shall never be forgotten They will live in the affections of their countrymen and their country's history. It is eminently proper that you who survive them have these annual reunions, where you can mingle your joys and your sorrows, and where, in your imaginations, you can live over again your happiest days of the war. The people of Xenia, therefore, greet you with that genial, overflowing welcome, which is due to friends and brothers, to patriots and benefactors. We greet you as champions of the eternal principle, that all men are created equal, and that every man beneath our flag has a perfect right to the enjoyment of life, liberty, and pursuit of happiness. Welcome, grand old patriots! Welcome to the hearts and hospitalities of the people of Xenia.

Comrade Holbrook, of Company F, responded:

Citizens of Xenia and Friends: — In response to your greeting and welcome, in behalf of the members of the Twelfth regiment, we tender our sincere thanks. We remember that from

Xenia came our colonel — whom we revere and honor — than whom upon the field, in the battle, there were none we respected more than Colonel Lowe. It is not proper for us to boast of what we have done; but we are not ashamed of our record in West and East Virginia, at Antietam, or Bull Run. We were of that kind that would not allow a goose to bite us or a pig to insult us. We are glad to be here together. Pardon us, if in our joy of meeting one another, we may seem to be unappreciative of your attentions or kindness as citizens of Xenia, but you know the object of our reunion is to live over the incidents of the war through which we served together as comrades. It may appear selfish in us, but I assure you that it is not selfishness. This is our second reunion. I am glad to see so many here; would like to see more. We hope to so deport ourselves as to be worthy of your reception Please accept our hearty thanks for your kind reception.

Sergeant Stockman, of Franklin, Ohio, the presiding officer, then announced that the minutes of the previous meeting would be read by the secretary. The regiment were banqueted at the St. George, where ample preparations were made.

DINNER.

The large dining-hall of the St. George was elaborately and tastefully decorated with flags, streamers, and evergreens, in reception of the Twelfth regiment. At about 1:30 P. M., the regiment was dismissed from the Opera House, and marched to the hotel for dinner, which was enjoyed as only ex soldiers know how to enjoy a good thing. After dinner they were again assembled in the Opera House for the afternoon exercises.

Sergeant L. Stockman, presiding officer, announced that the exercises would consist of short speeches, incidents, songs, etc., and urged the boys to take part in the proceedings freely.

RELICS.

H. S. Day was then called upon to exhibit the relics, which, fortunately, he had been thoughtful enough to save. Mr. Day thereupon ascended the stage, and, after some very appropriate introductory remarks, exhibited the flag of Company C, which was presented to the company by the ladies of New Richmond, Ohio, and which they had carried as far as "Flat Top." The old flag was saluted by three rousing cheers. The next relic called forth much amusement. It was a pen-made poster, announcing the appearance of the "Buckeye Minstrels," at Fayetteville, West Virginia, at the time that the regiment was winter-quartered there. The minstrel company was formed of the boys of the Twelfth Regiment, and the running remarks made about the poster, and the incidents related of the entertainment, were very enjoyable. The poster was executed by Joe Compton. Tickets of admission were also exhibited, and it was claimed that the boys had some way of counterfeiting tickets that annoyed the managers of the minstrel troupe very much. Mr. Day exhibited a pass issued to him while at Fayetteville, which he read, together with several official reports, and announced that he had at home a shoe, cast off by a fleeing rebel, when one of the Twelfth boys was after him; also, a piece of a flag-staff that belonged to one of the North Carolina regiments that fought the Twelfth so stubbornly. It was remarked that the Twelfth was at one time in an engagement with the Twelfth North Carolina, and in the same battle the Twenty-third Ohio was engaged with the Twenty-third North Carolina. The next relic was a flattened musket-ball that had killed Aaron Sayers at Meadow Bluffs. Photographs of Captain Channel and General J. D. Cox were also presented, together with many other interesting papers and official reports referring to the gallant action of the regiment in the field, in one of which Captain W. H. Glotfelter, of this county, with others, was recommended for promotion on account of gallant service. The papers and relics were then delivered to the secretary, to be placed in the archives of the regiment. Messrs. Holbrook, Rigor, Lyons, Steve Mitchell, Captain "Buck" Smith, Captain Hilt, Sergeant Stockman, and many others whose names we could not get, related incidents, eliciting amusement and applause.

A DEAD LIVE MAN.

Thomas E. Gaddis called attention to the fact that there was present in the hall Pat. Pedit, who was reported killed in one of the battles, and his funeral obsequies had been duly celebrated in Germantown, Ohio. Sergeant Stockman then related the strange occurrence substantially as follows: At the second battle of Bull Run we were compelled to retreat. I saw comrade Pedit leaning against a stump. I touched him on the shoulder, and told him to get away from there, the rebels were coming. He was wounded badly, and as he looked pale, and did not answer me I supposed him to be dead. Captain Sherwood wrote to Mrs. Pedit that her husband had been killed. The friends at his home in Germantown arranged for the funeral, the Odd Fellows conducted services, the minister preached the funeral, and the audience was very large. Some time after — I think it was while we were at Antietam — some one received a letter from Pat. Pedit, asking about his knapsack. Well! we all had some trouble about our knapsacks, but we all had supposed that Pedit would never care for his knapsack again. He was captured, and being wounded, was unable to send word home for a long time — this letter was the first heard of him. We are glad to see him here alive to-day, and I request him to stand up that we all may see him. Mr. Pedit, with a wounded arm in a sling, stood up and modestly bowed to his comrades, who greeted him with cheers. Mr. Holbrook was called upon to produce, if it was possible, a large knife which he had captured from the enemy. He said that he did not know where it was at present, but it was quite a large knife, like a corn-cutter, and had inscribed on it, "Death to Yanks." Some one added that Mr. Holbrook captured the knife from a six-footer.

"MARCHING THROUGH GEORGIA."

After frequent calls, Thomas Gaddis, Professor Holbrook, and Iliff, took the positon in front and led the regiment in this stirring song, whose strong chorus — in which the regiment joined — fairly shook the Opera House. After the song William Dingess, of Company D, from Jamestown, arose in the rear of the house and said, "Though we did not march to the *sea*, I am glad we had the honor of marching to what we did *see*."

Letters of regrets from the following absent members were read: J. W. Goldener, Greenville, Ohio; F. Gunkle, Dayton, Ohio; J. B. Homan, Blanchester, Ohio; E. K. King, Percival Hawes, Pike, Kansas, and H. F. Cramer. Captain B. Nesbitt, of this city, was then called upon and made a short address.

Resolutions thanking the comrades of Greene County, and the people of Xenia, for their kind reception, were passed with three hearty cheers and a *tiger*.

The following resolution was then offered by Thomas Gaddis:

Resolved, That we are acquainted with the facts in the case of our comrade, T. J. Sutton, of Company H, and that we hereby admit him to good standing in our association, and we also authorize our officers to attach their official signatures to his petition for an honorable discharge.

The resolution received a unanimous and emphatic approval. The executive committee was announced, namely, George A. Stivers, Isaac Boswell, and William Quickbaum.

The president then announced the next thing in order to be

the election of officers for the ensuing year, which was proceeded with, and the following were all elected unanimously: President, L. Stockman; Vice-president, J. L. Hill; Secretary and Treasurer, George A. Stivers; Corresponding Secretary, W. B. Nesbit.

Several places were named for holding the next reunion, but after considerable discussion, Ripley, Ohio, was selected, and the third Thursday in October, 1884, as the date.

MEMBERS PRESENT.

The following is a list of the members who were present:

COMPANY A.

James Phillips, Morrow; H. C. Parker, Morrow; James Ireland, Morrow; C. B. Riley, Blanchester; John Kline, Cincinnati; Edward Mader, Cincinnati; Elias Whitacre, Edwardsville; James Eagle, Clarksville; H. P. Kiphart, Clarksville; E. R. Grim, Morrow; G. N. Smith, Dayton; John Troville, Morrow.

COMPANY B.

I. M. Duncan, New Vienna; J. W. Matthews, New Vienna; W. H. Glotfelter, Alpha; W. W. B. Alexander, Lagonda; A. L. Wright, Xenia; Robert McCreight, Xenia; Ab. Keble, Xenia; H. L. Hay, Parkersville, Kansas; R. J. Johnson, Mt. Carmel.

COMPANY C.

J. A. Enson, Berrien Springs, Michigan; G. H. Slade, Bantam; Charles McMast, Moscow; Steve Mitchell, Cincinnati.

COMPANY D.

J. E. Brown, Jamestown; F. G. Barber, Garnet, Kansas;

R. B. Beard, Clinton County, Kansas; H. D. Kline, Cedarville; John Cordingly, Yellow Springs; John Davis, Mechanicsburg; W. A. Doyer, Jamestown; J. H. Davidson, Xenia; Michael Donelly, Yellow Springs; Ellis Dorriel; H. W. Ford, Cedarville; L. C. Ginn, Yellow Springs; J. S. Harper, Xenia; J. L. Harper, Eureka Springs, Arkansas; H. C. Huffin; J. F. Harris, Jamestown; W. H. Iliff, Cedarville; C. W. Stevenson, Xenia; I. H. Iliff, Cedarville; Alex. Turnbull, Cedarville; I. W. Irwin, Cedarville; John Kirkwood, Springfield; J. T. Willis, Straughn, Indiana; W. B. Smith, South Salem, Indiana; Fred Snively, Xenia.

COMPANY E.

J. L. Van Allen, Utica; J. M. Deboth, Utica; Wilson Lamb, Newark; James Houghy, Newark; Matthias Bigger, Newark; D. Weaver, Utica.

COMPANY F.

R. B. Wilson, Cincinnati; J. H. Smith, Lebanon; Irwin Snook, Lebanon; C. K. Dunham, Waynesville; E. K. Snook, South Lebanon; W. P. Bailey, Morrow; H. M. Cox, South Lebanon; Josiah Holbrook, Lebanon; John M. Snook, Lebanon.

COMPANY G.

J. T. Hilt, Middleton; J. N. Yager, Jacksonville; N. Miars, Piqua; John Vannote, Lebanon; Joe Pettitt, Germantown; Wm. Boore, Germantown; L. Stockman, West Carlisle; J. Van Tillbury, Germantown.

COMPANY H.

Samuel Yeaton, Ripley; George Stivers, Ripley; M. Creekbaum, Ripley; H. Fisher, Ripley; G. W. Shaw, Ripley; T. Lowry, Maysville, Kentucky; Tom Sutton, Aberdeen; T. C. Gaddis, Cincinnati; J. E. D. Ward, Dayton.

THE TWELFTH.

COMPANY I.

Sol. R. Smith, Lincoln, Illinois; John Schon, Dayton; Wm. Hink, Dayton; Jacob Yeider, Hartford City, Indiana; Charles Conner, Oxford, Iowa; J. Garruch, Greenville; P. Smith, Columbus.

COMPANY K.

R. M. Riley, Blanchester; D. M. Taylor, Hillsboro; W. H. Barker, Centerville; J. W. Eddington, Cincinnati; J. K. Church, Shelbyville, Illinois; E. E. Hixon, Martinsville; H. Earhart, Dayton.

Ninety-Fourth Regiment, O. V. I.

This regiment was organized at Camp Piqua, Miami County, Ohio, under the immediate supervision of Colonel J. W. Frizell. The officers were appointed on the 22d of July, 1862, and so vigorously was the recruiting prosecuted, that in just one month one thousand and ten men were mustered into the United States service.

On the 28th of August, without uniforms or camp equipage, and never having been drilled as a regiment, the Ninety-fourth was ordered to Kentucky — that state being then invaded by rebel forces under Kirby Smith. It proceeded via Cincinnati, and upon arriving in that city, was immediately ordered to Lexington. By great perseverance the colonel succeeded in obtaining three rounds of cartridges to the man; and being supplied with this very limited amount of ammunition, and sufficient clothing to supply immediate wants, the regiment took the cars for Lexington, arriving at 9:00 P. M., on Saturday night, where they heard, for the first time, an authentic account of the battle of Richmond.

After considerable search the colonel succeeded in finding the officer to whom he was to report, but in such a beastly state of intoxication as to be unable to rise from his bed, and perfectly incompetent to give intelligent instructions. With the assistance of some citizens, passable quarters were obtained for the men. Hungry, tired, and anxious for the morning, the regiment tried bivouacking for the first time.

Sunday morning dawned bright and beautiful, disclosing the

town full of stragglers from the Richmond battle-field, relating wild stories of defeat and disaster, and though but little confidence was placed in their reports, still this, together with the general gloom always attending such a state of affairs as then existed, caused the order for the regiment to proceed to Tate's Ford, on the Kentucky River, fifteen miles east of Lexington, on the Richmond road, to be received with fearful foreboding. However, the order was obeyed without a murmur, and after a hard day's march under a scorching sun, over a dry and dusty road, with water very scarce, the regiment arrived near the field just at dark. This being the first march the regiment had made, the men were much exhausted, and dropped to the ground as soon as the order to halt was given.

While the colonel was endeavoring — as best he could in the darkness — to select a position which could be easily defended, a fire was opened upon the regiment by a rebel scouting party, concealed in the thickets skirting the road, and it was afterward ascertained that the whole of Kirby Smith's army was encamped but a couple of miles north of the Ford. A veteran regiment could not have behaved better than did the Ninety-fourth on this occasion. The night was very dark, the men were lying down, and many had already fallen asleep, but after the confusion incident to their rude awakening, very little trouble was experienced in getting the regiment properly formed. The rebel fire lasted but a moment, yet two men were killed and six wounded.

After posting his men to the best advantage, Colonel Frizell remained with the advance picket-post — which, from the nature of the country, was but a short distance from the regiment — all night, Major King, Captain Drury, and the adjutant occupying intermediate positions between the colonel and the regiment. The night passed slowly and without further alarm, and as soon as daylight appeared the hungry men began looking in some wagons that had arrived during the night for the supplies, which the officer in command at Lexington had said he would send. The search revealed one hundred and twenty-five rounds of ammunition to each man, and three sacks of green coffee to the regiment.

While endeavoring to make a breakfast from these "supplies," the rebel army was reported advancing, and soon commenced shelling the regiment from a battery they had placed in position in the woods just across the river. Colonel Frizell watched the maneuvers of the rebels for a few moments, and then ordered his adjutant to form the regiment and march back until past the road, where it was supposed the rebels would attempt to form and prevent a retreat. The movement was effected in good order, but none too soon, as the rear guard had just passed the road when the rebels came trooping from it into the pike, and began firing upon Captain Drury's command, which had been selected as rear guard. Colonel Frizell remained in the rear until the advancing rebels were checked, when he directed the regiment to a certain point, and there to form for action. He knew that his force was greatly outnumbered, but his order was to contest every foot of ground back to Lexington. Just as the movement was begun a messenger arrived with an order from General G. C. Smith, dated the night before, for the Ninety-fourth to return to Lexington with all possible dispatch.

The regiment was now twelve miles from any support, with a fresh and victorious enemy, more than ten times superior in numbers, close in the rear, and to successfully conduct a retreat of raw troops under such circumstances, required the most thorough ability on the part of the commander, and the most undoubted confidence on the part of the men. The regiment toiled along the hot and dusty road, Colonel Frizell and Captain Drury fearlessly exposing themselves, together with the other officers, to prevent straggling; but their efforts could not prevent quite a number of the almost-exhausted men from falling by the wayside, and becoming an easy prey to the closely pursuing enemy. At four o'clock the regiment reached Lexington, greatly to the surprise of every one who knew that it had gone out on the expedition. The order sending it to the Ford was a blunder, and probably the only thing that prevented its capture was the very boldness of the movements made.

Our army that had retreated from Richmond had already left Lexington, still in retreat toward Louisville, and all stores that could not be easily transferred had been destroyed. With the exception of coffee and crackers on Sunday morning, the men of the Ninety fourth had had little to eat since Saturday morning, were tired and foot-sore, and in bad condition for further marching. In the absence of instructions to the contrary, it was Colonel Frizell's intention to remain in Lexington, unless driven out, until the men had procured the much-needed food and rest; but the order for continued retreat reached him, and was obeyed. At daylight the retreating army reached Versailles, and a halt for breakfast was ordered, but just as the coffee began to boil another order to fall in came from the officer in command. The season was very dry, and but little water could be obtained. The suffering in consequence of this may be inferred from the fact that the Ohio soldiers gave five dollars for a canteen full of muddy water — a dollar a drink — and many drank from standing pools the water that the horses refused to touch. The roads were almost ankle deep with dust, and the sun shone fiery overhead. The day's march began at from two to three o'clock in the morning, and continued until late in the night, and the only provisions issued — or to be obtained — were a few hard crackers each night and what green corn yet remained in the fields adjacent to the camping-grounds. The troops were all, or nearly all, newly enlisted, and being unused to such a life, it is not to be wondered at that they fell out of the ranks by the hundred, and were so easily captured by the force of rebels following.

Upon arriving at Louisville the Ninety fourth went into camp, without tents, in the woods, but the men were so utterly exhausted that their only need was rest, as best they could get it. Having been deprived almost entirely of sleep, water. and food tor seven days, marching night and day, with feet and limbs swollen almost to bursting, and every sense dulled with suffering, many of the men were pitiable objects. In a short time, however, all had regained comparative strength, health, and cheerfulness, and were ready to go where duty called.

The first regular report that the adjutant could make after arriving at Louisville, showed a loss of two hundred and eighteen men. With the exception of the two men killed at Tate s Ford, all eventually returned to the regiment, having been paroled by the rebels almost as soon as captured.

With the exception of some hard work in the trenches and on fortifications, and a participation in two or three "grand reviews." the regiment had very easy times until the first of October, when the movement began, which resulted in the battle of Perryville, and the driving of Bragg's rebel army from Kentucky. Previous to the battle of Perryville the Ninety-fourth had been assigned to Rosseau's division of McCook's corps, and took an active part in the engagement, being highly complimented in general orders. The regiment broke camp near Nashville on Christmas-day, 1862, and was in advance of the army marching on Murfreesboro, and during the battle of Stone River was engaged every day — from Wednesday until Saturday. The Ninety-fourth was again in advance on Tullahoma, participating in the fight at Hoover's Gap in June, 1863, had a skirmish at Dug Gap, and were engaged in the hard fought battle of Chickamauga. At Lookout Mountain and Mission Ridge the regiment again took a prominent part, participating in the grand charge upon the Ridge; was with Sherman on the march to Atlanta, taking part in the battles at Buzzard's Roost, Resaca, Kingston, Pumpkinvine Creek, Kennesaw Mountain, Chattahoochie River, Peach Tree Creek, Atlanta, and Jonesboro. After pursuing Hood, the Ninety-fourth participated in Sherman's grand march to the sea, arriving at Savannah before Christmas. On the 20th of January, 1865, it was again on the march through North and South Carolina, and after participating in the battle at Bentonville, North Carolina, arrived at Goldsboro on the 23d of March, 1865. The Ninety-fourth was the first regiment of infantry to enter Raleigh, North Carolina, and soon 'after the surrender of Johnston marched to Washington, via Richmond and Alexandria, participating in the grand review before the President, General Grant, and others, and was mustered out of the service at Washington on the 6th of June, 1865, with an aggregate of three hundred and thirty-eight men — all that were left of them — left of one thousand and ten!

One Hundred and Tenth, O. V. I.

This regiment was organized at Camp Piqua, Ohio, on the 3d of October, 1862. On the 19th of October the regiment moved by railroad to Zanesville, thence by steamer to Marietta, and from thence by railroad to Parkersburg, Virginia. On the 3d of November it marched to Clarksburg, where it remained until the 25th, and then took the cars for New Creek, where it arrived the next day. Here it remained in camp, fortifying, and drilling, and performing guard and picket duty, until December 13th, whence it marched, via Burlington and Petersburg, to Moorfield, Virginia. Three hundred men from the One Hundred and Tenth joined an expedition to move in the direction of Winchester, Virginia, while the remainder of the regiment moved with another expedition in the direction of Romney. The main portion of the regiment arrived at Winchester, without serious interruption, on the 1st of January, 1863, and joined the detachment which had arrived a week previous.

While at Winchester the regiment was assigned to the first brigade, second division, eighth army corps, and companies A and D were detailed as provost guard. The regiment was employed in guard and picket duty, in drilling, fortifying, and making raids and reconnoissances. At one time a detachment went to Front Royal and captured a large amount of stores. At another time a detachment proceeded to Summit Point and other places, dispersing bands of rebels and destroying stores; and in the early part of May the regiment marched to New Market and returned. On the 13th of June the regiment was moved out to Kernstown, and engaged Lee's advance. This is the first time the regiment was under fire, but they behaved bravely. On the morning of the 14th the One Hundred and Tenth occupied a small earthwork, about three-fourths of a mile from the main fort. In the afternoon the enemy opened on it with twenty-six pieces of artillery, and advanced in strong columns to the assault. The regiment held the works until it was driven out at the point of the bayonet by an overwhelming force. It attempted to retire in the night, but was met by the enemy, and a two hours' engagement ensued, in which the regiment succeeded in cutting its way through, and marched to Harper's Ferry.

On the 16th of June the regiment crossed the river and encamped on Maryland Heights. On the 1st of July it went by canal to Georgetown, D. C., then to Tenallytown, then to Washington, and from thence to Frederick City, Maryland. At this place the regiment was assigned to the second brigade, third division, third army corps, Army of the Potomac. Marched in pursuit of Lee to Williamsport, Loudon, Upperville, and Manassas Gap, where it skirmished with the enemy, and reached Fox's Ford, on the Rappahannock, on the 1st of August. On the morning of the 15th the regiment left the Ford, took the cars at Bealton Station for Alexandria, and from there to New York, where the regiment camped for awhile on Governor's Island, and then moved to Carrol Park, South Brooklyn. On the 6th of September the regiment returned, via Alexandria, to Fox's Ford, and marched from there to Culpepper, Virginia, in charge of an ammunition-train. On the 10th of October it moved out to meet an attack, and remained there all night under arms, and the next day marched across the Hazell and Rappahannock rivers, through Centerville, Bristow, Catlett's Station, and at last reached and occupied the first line, near the Rappahannock. On the 7th of November the regiment crossed the river, skirmishing with the enemy, and the next morning made a reconnoissance, and captured between thirty and forty prisoners. In the afternoon the One Hundred and Tenth, in advance of Brandy Station, was severely shelled by the artillery, and was the first to occupy the enemy's position.

Upon breaking camp at Brandy Station, four companies of the regiment were detached as train guard, and the others took a prominent part in the battle of Locust Grove, losing five killed and twenty wounded. The regiment returned to Brandy Station, December 3d, and occupied winter quarters.

During the month of March, 1864, the One Hundred and Tenth became a part of the second brigade, third division, sixth army corps. On the 4th of March the regiment crossed the Rapidan, at Germania Ford, and the next day took a position on the extreme right of the national line at the Wilderness. After brisk skirmishing it advanced to charge, and drove the enemy to their works. The regiment held its position until after dark, and only fell back when its ammunition was exhausted. The loss sustained was one officer killed, and six wounded; eighteen men killed, eighty-two wounded, and eleven missing. The next day the regiment occupied the second line, but was much exposed to artillery. In the evening, the brigade on the right being routed, the One Hundred and Tenth fell back about a mile, and held the new position all day on the 7th, and in the evening fell back through Chancellorsville to the vicinity of Spottsylvania C. H. Here the regiment was engaged in fortifying and skirmishing until the 14th, when it marched toward Spottsylvania, waded the Nye River after dark, and occupied the enemy's works, from which they had been driven. The One Hundred and Tenth was almost constantly engaging the enemy, marching via Guinea Station and Chesterfield Station, crossing the Pamunky, and throwing up fortifications on Dr. Palmer's farm.

On the 1st of June the regiment was engaged at Cold Harbor. In the assault on the enemy's works on the 3d, the regiment was in the front line, and was ordered to continue the advance after the line halted, which it did, and was exposed for two hours, when it was withdrawn. During the entire day the regiment was exposed to a heavy fire, losing one commissioned officer, four men killed, and thirty-four wounded.

On the 14th the regiment left the works, crossed the Chickahominy, passed Charles City, C. H., embarked on the transport Star, landed at Point of Rocks, and marched to Bermuda Hundred. In the evening of the 19th it crossed the Appomattox, and arrived near Petersburg. After resting a day it marched to the Norfolk and Petersburg Railroad, and charged the enemy's line, driving it in; and a few days later moved to the Petersburg and Weldon Railroad.

On the 30th of June the enemy commenced its return, and on the 2d of July occupied its former position near Petersburg. It embarked on the transport City of Albany, for Baltimore, where it arrived on the 8th, and took the cars for Monocacy Junction, and took part in the Monocacy battle. From there it went to Ellicott's Mills, where it arrived on the 10th of July. On the 11th the regiment went to Baltimore, and camped at Druid Hill Park until the 14th, when it took the cars to Washington, and the next day after marched through Tenallytown, waded the Potomac near Edward's Ferry, passed through Snicker's Gap to the Shenandoah, skirmished with the enemy, and rested awhile. On the 20th the regiment crossed the Shenandoah, then recrossed the river, and marched all night, arriving at Washington again on the 23d. Three days after it broke camp and marched through Hyattstown, Monocacy Junction, Frederick City, Maryland, and Harper's Ferry to Healltown, arriving on the 29th, and on the next day fell back through Harper's Ferry to Frederick City, Maryland. On the 3d of August the regiment resumed the march through Buckeyetown, crossed the Monocacy at Monocacy Mills, then moved by cars from Monocacy Junction to Bolivar, and marched from there to Healltown. On the morning of the 10th it marched through Charleston, Newtown, and Middletown, arriving at Cedar Creek on the 12th. Here it was engaged in several skirmishes, and on the 16th marched as train guard to Charleston. It fell back to Bolivar Heights, but again advanced to Charleston, and on the 29th, in an engagement, completely routed the rebels. On the 3d of September the regiment marched to Clifton Farm and fortified. On the 19th it crossed the Opequan, and engaged in the battle of Winchester. It engaged the rebels at Fisher's Hill, capturing four pieces of artillery and one hundred prisoners, then marched to Mount Crawford, and returned to Harper's Ferry. On the 6th of October it moved to Strasburg, and from there to the vicinity of Front Royal. On the 13th it marched to Ashby's Gap, and on the next day returned and camped at Cedar Creek.

On the morning of the 19th of October, when the eighth and nineteenth corps were driven back, the Sixth Corp, with the One Hundred and Tenth Ohio in the front line, was formed to arrest the advancing rebels, and in the final effort, which resulted in routing the rebels, no regiment took a more active part than the One Hundred and Tenth. It lost two officers wounded — one of whom died a few days after — five men killed, and twenty-seven wounded, and one officer and one man missing. In the evening the regiment occupied the camp from which it had been driven in the morning, and occupied it until November 9th, when it encamped one mile from Keinstown, and built winter quarters. On the 3d of December it marched to Stebbin's Station, took cars for Washington, proceeded thence to City Point by steamer, took cars near midnight on the 6th, and arrived at the front at daylight. It occupied the line east of the Weldon Railroad, and proceeded to build winter quarters.

On the 9th of February, 1865, the regiment took position between forts Fisher and Welch, and again erected winter quarters. On the 25th of March the entire brigade assaulted the strongly entrenched picket-line, and after a second charge, under a severe fire, carried it, capturing a large number of prisoners and small arms.

An assault was made on the enemy's works before Petersburg, on the 2d of April. Just before daybreak, and before it was fairly light, the Sixth Corps was in possession of the fortifications and many prisoners and guns. The regiment pursued the enemy, routing him at Saylor's Creek, and continuing the pursuit until the surrender of Lee.

The regiment marched to Burksville Junction, and on the 17th, at the presentation of captured flags to Major General Meade, the One Hundred and Tenth — having captured more flags than any other regiment in the corps — was selected as a guard of honor to escort them to General Meade's headquarters.

The regiment proceeded to Richmond, Virginia, and while passing through the city was reviewed by General Halleck; from there it proceeded to Washington City, where it was reviewed by the President and Cabinet at the Executive Mansion. During its term of service the regiment was in twenty-one engagements, and sustained a loss in killed, and wounded, and missing, of seven hundred and ninety-five men. It was mustered out at Washington City on the 25th of June, 1865, and was discharged at Todd's Barracks, Columbus, Ohio.

KEIFER LEADS THE VAN.

REGIMENTAL SONG, ONE HUNDRED AND TENTH, O. V. I.

BY LIEUT. H. Y. RUSH.

TUNE—UNCLE SAM.

Come, Buckeye boys, and let us sing, for now we've shouldered arms,
We've left our wives and sweethearts home, with all their love and charms.
The hills and dales, the old homestead, the lovely scenes of youth,
We've bid a sad farewell to all, to battle for the truth.

CHORUS.

Then march along, march along, for Keifer leads the van,
And Foster he will stick to us as long as there's a man;
Then march along, march along, for Binkley's with us, too;
And he will never square the books till Davis gets his due.

The traitors first shot down our flag that o'er proud Sumter stood,
And reared their filthy rebel rag, all stained with Union blood.
But Yankee boys can rear again that Banner of the Free,
Whose folds shall all be kissed again with zephyrs from the sea.

Chorus—Then march along, etc.

The rebels they would fain tear down this temple of the free,
And build instead their cushion'd homes of aristocracy.
But from this temple not a stone shall ever be removed;
For in her halls is justice found, as foreign lands have proved.

Chorus—Then march along, etc.

Our country is the best on earth, and bears the fairest name;
And she can boast of giving birth to men of deathless fame;
There's Washington, whose dauntless deeds still keep his mem'ry green,
And Jackson, too, who whipped John Bull, so nice at New Orleans.

Chorus—Then march along, etc.

Poor Jeff, he thinks he's very sharp, and Yancey boasts of wit;
But we can whet our tools, my boys, for Yankees have the GRIT.
They call us stupid "mud-sills," boys, and other curious names,
But we have logic in our guns, and more within our brains.

Chorus—Then march along, etc.

Ne'er let your hands grow weary, boys, while in this noble cause,
Till every rebel grounds his arms, submitting to our laws;
Till on a strong palmetto-limb, a curious fruit you see,
Jeff Davis to a strong hemp rope "a-dancing jubilee."

Chorus—Then march along, etc.

We now are in that "Dixie land," of which we often sing;
And now the music of that song shall from the musket ring.
We come with love within our hearts, but lead within our guns,
With sharp and tickling bayonets to make the rebels run.

Chorus—Then march along, etc.

Come, let us press with vigor on, and crush rebellion down,
Then union, peace, and plenty all, shall through the land abound.
Then wives and children left behind, and sweethearts brave and true
Will welcome back the Buckeye boys that put the rebels through.

Chorus—Then march along, etc.

Forty-Fourth Regiment, O. V. I.

This regiment rendezvoused at the fair grounds, near Springfield, Ohio, during the summer and autumn of 1861, and on the 14th of October, being fully organized, it moved, via Cincinnati, to Camp Piatt, West Virginia. On the morning of the 19th, having reached its destination, the regiment disembarked and pitched its tents for the first time on disputed ground. Two weeks after its arrival five companies were ordered to Gauley Bridge, and assisted in driving Floyd from his camp, and engaged in all the skirmishes during his retreat. Before their return two hundred men from the regiment crossed the Kanawha, marched to Platona, captured the place, and moved on against Colonel Jenkins, at Logan C. H. — but the colonel decamped before their arrival. After being absent six days they returned, bringing in seven prisoners, some horses, and one hundred head of cattle.

After these expeditions the regiment remained in camp for five months, quietly drilling. Winter quarters were built, and the men comfortably sheltered. During the month of November Captain John M. Bell, of Company K, with an orderly sergeant and six men, were drowned while crossing the river in a skiff, to relieve the picket on the other side. This sad accident cast a gloom over the whole regiment, and it was felt that a serious loss had been sustained. During the latter part of the winter companies A, B, and K were stationed on the opposite side of the river from Camp Piatt, for the better security of the camp.

On the 1st of May, 1862, the regiment moved up the river

to Gauley Bridge, and was brigaded with the Thirty-sixth and Forty-seventh O. V. I., under Colonel George Crook. The brigade moved to Lewisburg, and from there the Forty-fourth and another regiment penetrated as far as Dublin Depot, on the Jackson River Railroad, and destroyed a portion of the track. Hearing that a large force of rebels were trying to intercept their retreat, the two companies withdrew to Lewisburg, where the enemy appeared on the 23d of May, and was not only repulsed but routed, leaving most of their dead and wounded to fall into the hands of our troops, together with three pieces of artillery and many prisoners. They occupied the place for a short time after the fight, then fell back to Meadow Bluffs, where they encamped until the middle of August.

The Forty-fourth took up the line of march on the 15th of August, toward the Kanawha, halting a week at Camp Ewing, and then falling back to Camp Tompkins. A force of six thousand rebels was advancing against the four regiments in the valley, and on the 9th of September the two regiments on the right bank — the Forty-fourth and another — were attacked, and fell back on Gauley, where a stand was made until the teams could be removed from danger, when the retreat began in earnest. The Forty fourth marched in the rear all day and nearly all night, covering the retreating column until it reached Camp Piatt. The national forces fell back upon Charleston, and on the 13th the rebels made the attack and were firmly met. Superior numbers finally forced the Union lines back, but every foot of ground was hotly contested. Our forces withdrew across a deep tributary of the Kanawha, and with a few blows of an ax severed the hawsers that held the suspension bridge, and it fell with a crash into the stream. The retreat now continued in safety to Racine, on the Ohio River, and from that place the troops were taken by steamer to Point Pleasant. Transportation was procured, and they were sent forward into Kentucky. They encamped some time at Covington, watching the movements of Kirby Smith, and on his retreat they pursued as far as Lexington, where they were ordered into camp and assigned to the Second Brigade, Second Division, Army of Kentucky, commanded by General Gordon Granger. The regiment was actively engaged in scouting, taking in its field of operations Richmond and Danville.

On the 20th of December the regiment returned to Frankfort and was mounted, and from that time, until Burnside's advance into Tennessee, there was but little rest for man or beast. The men almost lived in the saddle. It was continual advance and retreat, with almost constant skirmishing. The regiment partook in the engagement of Dunstan's Hill, charging the rebels and contributing materially to their rout. The regiment was frequently engaged in chasing John Morgan, though with not very satisfactory results, as he generally proved the faster rider.

When General Burnside made his advance into Tennessee the Forty-fourth was dismounted and accompanied him. It can claim equality with any other regiment of all that took part in this expedition. Finally, falling back on Knoxville, and throwing up fortifications, it lay in the wet, chilly ditches day and night When the rebels retreated the regiment pursued, and on its return went into camp at Strawberry Plains.

On the 1st of January, 1864, the proposal to re-enlist was made to the regiment, accompanied by the promise that they should be armed and mounted as cavalry. Before the 5th — out of six hundred men — five hundred and fifty had re-enlisted. On the 7th they marched for Camp Nelson, Kentucky, and on the 21st took cars for Cincinnati, where they arrived the next day, and were quartered in the Fifth Street Bazaar, erected for the Sanitary Fair. Here they were obliged to wait until muster-out and muster in rolls could be made out. This was at last accomplished, and the men were mustered by the 29th, and started on a special train for Springfield. Their arrival was heralded by the booming of cannon, and they were received with joyous shouts and enthusiastic greetings. In a few days the men were paid off and furloughed, and when they again assembled it was under the name of the Eighth Ohio Cavalry, of which the following is a brief sketch :

On the 28th of March, 1864, the veterans and recruits of the Forty-fourth Ohio Infantry were ordered to report at Camp Dennison, where they went without delay, and were organized into the Eighth Ohio Cavalry. On the 26th of April six companies — not mounted — were ordered to Charleston, West Virginia, and on the 8th of May the detachment remaining in camp was ordered to march to Cincinnati, to be transported thence by steamer to Charleston. On the 10th they left camp for Cincinnati, mounted on horseback, with no rein but a rope, and each man leading two or three horses. They arrived in the city a little after noon, in a drenching rain, and by dark were on the boat on their way up the river. On the second morning after they started they landed at Guyandotte, and again mounting barebacked rode to Charleston, arriving on the 14th, very much exhausted.

At Charleston the Eighth was armed with carbines and drew-saddles, and on the 29th of May marched for Lewisburg, where they arrived on the 1st of June, and on the 3d started with Averill on the Lynchburg raid. The regiment was first assigned to General Duffie's brigade, and afterwards to Colonel Schoonmaker's Fourteenth Pennsylvania Cavalry. On the 9th they arrived at Staunton, formed a junction with General Hunter, and on the 13th moved to Buchannon, where they rested until the 15th. They had frequent skirmishes, doing good service, until they arrived at White Sulphur Springs, where they arrived on the 24th, and from thence moved to Beverly, arriving at noon on the 30th, having marched six hundred miles. On the 23d of August companies C, H, and K — eighty men in all — were surprised and captured at Huttonsville. The men were released, but all their equipments and horses taken by the rebels. Soon after Company A was captured, and the captain and some of the men taken to Richmond. About the 1st of December Colonel Moore joined the regiment. They were at Winchester, fought at Fisher's Hill, and barely escaped at Cedar Creek. On the 11th of January the rebels surprised the camp, killing and wounding twenty-five, and capturing five hundred and seventy men and eight officers. They were taken to Libby Prison, but afterwards paroled at Columbus, Ohio, and in August were mustered out of the service at Camp Dennison.

Tenth Ohio Battery.

This battery was organized at Xenia, Ohio, on the 9th of January, 1862, and was mustered into service on the 3d of March. It was ordered to St. Louis, Missouri, and on the 4th of April moved up the Tennessee River to Pittsburg Landing, where it arrived on the 9th. On the 13th it received some twenty men from the Thirteenth Ohio Battery.

With the rest of the army the Tenth moved upon Corinth, but during the siege it was held in reserve. The Battery remained at Corinth from the 25th of June to the middle of September. It then moved to Iuka, and remained at that post on garrison duty.

While at Iuka orders were received to procure forage from the country. A portion of the men, under command of Lieutenant Grossekoff, while in the performance of this duty, were attacked by Roddy's rebel cavalry, at a point five miles below Iuka, and lost, by capture, privates William F. Nixon, Richard Sparrow, John W. Shoemaker, Abe Hulsizer, and William Leslie. These men were taken to southern prisons, and afterward exchanged.

On the 1st of October the Battery moved toward Corinth, and on the 2d it passed through the town and halted for the night at a fort southwest of it. On the morning of the 3d it was ordered to take position near the Chewalla Road, where it crossed the Memphis Railroad. From this place the Battery was ordered into position north of Corinth. About eleven o'clock, on the morning of the 4th, the rebel lines advanced. The Battery opened with shell, and one piece was disabled after the first fire, by a shell getting fast half way down. Two shells were fired by each of the other three pieces, and canister — doubled — was used to the direct front. The ground was favorable for canister practice, and at each fire gaps of twenty, thirty, and forty feet wide were cut into the advancing columns. The Battery stopped three columns of rebels. Each piece was pouring out from eighteen to twenty rounds per minute, when the order was given to retire. The rebels had advanced on the right, and the Battery was without the support of a single musket, right or left. The pintle-key of the third piece had to be tied to its place, and the corporal, while tying it, discovered that the sponge-bucket was left. He called out, "Get the bucket, No. 2!" George S. Wright, a boy of eighteen, acting as No. 1, ran back towards the rebels, picked up the bucket when they were not more than twenty-five rods from him, and returned with it to the gun.

As fast as the pieces were limbered they went off at a gallop. They were unlimbered east of the town and south of the Decatur Railroad, but only for a moment, when they were returned to a point about one hundred yards in rear of the former position. In a short time the enemy retired. The Battery lost only three men wounded. A number of horses were also wounded, including those belonging to Captain White and the bugler. It pursued the enemy as far as Ripley, and then returned to Corinth.

In the latter part of October the Battery received forty men from an Iowa brigade, but about twenty of them were returned. In November it moved to Grand Junction, and marched with the army into Mississippi, along the Mississippi Central Railroad.

After the surrender of Holly Springs, the Battery returned to that point, and formed part of the garrison. It removed from there to Lafayette, and from Lafayette to Memphis On the 21st of January it moved to Milliken's Bend, and from there to Lake Providence. In April it returned to Milliken's Bend, and moved from there to Grand Gulf.

On May the 14th, while the Tenth was at Grand Gulf, General Dwight, of General Banks' army, arrived on a gunboat, on his way to General Grant's head quarters — then near Black River. There being no cavalry at the post, Captain White was detailed with thirty men of the Battery to act as an escort to the general. They left Grand Gulf May 16th, and rode all night. The battle of Champion Hills being in progress, they were unable to reach General Grant's head-quarters, and were compelled to remain on the road in their saddles until two o'clock in the morning of the 18th, without rations for themselves or forage for the horses. At six o'clock in the morning, when General McPherson's head quarters were reached, the men were completely exhausted, and the horses unfit for further travel.

Later in the day the escort commenced its return to Grand Gulf, having supplied themselves with horses and mules taken from citizens. On its march through the woods the escort ran into a brigade of Pemberton's rebel army, that had been cut off from the main force. Captain White so maneuvered his men as to make the rebels believe he had a large force of cavalry, and actually succeeded in capturing thirty-four rebels. On returning to camp some of the men of the escort were asleep in their saddles

On the 13th of June the Battery reached Vicksburg, and on the 18th it was posted in Fort Ransom. On the next day one of the guns broke its axle, and another its stock, leaving but two serviceable pieces. On the night of the 19th Quartermaster McPherson, with the wagon-master and Artificer Cline, procured another carriage from near the rebel lines, cutting it out, as it were, under fire of the rebel guns. On the 20th artificers Cline and Wheeler, while under fire from the enemy's sharp shooters, repaired the disabled guns.

The Battery remained in the fort until the latter part of June. It then moved to Big Black, and after the surrender of Vicksburg it marched to Jackson. As soon as it arrived it was ordered back to Champion Hills, to guard the communications. On the 28th of July the Battery entered Vicksburg.

In August — of seventy-two men present — only seventeen were reported for duty. The men were worn out with sickness and service. The well men did guard duty, took care of seventy horses and mules, went for forage and rations, hauled water, fixed shades, and at night cared for their sick comrades.

The garrison went into winter quarters on the bluffs south of Vicksburg — one section was sent to Red Bone Church, twelve miles south of Vicksburg; the other put on duty at Hall's Ferry Road.

During the winter the Battery received about ninety recruits. Thirty two men out of fifty four, who were eligible, re-enlisted, and on the 8th of April, 1864, the Battery, with one hundred and fifty men for duty, left Vicksburg for Cairo. The Battery was attacked on its way up the river by a portion of Forrest's forces, but it used its guns effectually, and drove off the rebels. Fort Pillow was held by the enemy. The Battery returned to Memphis, and remained on duty there until the latter part of April, when it moved to Cairo. The veterans proceeded to Ohio and were furloughed.

The Morgan raid through Kentucky prevented the veterans from joining their battery until the 23d of June. They were retained at Louisville, Kentucky. At Cairo the Battery received a new outfit. On the 9th of May it moved to Paducah, and on the 13th started up the Tennessee. On the morning of the 14th it disembarked at Clifton, and on the 16th began the march to Acworth, Georgia. The distance was about five hundred miles. The march occupied twenty-four days, and the route lay through Pulaski, Huntsville, Decatur, Rome, and Kingston. The weather was very warm, but the Battery did not lose a man.

At Acworth the Tenth was placed in the Fourth Division of the Seventeenth Army Corps. On the 10th of June it took position at the front, and with the exception of the Fourth of July, was engaged every day for a month, most of the time in front of Kennesaw Mountain, but most severely at Nickojack Creek. On the 12th of July it returned to Kennesaw, and after remaining a few days took position at Marietta, where it formed a part of the garrison until November.

During Hood's march in October the Battery was ordered out frequently, but it was engaged only once. About the last of October the horses and mules were turned over, and the Battery was ordered to Nashville. About seven recruits were received from Ohio. On the 2d of November the Battery left Marietta, and after more than a week's detention at Chattanooga, it procured transportation, and arrived at Nashville on the 14th. It was posted at Camp Barry, and about the middle of November the majority of the men in the Battery were sent about thirty miles up the Cumberland to get timber for winter quarters. They did not return until the 1st of December.

When Hood threatened Nashville the Battery was posted at Fort Gillen, but it was not called into action. About the last of December the Battery moved to Camp Barry, and erected winter quarters. The men were armed with muskets, and for two months acted as infantry.

On the 13th of March, 1865, the Fourth and Tenth Ohio batteries were consolidated, and sixty-four men were thus added to the Tenth, which retained its name and organization. The men from the Fourth were mostly Germans. About the 1st of April the Battery was ordered to East Tennessee, and after guarding the post of Sweetwater for two weeks, it was ordered to Loudon, where it remained until orders to muster out were received.

The Battery was mustered out at Camp Dennison on the 17th of July, 1865, and paid off and discharged on the 21st. The names of the officers were as follows:

Captains — H. Berlace White, Francis Seaman, J. R. Crain.

Lieutenants — W. F. Bardwell, Ambrose A. Blount, Edward Groosekoff, W. L. Newcomb, Joseph B Gage, James E Gilmore, George Kleder, Lanson Zane, James E. Bonticon, Samuel A. Galbreath.

TENTH OHIO BATTERY REUNION.

From Xenia Torchlight, October 6, 1883.

The gallant old Tenth Ohio Battery met in reunion at Cedarville, Ohio, October 3d and 4th, to the number of thirty-two, and had indeed a pleasant time and a happy reunion. In the evening, October 3d, they partook of a grand supper — grandly prepared by the good citizens of Cedarville. The Cedarville Brass Band discoursed splendid music. The large hall —

Mitchell's — was literally packed. After supper the exercises were as follows:
1. Welcome address, by Professor Van Fossen.
2. Response, by Comrade Greene.
3. Letters were read from absent members by Lieutenant J. B. Gage; also a history of the Battery's part in the battle of Corinth.
4. Resolutions and reading "Sheridan's Ride," and "A District School," by Comrade Greene.
5. A short address by Comrade Ramsey. Mr. I. S. Owens, of the Seventy-fourth, was introduced, and was proceeding to make some remarks, when it was announced that Marshal Harris had been shot on the street, which produced so much excitement that further proceedings were dispensed with, and the assembly adjourned.

A meeting was held in Firemen Hall, at 9:00 A. M., October 4th, when other business was transacted and other letters were read by Lieutenant J. B. Gage. Officers were then elected for the ensuing year, namely, all the former officers, with the addition of Billy Williams as recording secretary. The members then repaired to the street, where a picture of the Battery was taken by Artist Biddle, of Xenia. At one o'clock the meeting re assembled, and transacted other business. A resolution was passed fixing the time for next meeting the first Wednesday in October, at West Liberty, Ohio. The meeting then adjourned.

By request of members the roll was called, after which the letters were read by Lieutenant J. B. Gage, one from Lieutenant Mong, after which a resolution, by Lieutenant Gage, as folows:

That the members of the Tenth Ohio Battery, assembled at its second reunion, held at Cedarville, Ohio, October 3 and 4, 1883, regret that Lieutenant W. J. Mong could not be present at the reunion, and thank him for his letter and for the copy of the company's receipt for clothing forwarded by him, and extend to him a special invitation to be present at the next reunion.

Resolved, That a copy of this resolution be forwarded to Lieutenant W. J. Mong, at Minerva, Stark County, Ohio.

RESOLUTIONS.

At a meeting of the Tenth Ohio Battery, held at Cedarville, Ohio, October 3 and 4, 1883, the following preamble and resolutions were adopted:

WHEREAS, The citizens of Cedarville — and especially the ladies thereof — have given to the members of the Tenth Ohio Battery, at its second reunion, held at Cedarville, Ohio, October 3 and 4, 1883, cordial and friendly greeting; therefore, be it

Resolved, That we extend to them our heart-felt thanks, and to Miss Blake and Miss Hudson we are especially under obligations for the button-hole bouquets, and also the pleasure of having them pinned on by such lovely young ladies.

WHEREAS, Death has taken from our ranks Samuel A. Barr, John W. Shoemaker, Thomas Fryer, Fred Maurer, and James Worthington, friends and comrades of the war; be it

Resolved, That we grieve in the death of these comrades, and extend to the families of the deceased our sincere sympathy in their loss.

That a copy of this resolution be forwarded to the families of each of the members who have passed to rest, and that it be published in the *Cedarville Herald* and *Xenia Torchlight*.

MEMBERS PRESENT.

Lieutenant J. B. Gage, Brooklyn, New York; William A. Byrd, Alconey, Miami County, Ohio; Reese Underwood, West Liberty, Ohio; J. B. Crain, Jamestown, Ohio; John W. Randall, Guard, O. P.; Nathan Wike, Springfield, Ohio; George L. Johnston, La Fontaine, Indiana; Dinsmore Randall, Springfield, Ohio; Samuel J. Knott, Springfield, Ohio; Walter A. Keith,

West Liberty, Ohio; William Myers, Springfield, Ohio; Jacob M. Beemer, Cedarville, Ohio; P. G. Clevell, Dayton, Ohio; William H. Elwell, Springfield, Ohio; Samuel Galbreath, Cedarville, Ohio; G. N. Randall, Cedarville, Ohio; Frank Dillmore, Soldiers' Home, Dayton, Ohio; Edward Spencer, Cedarville, Ohio; G. N. Shrods, Cedarville, Ohio; L. N. Luce, Mt. Etna, Huntington County, Indiana; C. N. Ramsey, Washington C. H., Ohio; Pellegro Leuchesey, Madison County, Ohio; John A. Mitchell, Cedarville, Ohio; James Judy, Bloomington, Fayette County, Ohio; George S. Wright, Mad River P. O., Clark County, Ohio; Joseph W. Randall, Cedarville, Ohio; O. V. Flora, Madison, Indiana; William K. Byrd, Xenia, Ohio; Joseph Cline, Cedarville, Ohio.

Others were present who did not register their names.

One Hundred and Fifty-Fourth O. V. I.

The One Hundred and Fifty-fourth Regiment, Ohio Volunteer Infantry, National Guards, was formed by consolidating the twenty-sixth and sixtieth battalions of Ohio National Guards. It was organized at Camp Dennison, and was mustered into the service on the 9th of May, 1864, with an aggregate of eight hundred and forty two men. Colonel, Robert Stevenson, Assistant Surgeon, Leigh McClung, Quartermaster, A. L. Trader. Several of the line officers, non-commissioned officers, and many of the privates had seen service in other organizations.

On the 12th of May the regiment proceeded, via Columbus and Bellaire, to New Creek, West Virginia, arriving on the evening of the 14th. The next day — in one of the most violent storms of the season — it laid out its camp and pitched its tents. On the 22d Company F was ordered to Piedmont, West Virginia, where it remained until the regiment started for Ohio for muster-out.

The One Hundred and Fifty-fourth performed guard, picket, and escort duty until the 29th of May, when one company moved to Youghiogheny Bridge, and the remaining eight companies to Greenland Gap. Scouting parties were out almost constantly, and on the 4th of June a detachment of the regiment had a skirmish with McNeil's battalion, near Moorfield, in which the rebels were defeated.

About the 12th of June three hundred men from the One Hundred and Fifty-fourth, with a cavalry force, were engaged in a ten-day's scout. Skirmishing was frequent, but the enemy kept so securely in the mountains that only three rebels were captured in the ten days. On the 23d another scout — of one hundred men and a small force of cavalry — was ordered out, with three days' rations, but no enemy was discovered.

On the Fourth of July the regiment fell back to New Creek, expecting an attack, but the enemy having retired it returned again to Greenland Gap, arriving on the 7th. Company H — until this time at Oakland — joined the regiment at New Creek, and returned with it to the Gap. On the 25th the regiment again fell back to New Creek, and Greenland Gap ceased to be held as a military post.

On the 4th of August the rebels, under McCausland and Bradley Johnson, attacked the force at New Creek, but at night they were compelled to withdraw, leaving their killed and wounded on the field.

On the 10th of August a detachment of the One Hundred and Fifty-fourth proceeded to Camp Chase, in charge of prisoners, and remained there until the regiment returned to the state. On the evening of the 22d the regiment started for Ohio, arriving at Camp Chase on the 27th, where it was mustered out of the service on the 1st of September, 1864.

Fifty-Fourth O. V. I.

Recruiting for this regiment began in the latter part of the summer of 1861, the place of rendezvous being Camp Dennison, where the regiment was organized and drilled during the fall and winter of 1861. The men composing this command were from the counties of Allen, Auglaize, Butler, Cuyahoga, Fayette, Greene, Hamilton, Logan, and Preble.

On the 17th of February, 1862, the regiment went into the field with an aggregate of eight hundred and fifty men. The Fifty-fourth reached Paducah, Kentucky, February 20, 1862, and was assigned to a brigade commanded by General Sherman. On the 6th of March the command ascended the Tennessee River, disembarked at Pittsburg Landing, and camped near Shiloh Church. On the 6th of April the regiment engaged in the battle of Pittsburg Landing, its position being on the extreme left of the army; but on the second day it was assigned a new position, near the center of the line. In the two days' fighting the regiment lost one hundred and ninety-eight men killed, wounded, and missing. On the 29th of April the regiment moved upon Corinth, skirmishing severely at Russell House, May 17th, and engaging in the movement upon the works at Corinth, May 31st.

On the morning of the evacuation the Fifty-fourth was among the first organized bodies of troops to enter the town. The regimental colors were unfurled from a public building, and the regiment was designated to perform provost duty — the commanding officer of the regiment being appointed commandant of the post of Corinth. The regiment moved with the army to La Grange, Tennessee, and from there to Holly Springs, Mississippi, and then returned to Corinth. Soon after it again marched to Holly Springs; from there to Moscow, Tennessee, and thence to Memphis, where it arrived July 21, 1862.

During the summer the regiment was engaged in several short expeditions, and on the 26th of November it moved with the army toward Jackson, Mississippi, by way of Holly Springs. The regiment soon returned to Memphis, and with a portion of the army under General Sherman moved down the Mississippi, and went into position before the enemy's lines at Chickasaw Bayou. It was engaged in the assault on the rebel works December 28th and 29th, with a loss of twenty men killed and wounded. On the 1st of January, 1863, the regiment withdrew, ascended the Mississippi and Arkansas rivers, and engaged in the assault and capture of Arkansas Post. The Fifty-fourth again descended the Mississippi River, and disembarked at Young's Point, Louisiana. Here it was employed in digging a canal, and in other demonstrations connected with the Vicksburg campaign, which resulted in the rescue of the fleet of gunboats which was about to be abandoned and destroyed.

On the 6th of May the regiment began its march to the rear of Vicksburg, by way of Grand Gulf, and was engaged in the battles of Champion Hills and Black Ridge. It was engaged in a general assault on the enemy's works in the rear of Vicksburg, on the 19th and 22d of June, losing in the engagements forty-seven killed and wounded. It was continually in skirmishing and fatigue duty during the siege of Vicksburg, except for six days, which were consumed in a march of observation toward Jackson, Mississippi.

After the fall of Vicksburg the Fifty-fourth moved with the army upon Jackson, Mississippi, and was constantly engaged in skirmishing from the 9th to the 14th of July. After the capture of Jackson the regiment returned to Vicksburg, and remained until October, 1863, when, forming a part of the Fifteenth Army Corps, it ascended the Mississippi River to Memphis, and from there proceeded to Chattanooga. It was engaged in the battle of Missionary Ridge, November 26th, and the next day marched to the relief of the garrison at Knoxville, Tennessee. It pursued the enemy's wagon-train from Knoxville through the south-eastern portion of Tennessee, and a short distance into North Carolina, and then returned to Chattanooga, and moved thence to Larkinsville, Alabama, where it went into winter quarters, January 12, 1864.

The regiment was mustered into the service as a veteran organization on the 22d of January, and at once started to Ohio on furlough. It returned to camp in April, with an addition of two hundred recruits, and entered on the Atlanta campaign, on the 1st of May. It participated in a general engagement at Resaca and Dallas, and in a severe skirmish at New Hope Church, June 6th and 7th. It was in the general assault upon Kennesaw Mountain, June 27th, losing twenty-eight killed and wounded; was engaged in a severe skirmish at Nickojack Creek, July 3d, losing thirteen killed and wounded, and was in a battle on the east side of Atlanta, July 21st and 22d, sustaining a loss of ninety-four killed, wounded, and missing. The Fifty-fourth lost eight men killed and wounded at Ezra Chapel, on the 28th of July, and from the 29th of July to the 27th of August it was almost continually engaged in skirmishing before the works of Atlanta. It was in a heavy skirmish at Jonesboro, August 30th, and in a general action at the same place the two days immediately following.

After resting a few weeks in camp near Atlanta, the regiment started in pursuit of Hood, and followed him within sixty miles of Chattanooga, and from there to Gadsden, Alabama, when it returned to Atlanta, and prepared for the march to

Savannah. The Fifty fourth started on that wonderful march on the 15th of November, and on the 15th of December was engaged in the assault and capture of Fort McAllister, near Savannah. The regiment assisted in the destruction of the Gulf Railroad, toward the Altamaha River, and on the 7th of January, 1865, marched into Savannah.

After a rest of several weeks it moved with the army on the march through the Carolinas, skirmishing at the crossing of the South Edisto and North Edisto rivers, on the 10th and 12th of February, respectively. It was closely engaged in the vicinity of Columbia, and participated in its last battle at Bentonsville, North Carolina, March 21, 1865. The regiment marched to Richmond, Virginia, and from there to Washington City, where it took part in the grand review of the Western Army. On the 2d of June it was transported by railroad and steamboat to Louisville, Kentucky, and after remaining two weeks there it proceeded to Little Rock, Arkansas, and there performed garrison duty until August 15, 1865, when it was mustered out.

The regiment returned to Camp Dennison, Ohio, where it received final pay, and was disbanded on the 24th of August, 1865. The aggregate strength of the regiment at muster-out was two hundred and fifty five — twenty four officers, and two hundred and thirty-one men. It marched during its term of service a distance of three thousand six hundred and eighty-two miles, participated in four sieges, ninety-seven skirmishes, fifteen general engagements, and sustained a loss of five hundred and six men killed, wounded, and missing.

Seventeenth O. V. I.

Dr. John Turnbull, of Bellbrook, Ohio, deserves a notice in this work. He enlisted as private in Company A, Seventeenth Regiment, O. V. I., April, 1861; served four months in said regiment, and afterward as acting assistant surgeon of the Sixty-fifth Regiment, O. V. I., nearly one year; and lastly as assistant surgeon of the One Hundred and Fifth Regiment, O. V. I.

Thirty-Fourth O. V. I.

This regiment was organized at Camp Lucas, Clermont County — Company F being largely composed of men from Greene County, therefore I give it a place in this work — during the months of July and August, 1861, the first detachment entering camp July 15th, and the first regular companies, under captains Broadwell and Evans, July 21st.

On the morning of September 1st it moved to Camp Dennison, and was there prepared for the field, adopting as its uniform — a license allowable at the early period of the war — a light-blue Zouave dress. In compliment to their colonel the name of "Piatt Zouaves" was adopted.

The regiment left Camp Dennison on the 15th of September, 1861, for western Virginia, with full ranks, and arrived at Camp Enyart, on the Kanawha River, on the 20th of the same month. On the 25th it fought its first battle, in a gap near Chapmanville, Logan County, Virginia, whipping a Virginia regiment, inflicting considerable loss to the rebels in men, and badly wounding their commander, Colonel Davis. The loss of the Thirty-fourth was one killed and eight wounded. During the remainder of the autumn the regiment was engaged in the arduous duty of guarding the rear of General Rosencranz' army, and the counties of Cabell, Putnam, Mason, Wayne, and Logan were kept pretty free from guerrillas, by continual scouting.

In March, 1862, the Thirty-fourth was ordered to Gauley Bridge, to join General Cox in his demonstration on the Virginia and Tennessee Railroad. The regiment participated in the battle of Princeton, on the 17th and 18th of May, losing several men. Lieutenant Peck and Peters were wounded, and Captain O. P. Evans taken prisoner. Humphrey Marshall commanded the rebels.

When General Cox was ordered to join General McClellan, in August, 1862, there were six regiments left to guard the Kanawha Valley. The Thirty-fourth and Thirty-seventh held the outposts at Fayetteville, where, on the morning of September 10th, they were attacked by a rebel force under General Loring, ten thousand strong. With the aid of breastworks, previously constructed by General Scammon, two two-pound brass field-pieces, and four six-pound mountain howitzers, the position was held until midnight, when the place was evacuated. Part of the time the Thirty-fourth was in the open field, and repeatedly charged on the enemy. Its loss was necessarily heavy. Of six companies engaged—the other four, under Major Franklin, being on a scout—the loss was one hundred and thirty, or fully one third. One half of the officers were either killed or wounded. Cutting their way out under a heavy fire, the national troops fell back towards the Kanawha River, made a stand at Cotton Mountain the next day, and Charleston on the 12th, where a severe engagement took place. From this point the entire Federal force fell back to Point Pleasant, leaving the entire valley in the hands of rebels. In October General Cox returned with his command, when another advance was made, and the valley regained. From this time, until May, 1863, nothing of moment occurred to vary the monotony of garrison duty. During May the regiment was furnished with horses, and transformed into mounted rifles.

On the 13th of July, 1863, an expedition, consisting of the Thirty-fourth, two companies of the First, and seven companies of the Second Virginia Cavalry, under command of Colonel Toland, made a demonstration on the Virginia and Tennessee

Railroad, striking it on the evening of the 18th, at Wytheville. A desperate fight ensued, the enemy occupying the house, barns, yards, etc., on a slight elevation to the rear of the town. About dark the national forces succeeded in capturing the enemy's artillery, and driving him in all directions. Captain Delaney, commanding First Virginia, was killed, and Colonel Powell, Second Virginia, badly wounded. The Thirty-fourth Ohio lost four killed—including Colonel Toland—thirteen wounded, and thirty three missing. Colonel Toland was shot from a window of a house in his immediate vicinity, while seated on his horse, engaged in giving orders, surrounded by a few of his staff. The ball passed through his left breast. The colonel did not fall from his horse, but caught the mane with his right hand, when his orderly, who was about fifty yards distant from him, ran and caught him before he had time to reach the ground. With his last breath he requested that his horse and sword be sent to his mother.

The brigade left Camp Piatt with nearly one thousand men; marched six hundred and fifty two miles in eleven days, traversing some of the highest mountains in West Virginia, capturing over two hundred and fifty horses, and three hundred and sixty prisoners, two pieces of artillery, and a large amount of commission stores; destroyed between three and five thousand stand of arms, a bridge of importance, and partially burned one of the wealthiest cities in Virginia Upon the fall of Colonel Toland, the command devolved upon Lieutenant Colonel Franklin, who decided on a retrograde movement. This he found it difficult to execute, from the fact that the rebel General Mc-Causland had blockaded the roads in the most effectual manner. For several days the command was moving in the mountains, destitute of food for themselves or fodder for their horses, and continually harrassed by rebel cavalry. On the day previous to the arrival of the regiment at Wytheville, Company C, acting as rear guard, was attacked by a superior force of rebel cavalry. A number were killed and wounded, and Captain Cutler and fifteen men were taken prisoners. Several expeditions, under General Duffie — who had assumed command of the Kanawha Cavalry — to Lewisburg and vicinity, completed this year's campaign.

In January, 1864, about two thirds of the regiment reenlisted as veterans. On the 29th of April, 1864, the regiment was divided into two detachments. The mounted portion was to operate with the cavalry, under General Averill; the dismounted with the Thirty-sixth Ohio Volunteer Infantry, in General Crook's division of infantry. On the 1st of May, 1864, the second expedition, for the destruction of the Virginia and Tennessee Railroad, left Charleston. On the 9th the cavalry arrived at Wytheville, encountered the rebels under General Morgan, were repulsed, and were compelled to fall back with considerable loss. The infantry under General Crook were more successful. On the same day that Averill was defeated Crook achieved a solid victory over General Jenkins, at Cloyd Mountain, near Dublin Depot, which was captured the same evening.

On the day following the enemy was again encountered and defeated at the railroad bridge, over New River, and the bridge totally destroyed. From this point the command returned to Meadow Bluffs, crossing Salt Pond, and Peters Mountains, and the Greenbrier River, arriving at their destination on the 19th of May, completing a distance of four hundred miles marched during the month. From Meadow Bluffs the Thirty-fourth started to join General Hunter, at Staunton, in the Shenandoah Valley, passing through White Sulphur Springs, Callahan's Stand, and crossing Panther Gap Mountain, where a skirmish ensued.

On the 5th of June the regiment reached Goshen, on the Virginia Central Railroad, and skirmished with a body of cavalry at Cow Pasture River. The day after the rebels were met at Buffalo Gap, in a position secure from attack, but General Hayes' brigade succeeded in flanking and driving them out of it. Staunton was reached on the 8th of June, where the Thirty-fourth made its final preparations to join General Hunter on his disastrous raid to Lynchburg. General Hunter, now re-enforced by Generals Crook, Averill, and Duffie, left Staunton on the 9th, and passing through Brownsburg reached Lexington on the 11th. The evening of the 14th found the regiment at Buckhannon, on the James River, at which point a few shots were exchanged with a small rebel force that had been driven out of Lexington. Crossing the Blue Ridge, near the Peaks of Otter, the town of Liberty was reached on the 16th, when another skirmish occurred. From this point General Crook's command, with the dismounted members of the Thirty-fourth, were sent on a flanking expedition across the James, for the purpose of attacking Lynchburg in the rear, the cavalry on the left to make a diversion in their favor. The attack was made late in the afternoon of the 18th of June, was partly successful, and in the opinion of the Thirty-fourth, would have been entirely so had General Crook been allowed to occupy the city that night, according to his wish, but orders from his superior officers forbade it. The enemy were re-enforced that night by about twenty thousand men, from the vicinity of Richmond, under the command of General Early, which, of course, so strengthened the city that it was impossible, with the small and illy-appointed force under General Hunter, to cope with the rebels The situation was fully developed early the next morning, by a fierce cannonade from the rebels, which was promptly replied to by the national forces. In the afternoon an engagement occurred in which the Thirty-fourth severely suffered. The retreat of the national forces commenced at dark, on the 19th of June. The rear, heavily pressed by the pursuing enemy, the second skirmish occurred at Liberty. At Salem, on the 21st, while the artillery of Hunter's command was passing through a narrow defile, totally unsupported, a party of rebels made a sudden descent from the hills, and dispersing the drivers and gunners, commenced the work of destruction by shooting horses, cutting spokes and harness, and blowing up caissons. The mounted portion of the Thirty-fourth being a few miles in the rear, hurried to the scene of action, dismounted, and with Lieutenant Colonel Shaw as their leader, encountered the rebels. After a sharp fight the rebels were driven off, and the artillery regained. The retreat was continued. Big and Little Sewell mountains were crossed, and Charleston reached on the 1st of July, where the exhausted, ragged, and starved troops were permitted to rest. Thus ended this most disastrous expedition. The constant skirmishing, the starved bodies, and blistered feet of those who participated in it, made "Hunter's retreat from Lynchburg" an event long to be remembered.

The Thirty-fourth lay at Charleston on the 10th of July, when it embarked on transports for Parkersburg. A day or two previous to this move the whole regiment was dismounted, and horses and equipments turned over to the cavalry. From Parkersburg the regiment moved by rail to Martinsburg, arriving there on the 14th of July, 1864. The regiment was now in the Shenandoah Valley. On the 20th of July, while General Crook, with his main force and the Sixth and Nineteenth corps were pressing Early back on Winchester, General Duval's brigade, of which the Thirty-fourth was a part, attempted to occupy the place in advance of the rebels, by a forced march from Martinsburg. Early, anticipating the movement, had sent forward his old division, under General Ramseur, to check it. The national force, only twelve hundred strong, met and attacked the rebels two miles from Winchester, completely routing them, capturing their artillery, and killing and wounding all their brigade commanders. The loss of the Thirty-fourth was ten killed and twenty wounded.

Four days later occurred the fourth battle of Winchester, in which General Early, taking advantage of the absence of the Sixth and Nineteenth corps, overwhelmed General Crook — the latter, however, effecting an orderly retreat with the loss of only a few wagons. In this battle General Duval's brigade had the honor of bringing up the rear, and the Thirty-fourth suffered severely, losing their commander, Lieutenant Colonel Shaw, a cool, determined soldier and Christian. He was struck in the abdomen by a musket-ball, and was borne from the field by a few faithful men of his regiment, placed in an ambulance, and carried eleven miles distant, to a place called Bunker Hill, where he died. His last words were, "Welcome, welcome death!" Captain G. W. McKay was wounded, about the same time, in the leg, and would have fallen into the hands of the enemy, but for the heroic devotions of some of his men, who carried him on a litter, fifteen miles, to Sandy Hook, Maryland, where he died. The command of the regiment devolved upon Captain S. R. S. West, who fully sustained his reputation as a brave and gallant officer.

The next day, July 25th, another stand was made at Martinsburg, the Thirty-fourth being the last regiment to leave the field, which it did under a galling fire. The time of the regiment, between the 25th of July and the 3d of September, was occupied as follows: July 26th, forded the Potomac at Williamsport; 27th, marched to Sandy Hook, Maryland, opposite Harper's Ferry; 28th, crossed the Potomac at Halltown; 30th, re-crossed to Sandy Hook; 31st, marched through Middletown, towards Pennsylvania state line. August 1st, continued the march to Wolfville, Maryland; 3d, returned by same road to Frederick City, Maryland, and encamped on the Monocacy;

6th, returned to Harper's Ferry; 8th, re-crossed the Potomac, and moved in the direction of Halltown; 10th, reached Berryville, Virginia; 11th, marched in line of battle in the direction of Port Royal — heavy skirmishing with Early, who was falling back on Fishers Hill; 12th, reached Cedar Creek, found the enemy had burned the bridge, and was intrenched on the south bank of the stream. The Thirty fourth lay here until the evening of the 17th, skirmishing heavily in the meantime. It then fell back, marching all night, passing through Winchester, and camping at Berryville early next morning.

The 20th of August found the Thirty-fourth at Charlestown, with the enemy close in its rear. In the expectation of an attack breastworks were thrown up, but after waiting in vain until ten o'clock at night, the regiment fell back to Halltown. The enemy still followed, and taking a position in the immediate front of the regiment, heavy skirmishing ensued until the 27th, when they withdrew, to demonstrate on the upper Potomac.

On the day following the Thirty-fourth again occupied Charlestown, where the regimental officers were busily engaged making up the necessary papers for discharge of the non-veterans, who, on the morning of the 3d of September, proceeded to Columbus, Ohio, in charge of Captain West. During the few months previous to this time the Thirty fourth had been largely re-enforced by new recruits. Counting the veterans and the men of 1862 it still numbered between four and five hundred, present and absent. On the evening of the day on which the non-veterans left, the regiment participated in the battle of Berryville; the non-veterans were near enough to hear the booming of cannon. The enemy fell back to Winchester and Bunker Hill. The Thirty-fourth marched to Summit Point, and lay in camp until the morning of the 19th of September, the day on which occurred Sheridan's famous battle of Winchester, it being the third time the regiment had fought over nearly the same ground. It suffered terribly that day, the color guard having no less than six men, in quick succession, killed and wounded, while carrying the flag. It was finally brought through safe by George Rynals, of Company A. All know the result of that glorious battle, and remember Sheridan's celebrated dispatch, commencing, "I am moving up the valley to-night." In accordance with this announcement, the next evening found the regiment at Cedar Creek, where it lay until the 22d, when occurred the battle of Fishers Hill. Here, again, by the excellent management of General George Crook, the enemy was successfully flanked, which resulted in his total rout and the capture of all his artillery. The loss of the Thirty-fourth, in the last two engagements, was sixty one killed.

The national forces followed the retreating and demoralized enemy to Harrisonburg, where they lay until the 6th of October. In the meantime the cavalry were busily engaged in burning barns filled with grain, driving in stock of all kinds, and otherwise rendering the valley untenable as a base of supplies — literally fulfilling Grant's order to Sheridan, to render it so desolate and provisionless that a "crow, in passing over it, would be compelled to carry his rations with him."

By the 6th, the work of devastation was completed, and the national army again fell back to Cedar Creek, while the enemy, following at a respectful distance, once more resumed his old position at Fishers Hill. Of General Early's desperate attempt to regain his lost laurels on the 19th of October, and of his partial success on the morning of "Sheridan's ride" to the scene of action, and the irretrievable disaster of the rebels in the afternoon, much has been said and sung The brunt of the morning's surprise and attack fell on the left flank, composed of General Crook's corps, which, with the Nineteenth Corps, occupying the center of the line, was badly shattered. The Sixth Corps, on the right, had time to fall back in good order. The troops were rallied near Middletown, from whence the final advance was made which swept everything before it. It is sufficient to say that the day was won.

The evening before the battle the regiment, under command of Lieutenant Colonel L. Furney, was sent on picket. In the morning, before dawn, when the surprise occurred, the colonel and eighteen of his men were taken prisoners. The colonel escaped at Mount Jackson, and joined his command a few days afterward. The loss of the Thirty-fourth in this affair was two killed, twelve wounded, and eighteen prisoners. From this time until the latter part of December, 1864, the regiment lay in the neighborhood of Kernstown, when it marched to Opequan Crossing, and from thence to Martinsburg.

On the evening of the 22d of December, as the regiment was leaving Martinsburg, on its way to Webster, by rail, the train on which it was being transported came in collision with one loaded with coal, killing two men and wounding fourteen. It reached Webster on the 25th, and Beverly on the 28th.

On the 11th of January, 1865, the post of Beverly, garrisoned by the Thirty-fourth — which by this time was reduced to three hundred men present for duty — and the dismounted portion of the Eighth Ohio Cavalry, was attacked by the enemy, under the command of General Rosser. So secret and sudden was the attack — no alarm whatever being given until the enemy were in the quarters — that resistance was out of the question, and nearly every man was at one time a prisoner, though subsequently a great many escaped, favored by the darkness and intense excitement of the occasion. Colonel Youart, of the Eighth, commanding the post, and Colonel Furney, were both captured, but afterward escaped. The survivors of this unfortunate and disgraceful affair fell back to Phillippi, and from thence were ordered to Cumberland, Maryland, where they were consolidated with the Thirty sixth Ohio — General Crook's old regiment — commanded by Colonel H. F. Duval.

The union of the separate organizations dates from the 22d of February, 1865, in which the old Thirty-fourth loses its identity, the coalition being known as the Thirty-sixth Ohio Veteran Volunteer Infantry.

One Hundred and Eighty-Fourth O. V. I.

This was one of the regiments raised under the last call of President Lincoln, to serve for one year. As there were Greene County soldiers in it, I give it a place.

It was organized on the 21st of February, 1865, at Camp Chase, and immediately after muster it received orders to move for Nashville without delay. It remained there a short time, doing garrison duty. From Nashville it proceeded to Chattanooga; thence to Bridgeport, Alabama, which point it reached about the 21st of March, and was engaged in protecting an important railroad bridge over the Tennessee River. It also guarded the track of the railroad between Bridgeport and Chattanooga, a distance of about thirty miles. In the performance of this duty, detachments of the regiment stationed in the blockhouses and forts along the road had frequent encounters with rebel guerrillas and squads of rebel cavalry. A number of prisoners were taken, at the expense of some few casualties.

On the 25th of July the One Hundred and Eighty-fourth was ordered to Edgefield, for garrison duty, and remained at that place until it was mustered out of service on the 20th of September. It at once proceeded, under orders, to Camp Chase, Ohio, and on the 27th of September, 1865, the men were paid and discharged.

The One Hundred and Eighty-fourth, like the majority of the one-year's regiments, was composed of excellent material—

the most of the men having seen service. Although the regiment did not participate in any general engagement, yet it is fair to presume that had they been called on to fight, they would have acquitted themselves with bravery and distinction.

ROSTER OF THE SEVENTY-FOURTH REGIMENT, O. V. I.

RANK.	NAME.	DATE OF RANK.	COM. ISSUED.	REMARKS.
Colonel	Granville Moody	Dec. 10, 1861	Mar. 28, 1862	Resigned May 16, 1863.
Colonel	A. Von Schroeder	May 16, 1863	May 22, 1863	Declined.
Colonel	Josiah Given	May 16, 1863	June 2, 1863	Resigned September 29, 1864.
Colonel	R. P. Findley	July 12, 1865	July 12, 1865	Mustered out as lieut. colonel.
Lieut. Colonel	A. Von Schroeder	Dec. 10, 1861	Mar. 28, 1862	Resigned April 8, 1865.
Lieut. Colonel	Thomas C. Bell	May 16, 1863	May 25, 1863	Revoked.
Lieut. Colonel	Robert P. Findley	May 18, 1865	May 18, 1865	Promoted to colonel.
Lieut. Colonel	Cornelius McGreavy	July 12, 1865	July 12, 1865	Mustered out as major.
Major	A. S. Ballard	Oct. 5, 1861	Mar. 28, 1862	Resigned June 7, 1863.
Major	T. C. Bell	Nov. 22, 1862	Nov. 27, 1862	Resigned June 7, 1863.
Major	Joseph Fisher	May 16, 1863	May 26, 1863	Revoked.
Major	Robert P. Findley	June 7, 1863	Sept. 9, 1863	Promoted to lieut. colonel.
Major	C. McGreavy	Nov. 12, 1862	Nov. 12, 1863	Promoted to lieut. colonel.
Major	M. H. Peters	May 18, 1865	May 18, 1865	Mustered out as adjutant.
Major	Joseph Fisher	July 12, 1865	July 12, 1865	Mustered out.
Surgeon	J. R. Brelsford	Nov. 5, 1861	Mar. 28, 1862	
Surgeon	M. W. Dickson	Dec. 7, 1864	Dec. 7, 1864	Mustered out with regiment.
Ass't Surgeon	E. W. Steele	Jan. 9, 1862	Mar. 28, 1862	Resigned June 4, 1862.
Ass't Surgeon	Wm. Arnold	June 4, 1862	June 17, 1862	Resigned November 22, 1862.
Ass't Surgeon	A. L. Williams	July 4, 1862	July 23, 1862	Discharged Dec. 31, 1862.
Ass't Surgeon	Matthew W. Dickson	Dec. 23, 1862	Dec. 31, 1862	Promoted to surgeon.
Ass't Surgeon	Wm. Hayes	June 9, 1863	June 10, 1863	
Ass't Surgeon	C. A. Moore	June 8, 1865	June 8, 1865	
Chaplain	Samuel Marshall	Mar. 12, 1862	Mar. 18, 1862	Resigned September 8, 1862.
Captain	T. C. Bell	Nov. 2, 1861	Mar. 28, 1862	Promoted to major.

THE SEVENTY-FOURTH. 189

Rank	Name	Date			Date			Remarks
Captain	S. A. Bassford	Dec.	5,	1861	Mar.	28,	1862	Resigned July 28, 1862.
Captain	Samuel T. Owens	Dec.	23,	1861	Mar.	28,	1862	Resigned December 22, 1862.
Captain	Austin McDowel	Dec.	28,	1861	Mar.	28,	1862	Resigned February 10, 1863.
Captain	Joseph Fisher	Dec.	31,	1861	Mar.	28,	1862	Promoted to major.
Captain	Walter Crook	Jan.	7,	1862				Mustered out.
Captain	A. W. Bostwick	Feb.	18,	1862	April	2,	1862	Resigned November 19, 1869.
Captain	R. P. Findley	Feb.	27,	1862	April	2,	1862	Promoted to major.
Captain	Joseph H. Ballard	Feb.	20,	1862	April	4,	1862	Resigned February 20, 1862.
Captain	Patrick Droyer	Dec.	31,	1861	April	17,	1862	Resigned February 17, 1863.
Captain	William Mills	Sept.	1,	1862	Dec.	20,	1862	On detached service.
Captain	William McGinnis	Nov.	22,	1862	Dec.	27,	1862	Resigned April 26, 1864.
Captain	William T. Armstrong	Dec.	22,	1862	Jan.	14,	1863	Resigned November 6, 1864.
Captain	F. L. Tedford	Nov.	19,	1862	Jan.	16,	1863	Mustered out June 14, 1865.
Captain	T. C. McIlravy	Feb.	10,	1863	Feb.	17,	1863	Mustered September 20, 1864.
Captain	Robert Cullen	Feb.	17,	1863	Mar.	6,	1863	Revoked.
Captain	David Snodgrass	Feb.	20,	1863	April	9,	1863	Resigned April 26, 1864.
Captain	H. H. Herring	Feb.	1,	1864	Feb.	13,	1864	Resigned November 8, 1864.
Captain	C. McGreavy	Feb.	17,	1863	Jan.	10,	1864	Promoted to major.
Captain	J. W. McMillen	June	14,	1864	June	14,	1864	Mustered out with regiment.
Captain	Robert Hunter	June	14,	1864	June	14,	1864	Declined.
Captain	M. H. Peters	July	13,	1864	July	13,	1864	Promoted to major.
Captain	J. Q. Hutchison	Nov.	12,	1864	Nov.	12,	1864	Declined.
Captain	Perry A. Weaver	Nov.	12,	1864	Nov.	12,	1864	Mustered out with regiment.
Captain	Robert Hunter	Nov.	10,	1864	Nov.	10,	1864	Resigned as first lieutenant.
Captain	Joseph Hamill	Nov.	18,	1864	Nov.	18,	1864	Mustered out with regiment.
Captain	Thomas Kirby	Jan.	28,	1865	Jan.	18,	1865	Mustered out with regiment.
Captain	William T. Drummond	May	18,	1865	May	18,	1865	Mustered out with regiment.
Captain	M. K. McFadden	May	18,	1865	May	18,	1865	Mustered out as first lieut.
Captain	William C. Galloway	June	6,	1865	June	6,	1865	Mustered out as quarter mast.
Captain	Philip W. Stumm	June	6,	1865	June	6,	1865	Mustered out as first lieut.
Captain	Martin Ryan	June	16,	1865	June	16,	1865	Mustered out as first lieut.
Captain	John N. Haynes	July	12,	1865	July	12,	1865	Mustered out as first lieut.
First Lieut	T. G. Bell	Oct.	24,	1861	Mar.	28,	1862	Promoted to captain.

ROSTER—Continued.

RANK.	NAME.	DATE OF RANK.	COM. ISSUED.	REMARKS.
First Lieut	William McGinnis	Nov. 8, 1861	Mar. 28, 1862	Promoted to captain.
First Lieut	F. L. Tedford	Dec. 5, 1861	Mar. 28, 1862	Promoted to captain.
First Lieut	W. T. Armstrong	Dec. 23, 1861	Mar. 28, 1862	Promoted to captain.
First Lieut	John W. McClung	Dec. 28, 1861	Mar. 28, 1862	Resigned November 25, 1862.
First Lieut	H. H. Herring	Dec. 31, 1861	Mar. 28, 1862	Promoted to captain.
First Lieut	M. H. Peters	Jan. 7, 1862	Mar. 28, 1862	Promoted to captain.
First Lieut	J. H. Cochnower	Dec. 21, 1861	April 2, 1862	Discharged.
First Lieut	T. C. McIlravy	Feb. 18, 1862	April 2, 1862	Promoted to captain.
First Lieut	David Snodgrass	Feb. 20, 1862	April 4, 1862	Promoted to captain.
First Lieut	Henry M. Cist	Feb. 22, 1862	April 17, 1862	Promoted to capt. and A. A. G.
First Lieut	William Mills	Oct. 5, 1861	April 17, 1862	Promoted to captain.
First Lieut	Robert Cullen	Dec. 31, 1861	Nov. 28, 1862	Honorably dis. Dec. 26, 1863.
First Lieut	Robert Hunter	Nov. 25, 1862	Dec. 4, 1862	Promoted to captain.
First Lieut	J. W. McMillen	Nov. 22, 1862	Dec. 27, 1862	Promoted to captain.
First Lieut	Robert Stevenson	Dec. 22, 1862	Jan. 14, 1863	Resigned February 10, 1863.
First Lieut	Benjamin A. Weaver	Jan. 23, 1863	Feb. 11, 1863	Dis. April 6, 1865 (time out.)
First Lieut	J. Q. Hutchison	Dec. 22, 1862	Mar. 6, 1863	Promoted to captain.
First Lieut	G. W. Bricker	Feb. 10, 1863	Feb. 17, 1863	Died of wounds, Sept. 12, '64.
First Lieut	C. McGreavy	Dec. 31, 1862	Mar. 6, 1863	Promoted to captain.
First Lieut	W. H. Moody	Feb. 20, 1863	April 9, 1863	Died September 28, 1864.
First Lieut	J. Hamill	Mar. 21, 1864	Mar. 21, 1864	Promoted to captain.
First Lieut	Thomas Kirby	June 14, 1864	June 14, 1864	Mustered out Oct. 17, 1864.
First Lieut	Thomas H. Adams	June 14, 1864	June 14, 1864	Promoted to captain.
First Lieut	Wm. T. Drummond	June 14, 1864	June 14, 1864	Killed at Jonesboro.
First Lieut	John Scott	July 27, 1864	July 27, 1864	Promoted to captain.
First Lieut	M. K. McFadden			Promoted to captain.

THE SEVENTY FOURTH.

Rank	Name	Date commissioned	Date mustered	Remarks
First Lieut.	Michael McGreavy	Oct. 12, 1864	Oct. 12, 1864	Declined promotion.
First Lieut.	John W. Baldwin	Oct. 12, 1864	Oct. 12, 1864	Declined promotion.
First Lieut.	Richard Powell	Oct. 12, 1864	Oct. 12, 1864	Mustered out May 15, 1865.
First Lieut.	W. C. Galloway	Nov. 12, 1864	Nov. 12, 1854	Promoted to captain.
First Lieut.	Philip W. Stumm	Nov. 12, 1864	Nov. 12, 1864	Promoted to captain.
First Lieut.	Martin Ryan	Nov. 12, 1864	Nov. 12, 1864	Promoted to captain.
First Lieut.	J. N. Haynes	Nov. 18, 1864	Nov. 18, 1864	Promoted to captain.
First Lieut.	C. C. Dodson	Jan. 6, 1865	Jan. 6, 1865	Mustered out with regiment.
First Lieut.	Wm. M. Snyder	Jan. 6, 1865	Jan. 6, 1865	Mustered out as adjutant.
First Lieut.	J. B. Gundy	May 11, 1865	May 11, 1865	Mustered out as Q. M. serg't.
First Lieut.	James McCann	May 11, 1865	May 11, 1865	Mustered out with regiment.
First Lieut.	C. L. Gallaher	May 18, 1865	May 18, 1865	
First Lieut.	R. P. Findley	May 18, 1865	May 18, 1865	Mustered out with regiment.
First Lieut.	E. S. Barnett	May 31, 1865	May 31, 1865	Mustered out with regiment.
First Lieut.	Isaac Miller	June 6, 1865	June 6, 1865	Mustered out with regiment.
First Lieut.	A. Flannigan	June 6, 1865	June 6, 1865	
First Lieut.	T. C. Hook	June 6, 1865	June 6, 1865	
First Lieut.	Saul Poland	July 12, 1865	July 12, 1865	Mustered out as serg't major.
Second Lieut.	Robert Stevenson	Oct. 10, 1861	Mar. 10, 1862	Promoted to first lieutenant.
Second Lieut.	J. W. McMillen	Oct. 24, 1861	Mar. 28, 1862	Promoted to first lieutenant.
Second Lieut.	Benjamin F. Shickly	Nov. 14, 1861	Mar. 28, 1862	Resigned September 25, 1862.
Second Lieut.	Richard King	Dec. 5, 1861	Mar. 28, 1862	Resigned January 23, 1863.
Second Lieut.	J. R. Hitesman	Dec. 16, 1861	Mar. 28, 1862	Resigned June 6, 1863.
Second Lieut.	Robert Hunter	Dec. 28, 1861	Mar. 28, 1862	Promoted to first lieutenant.
Second Lieut.	William H. Reed	Dec. 2, 1861	April 2, 1862	Resigned April 28, 1863.
Second Lieut.	George W. Bricker	Feb. 18, 1862	April 2, 1862	Promoted to first lieutenant.
Second Lieut.	William H. H. Moody	Jan. 4, 1862	April 4, 1864	Promoted to first lieutenant.
Second Lieut.	B. J. Connaughtin	Dec. 31, 1861	April 17, 1862	Resigned June 24, 1862.
Second Lieut.	Wm. T. Drummond	Nov. 25, 1862	Dec. 4, 1862	Promoted to first lieutenant.
Second Lieut.	M. McGreavy	June 24, 1862	Dec. 8, 1862	Revoked.
Second Lieut.	Joseph Hamill	Dec. 15, 1862	Dec. 15, 1862	Promoted to first lieutenant.
Second Lieut.	Thomas H. Adams	Nov. 22, 1862	Dec. 27, 1862	Promoted to first lieutenant.
Second Lieut.	Thomas Kirby	Sept. 25, 1862	Dec. 27, 1862	Promoted to first lieutenant.

ROSTER — Continued.

RANK.	NAME.	DATE OF RANK.	COM. ISSUED.	REMARKS.
Second Lieut..	John Q. Hutchison....	Dec. 22, 1862..	Jan. 14, 1863..	Promoted to first lieutenant.
Second Lieut..	John Scott.........	Jan. 23, 1863.	Feb. 11, 1863	Promoted to first lieutenant.
Second Lieut..	C. McGreavy	June 24, 1862	Feb. 16, 1863	Promoted to first lieutenant.
Second Lieut..	James A. Worden......	Feb. 10, 1863	Feb. 18, 1863	Resigned May 21, 1863.
Second Lieut..	John I. Barrows..	Dec. 22, 1862	Mar. 6, 1863	Resigned August 5, 1863.
Second Lieut..	Ed. Ballard.......	Feb. 20, 1863	May 1, 1863	Resigned December 16, 1863.
Second Lieut...	John A. McKee......	April 28, 1863.	May 19, 1863	Drowned.
Second Lieut..	M. K. McFadden.....	May 21, 1863	June 26, 1863	Promoted to first lieutenant.
Second Lieut...	M. McGreavy........	Jan. 21, 1863	June 10, 1864	Declined promotion.
Second Lieut...	John W. Baldwin.....	Mar. 19, 1864	Mar. 19, 1864	Declined promotion.
Second Lieut..	Richard Powell.....	Mar. 21, 1864	Mar. 21, 1864	Promoted to first lieutenant.
Second Lieut..	John W. Devoe.......	July 9, 1865	July 9, 1865	Mustered out as first sergeant.

COMPANY A.

Captain Robert Hunter,   First Lieut. John N. Haynes.

SERGEANTS.

Geniah F. St. John,   Isaac N. Pickering,
George H. Cullumber,   Patrick H. Sudduth,
Lisbon Lucas.

CORPORALS.

Charles Humler,   Levi Beebe,
Jesse Curry,   Hezekiah F. Evans,
William L. Ford,   Isaac N. Quinn,
James Hulzler,   Leroy Clemons.

TRANSFERRED.

Corporal Walter S. Schull,   Wesley Thomas,
John Rose,   Artemus Henderson,
Richard Brady,   Henry Hopping,
William Sesler,   George Barringer,
Horace Ballard,   David Wilson,
Alfred Dean,   Samuel Calhoun,
Michael McManah,   Henry Turner,
Samuel H. Brouse,   Robert Walthal,
Isaac Blocher,   John H. Haughey,
Alexander Walthal,   Henry H. Todd,
Edward Jordan,   Philander Mahin,
James A. Smith,   Benjamin F. Shickley,
James Cummins.

DEATHS.

First Lieut. Clinton W. Strong,   W. H. Griffith,
Corporal Joseph R. Carper,   James Shirk,
Corporal Isaac J. Smith,   Joseph H. Crow,

Corporal George Hutson,
Jacob Bushart,
Wiatt H. Jones,
Philip Harness,
Palmer Martin,
Charles M. Wilson.

David T. Ford,
Lemuel H. Sires,
Robert M. Atkinson,
Henry Haynes,
J. C. Chalmers,

DISCHARGED.

Sergeant Felix P. Iman,
Corporal Thomas Moon,
John W. James,
John M. Syphers,
Peter Shickley,
Silas B. Shaner,
Joseph M. Baker,
Charles N. Smith,
Albert Wickersham,
William J. Loy,
George Shaner,
Captain Thomas C. Bell,
Captain William McGinniss,
Captain John M. McMillan,
Barney Walters,
David Ford,
Daniel J. Browder,
Philip A. Iman,
George W. Harness,
William Dedrick,

Gustave Humler,
David A. Johnson,
Michael Sheely,
Jacob Shirk,
J. C. Reeder,
Barkly T. Baily,
John L. Woods,
E. L. Rife,
William Havey,
Joseph Hyde,
Bernard McDaniel,
First Lieut. Thomas H. Adams,
Cornelius Perkins,
Macy Beason,
Joseph Ortman,
Daniel D. Buckles,
James A. Powers,
Joseph C. Wilkerson,
George Bowermaster,
Samuel Barnes.

DISCHARGED BY EXPIRATION OF SERVICE.

Eli Dean,
Thomas Donaldson,
John Dodson,
George W. Boop,
Harvey A. Miller,
Robert N. Miller,

William H. Hopping,
Martin V. Lucas,
James McBride,
Henry H. Long,
Lawrence Sanders,
Samuel H. Zartman,

Samuel Schooley,
William H. Ford,
Jacob Neal,
Jerry B. Shickley,

Jehu More,
John L. Glotfelter,
David B. Tiffany,
William R. Baker.

VETERANS.

Frank M. Bayless,
William Brown,
Francis Bryan.

Nathaniel Rife,
Sylvester Wilson,

THREE-YEAR RECRUITS.

Samuel T. Baker,
Thomas D. Bone,
Adam Bain,
Charles Carrol,
John M. Crambles,
William Dawson,
Jenkins Evans.

Philip M. Fudge,
William P. Fulton,
Garrett Fowler,
Enos Fisher,
Laban Glass,
Anderson J. Gulhire,

TRANSFERRED.

First Sergeant Jos. H. Ballard,
Sergeant Raper A. Sharp,
Sergeant Thomas C. Hook,
Sergeant James W. Zartman,
Sergeant Asa Mahin,
Sergeant John A. Quinn,
Sergeant James R. Hayslett,
David A. Guthrie,
William P. Green,
Benjamin F. Gilbert.

George Johnston,
James R. Milner,
Matthew Osborn,
John W. Smith,
William Shirk,
George Stewart,
Elijah C. Ward,
Valentine Wolf,
Theodore Wells,

ONE-YEAR RECRUITS.

Dennison Ballard,
William Downing,

Francis Johnson,
Wilson St. John.

COMPANY B.

Captain Stephen A. Basford, Second Lieut Richard H. King,
First Lieut. Frank J. Tedford.

SERGEANTS.

William L. Taylor,
Perry A. Weaver,
James McCann.

Thomas Giff,
John Scott,

CORPORALS.

Charles King,
John S. Watts,
Daniel H. Gist,
James B. Iliff,

Coleman Heaton,
David M. Reeves,
William Gano,
Edwin Sweet,

Musician — Jasper Anthony.

PRIVATES.

William Anderson,
Robert Arnett,
Enoch P. Arnett,
Joshua E. Arnett,
Charles F. Bull,
Alfred O. K. Bennett,
William L. Bone,
James A. Bone,
Moses Bone,
William R. Baker,
Thomas Bush,
James A. Blessing,
John H. Bolan,
Martin Bloom,
James L. Bottsford,
Lemuel Cline,

Ephraim Dickerson,
Patrick Davis,
James Elam,
Stephen Faulkner,
Thomas Faulkner,
William Fisher,
Thomas Grindle,
John Glassinger,
William Gano,
Thomas Giffe,
William Gordon,
Daniel H. Gist,
George H. Hoffman,
Coleman Heaton,
Euclid Harris,
Eli Houston,

THE SEVENTY-FOURTH.

David B. Cline,
John M. Clark,
William Campbell,
Wooly Combs,
Abraham Carl,
Charles Cammer,
Austin Lyman,
Horace B. Larkin,
Charles Lucas,
James McCann,
Samuel Mulford,
Masur Martin,
Wilson McFarland,
Patrick McNary,
Michael Oswold,
Ira S. Owens,
Michael Powers,
William A. Powers,
Alexander Pepper,
William H. Pratt,
Franklin Pratt,
Marion Ryan,
David M. Reeves,
William S. Reeves,
William Richardson,
John Shane,
John Scott,
William Roberts,
James B. Iliff,
John Gowdy,
Addison Jones,
John Kilpatrick,
Richard H. King,
Samuel Kyle,
Jesse Severs,
Edwin Sweet,
John Starr,
William A. Smith,
Lewis Starr,
John A. Sciss,
David Stipe,
James M. Smith,
Vinton C. Smith,
William L. Taylor,
Arthur Truman,
Charles Ulry,
John S. Watts,
Perry A. Weaver,
John F. Walton,
Jacob Wildermott,
James Whalen,
Joseph Williams,
William Zellers,
Charles Shambaugh,
John Elliott,
Jeremiah Fagerty.

COMPANY C.

Captain John Q. Hutchison,   First Lieut. Wm. C. Galloway.

SERGEANTS.

John W. Hedges,
John Norwood,
Edward H. Wright.
William Baker,
Jonathan Wood,

CORPORALS.

George Kempher,
Franklin McGinnis,
Benjamin Crossey,
William L. Wright,

Charles Holsman,
Ira S. Owens,
James H. Johnston,
Merritt R. Owens,

Musician — William Keinborts.

PRIVATES.

John J. Allison,
James Archibald,
George T. Copeland,
George W. Duffield,
James Handlon,
Hiram Hooten,
Matthew H. Hutchison,
Alexander Jones,
Samuel Jones,
Michael Jones,
Samuel Kildow,
James Lucas,
James Lynch.

John Long,
Simeon H. Mullen,
Columbus McDonald,
James Penrod,
Thomas Price,
Joel Perkins,
Clinton Randolph,
John A. Seldomridge,
Benjamin Smith,
John L. Thorn,
Daniel Teer,
Henry Wetlers.

TRANSFERRED.

First Serg't Edward S. Barnett,
Corporal Robert Gossard,
Isaac N. Laughhead,
William McDonald,
John A. Brown,
Thomas Burney,
David Perkins,
Ewell P. Drake,
James Rodgers,
Henry Simpson,
Ebenezer Turner.

Calvin Curl,
Mills Conwell,
Joseph Clemens,
William Evans,
William Gano,
John W. Devoe,
Jeremiah Williams,
John Coren,
Edward Clark,
Aseph Hollingsworth.

DISCHARGED.

Captain Samuel T. Owens,
Captain William F. Armstrong,
Second Lieut. Robt. Stevenson,
Second Lieut. John I. Barrows,
Second Lieut. William Baldwin,
Corporal Edward R. Bennett,
Corporal Abraham Cosler,
William Anderson,
William L. Beason,
James M. Howard,
James W. Dehaven,
Edward W. Johnson,
John G. Brewer,
Patrick W. McLaughlin.

Joseph J. Baldwin,
Elijah C. Humphrey,
Absolom Brandon,
James A. Brown,
Mercer Beason,
Charles M. Wolf,
James Allison,
Chancy White,
James G. Stevenson,
Charles Owens,
Henry Forbes,
George W. Seldomridge,
Barton Chaney,

DISCHARGED BY EXPIRATION OF SERVICE.

Sergeant John M. Smalley,
Corporal John H. McPherson,
Corporal George G. Sargeant,
Samuel W. Collins,
Smith A. Stow,
Joseph H. Clemens,
John T. Reed,
James B. Marshall,

James Sheffield,
Elias Vickers,
Creighton Erwin,
Philip Tracy,
Alfred Erwin,
Samuel T. Miller,
William Stewart,
Thomas Bethard.

DEATHS.

Corporal James H. Moore,
Corporal John Alexander,
Corporal Joseph Hedges,
Corporal George Schenebly,
Corporal John H. Forbes,
Thomas Harp,
John Hennessey,
William Funderburg.

Albert Harold,
John A. Sweeny,
David Seldomridge,
Harvey White,
Melville Davis,
James H. Seldomridge,
Addison Talbott,

COMPANY D.

Captain William Mills.

SERGEANTS.

Samuel I. Poland,
William N. Watt,
Thomas Hunter.

Joseph H. Bigger,
Robert S. Jacoby,

CORPORALS.

William H. Belt,
Absalom Ames,
Samuel G. Stewart,
Andrew C. Cottrill,

George W. King,
Samuel D. Focht,
Jacob Steen,
John Gallagher,

Musician — Aseph Hollingsworth.

VETERANS.

William H. H. Bridgeman,
Daniel Gallagher,
Thomas Grimes,
James Hamilton,

William Kiernan,
Josiah M. Lamme,
Joseph S. Loy,
George M. Moore.

RECRUITS.

John Ames,
Hezekiah V. Brown,
William A. Dodd,
Jacob C. Filbert,
John Gentleman,

Bazel V. Lucas,
James Maxwell,
George Nisonger,
David Patterson,
John G. Smart.

TRANSFERRED.

Sergeant William Collins,
Sergeant James A. Worden,
Sergeant Samuel Galloway,

First Lieut. Wm. T. Drummond,
Joseph Hamill,
William Connelly,

Sergeant William C. Galloway,
Arthur Chase,
James W. Reynolds,
Charles Kernon,
Samuel Stewart,
First Lieut. Robert Hunter.

William McAfee,
Gilbert Nesbitt,
John B. Gowdy,
Jacob H. Eichelberger,
James S. Thropp,

DISCHARGED.

Captain Austin McDowell,
First Lieut. John N. McClung,
Sergeant John C. Hale,
Sergeant Philip Meredith,
Corporal George Robinson,
Corporal James A. Gowdy,
Corporal George Thompson,
Corporal Benjamin Horner,
Corporal Samuel Dodd,
John McCrossen,
John A. Bower,
Mark Drummond,
Thomas Seavon,
Andrew J. Gregory,
Robert E. Games,
Jacob Greeser,
Wilson Pennyweight,
Samuel C. Hook,
Elijah Teach,
Richard S. Galloway,
John Q. Collins,
John Andrew,
Patrick Costello,
John Jelly.

Daniel Brannam,
Charles A. Haynes,
William F. McFadden,
Perry Horner,
Cornelius Beason,
William Andrew,
William G. Winter,
James Maxwell,
Albert T. Marshall,
Joseph W. Stewart,
Harrison A. Galloway,
Joseph Rippetoe,
John W. Sinnard,
Burgess Morgan,
Henry Ashton,
William C. Rippetoe,
Henry Frock,
Andrew J. Lennox,
Henry Henderson,
Amos W. Prugh,
Joseph H. Black,
William H. Collins,
Elisha Mills,

DISCHARGED BY EXPIRATION OF SERVICE.

Robert Duckson,
Robert M. Deen,
Robert M. Smart,
David Ewery,

John W. Fairchild,
Michael Illigs,
Orange H. Marshall.
Samuel S. Wingett.

DEATHS.

Sergeant John H. McClung,
Bowen Hale,
Emory Holt,
John Coppie,
John McCune,
Nile Drummond,

Corporal Cyrus N. McClure,
George Townsley,
Philip Minehart,
Francis Humphry,
Thomas W. Thompson,
Thomas Paxton.

DESERTED.

John S. Caddemy,
Peter Burkhamer,
S. P. Worden,

Isaac Crites,
George W. Streets,
William Williams.

COMPANY E.

PRIVATES.

Peter Benham,
Milton Bennett,
James Barrett,
George W. Cain,
Hiram J. Cahill,
John Cox,
John Carroll,
Amos Coy,
John Conner,
Jacob Cullenberg,
William Duffey,
—— Davis,
William Dixson,
Thomas Davis,
James Demint,
William Davis,
Henry C. Davis,
John Fitzgerald,

James John,
Isaac M. Krise,
Thomas Kirby,
John Kirby,
Samuel Lenibaugh,
Francis Lammel,
Jeremiah Linscott,
Garrett Linscott,
John Murphy,
John Mason,
Daniel M. Cornell,
Samuel Mendenall,
Daniel M. Canless,
John Newland,
Wesley Owens,
Thomas O. Donald,
Garrett Patterson,
John W. Passon,

THE SEVENTY-FOURTH. 203

John Feely,
Robert Finley,
Charles R. Finley,
John B. Fisher,
Edward Fest,
John L. Furguson,
Caserow Fest,
George Funk,
Enos Furguson,
Patrick Gibbons,
William C. Grooves,
Thomas Ginn,
John H. Garrett,
John H. Glotfelter,
Clayton Haynes,
Charles Hanison,
Samuel Hill,
John N. Haynes,
George W. Horner,
Joshua Holland,
William Holsten,
Daniel Harner,

John Rose,
Andrew Rovell,
Amer Reese,
Isicar Reese,
Benjamin Romspert,
John A. Shauk,
Isaac Sollers,
William Smith,
Edward C. Snyder,
Peter Snyder.
George A. Snyder,
Wesley Snyder,
Henry Snyder,
Henry Sellers,
Albert Swadner,
Mortimer Stenneth,
Eli Truly,
Samuel Tobam,
Josiah A. West,
John W. Watts,
Moses West,
Andrew Young.

COMPANY F.

Captain Walter Crook,
First Lieut. Matthew H. Peters,
Second Lieut. J. R. Hitesman,
First Sergeant Daniel Staly,
Second Sergeant Enos Wallers,
Third Sergeant Isaac Miller,
Fourth Serg't J. R. McCarter.
Fifth Serg't Charles C. Dotson,
Corporal Cyrus Phillips,
William H. Smith.

David Bausman,
Isaac Harshman,
Charles N. Harper,
Samuel Shellebarger,
Nathan Rasor,
Johnson Williams,
Musician, Isaac P. Foster.
Musician, Leon'd Peckenpaugh,
Teamster, H. N. Roberson,

PRIVATES.

David Bennett,
Martin Bowman,

Steven Lever,
Jacob Lenegar,

George W. Peck,
Jacob Bowman,
George Bausman,
Lewis Button,
Michael Benert,
Peter Brant,
R. H. Brooken,
William H. Barton,
John Boughner,
Henry H. Cassel,
Jacob H. Circle,
Joseph Coner,
John Constable,
Samuel Campbell,
Jacob Candle,
William Douglass,
John M. Drill,
Abraham Doughman,
John Epperd,
John Elliott,
David N. Elder,
William Ford,
William Fitzwater,
John W. Glover,
John Gillen,
William Huffman,
Benjamin G. Hughes,
William H. Huffman,
M. A. Harker,
Theodore Hoover,
Johnson Hadder,
Thomas B. Howard,
George M. Hause,
Thomas Hogland,
David E. Hooven,
Aaron S. Hull,
John H. Jacobs,
John Jones,

John M. Carter.
Patrick McCain,
James R. Martin,
James Miller,
Edward Moon,
John M. Mahon,
William Muns,
John Obrine, sen,
John Obrine, jun,
William Pearpoint,
George M. Perrine,
William Phillips,
George Reed,
Ranthus M. Runyan,
John M. Runyan,
J. R. Sample,
Eden Sherman,
Wesley Sheets,
George M. Stokes,
George L. Swentz,
Benjamin F. Shor,
John B. Sweney,
Jacob Steffer,
Steven Shaler,
John Shields,
John H. Tonkenson,
James Taylor,
Hugh Thompson,
Jonathan R. Townsend,
David Williamson,
Milton Weaver,
Squire White,
William H. Wilson,
Andrew J. Hyland,
John Walter,
Luther Wessinger,
Thomas Wright,
Andrew G. Wickham,

Frank Kramer,
Robert Kirkpatrick,
John Kipp,
William Constable.

Benjamin Wood,
Michael Welsh,
Charles Bealey,

COMPANY G.

Captain Albion W. Bostwick,
First Lieut. Thos. C. McElravey,
Second Lieut. Geo. W. Bricker,
First Serg't M. K. McFadden,
Theodore Ligget,
William H. Jones,
William V. B. Crosky,
John B. Pope,
Nathaniel Brindley,
Corporal Bennonia S. Hall.

Corporal Andrew F. Clark,
Corporal William G. Barnes,
Corporal William McCollough,
Corporal Leander Baker,
Corporal William C. Welling,
Corporal Jasper Denning,
Fifer, Thomas Wenfield,
Drummer, Frank Hatton,
Wagoner, Robert P. Canus,

PRIVATES.

John A. Askren,
Amos P. Barnes,
John F. Boles,
Thomas Burton,
James Beaty,
Samuel Browning,
Amos Brough,
Samuel Bridgman,
John W. Case,
Hiram Cox,
Jeremiah Gughan,
Isaac W. Campbell,
Thomas H. Channel,
Benjamin Cox,
George W. Cunningham,
David Copeland,
William Chambers,
William H. Crouch,.

Joshua Lowenmiller,
Kennedy Lyons,
John Luster,
George W. Legget,
Sheridan Loslin,
Isaac Liggit,
George B. Liggit,
George A. McAdamas,
Albert McFadden,
Thomas McFarland,
William S. Maxwell,
Joseph C. Mansfield,
John F. McFadden,
Thomas Miller,
David Miller,
John H. McGarvin,
James McGeary,
Alexander W. Osborn,

William Case,
William Denning,
Newton Denning,
Abraham Dennis,
Nathaniel Elliott,
Dundas Fisher,
William P. Frigar,
John Handy,
John A. Handlus,
Israel Howell,
Elias Hirl,
Benjamin Howes,
James Johnston,
John A. Jones,
Daniel Kimmel,
Samuel Handley.

Thomas W. Poland,
Richard Powell,
Joshua Timmons,
William Shires,
Franklin Shilling,
Solomon Sinsel,
John Scott,
Admardine Wood,
Joseph Walker,
Harvey B. Wright,
George Welling,
Parker S. Watson,
Samuel Wiggins,
Michael Wharton,
John S. Leister,

COMPANY II.

Captain Joseph H. Ballard,
First Lieut. David Snodgrass,
Second Lieut. W. H. H. Moody,
First Serg't Raper A. Spahr,
Second Serg't Farey Q. Bissett,
William H. Evans,
J. Will Conwell,
William H. Sesler,
Corporal Philip Stumm,

Luther Wissinger,
Henry Hooper,
Artemus Hendrickson,
William A. Brouse,
Israel Randall,
David H. Foster,
James Taylor,
Bugler, Horace L. Romey,

PRIVATES.

Horace Ballard,
George S. Baringer,
Richard Brady,
Thomas Buchett,
Melvin Barnhard,
Virgil T. Barnhard,
Richard H. Brookens,

Henry Romey,
Jules Romey,
J. M. Reynold,
Samuel Rodgers.
Xavier Ruegge,
Joseph St. John,
Daniel Shindledecker,

THE SEVENTY-FOURTH.

Peter Bostwick,
Christopher Cline,
Calvin Curl,
Joseph H. Clemons,
James Clark,
William Connelly,
Ezra Carpenter,
Henry H. Comesford,
John Close,
John Clippinger,
John W. Devoe,
Joseph Daughterly,
John A. Donard,
Henry Duncan,
William Douglass,
Philip Dencler,
Daniel Day,
Dudley Day,
William Day,
Solomon Ellis,
Adam Fisher,
John Glover,
Morris Haley,
John House,
Augustus Herman,
William Miller,
John Moon,
Ferdinand Moy,
Andrew McGinnis,
Erastus McInlin,
Daniel Wallet,
William Pierpoint,

Frederick Shuli,
William Skinner,
Harvey Snyder,
William Harness,
John Haner,
William H. Holden,
Albert F. Johnston,
John Jennings,
Israel Kirk,
Francis A. Snyder,
Thomas M. Lesler,
Benjamin F. Sher.
Warlsel Lent,
Jesse Snodgrass,
Alfred P. Snodgrass,
James H. Scott,
Vanransaler Thompson,
David B. Tiffany,
George W. Tiffany,
Owen Thompson,
Elijah C. Taylor,
Wesley Thomas,
Eli Turner,
Harvey R. Tinsley,
Jesse Williams,
George S. Wise,
George W. Wyburn,
Joseph Wyburn,
Curtis Harner,
George M. Wimwood.
Urs Yagge.

COMPANY I.

Captain Patrick Dwyer,
First Lieut. Robert Cullen,
Sec. Lieut. B. F. Connoughton,

First Serg't Corn. McGreavey,
John Tohee,
Bernard W. Neil,

Martin Ryan,
Corp. Rodger McDonnaugh,
Thomas Kennedy,
William Burns,
Michael McGreavey.

Morgan Evan,
Musician, Philemon E. Jones,
Musician, John Smith,
Wagoner, Michael Finegan,

PRIVATES.

Ambrose Edward,
William Anderson,
Michael Brannon,
Hugh Brady,
Frank Brady,
Edward Buffin,
John Birny,
James Bolger,
Michael Connell,
Anthony Cline,
James Corcoran,
Michael Canen,
Patrick Condon,
James Carrigan,
Thomas Cox,
Timothy Cronen,
John Creedon,
James Douces,
John Dervine,
Edward Donavan,
Michael Donavan,
John Donagheu,
James Dowling,
John Dowd,
Patrick Doyle,
John Dwyer,
James Dayley,
Patrick Flinn,
James Fayhey,
Hugh Fox,
Patrick Fogerty,

John Hawkins,
William Han,
Peter Johnston,
Martin Kenehan,
Edward Keating,
James Keating,
Thomas Lynch,
William Lyons,
Daniel Lane,
James Lyans,
Edward Lenehan,
James Lee,
James Lynham,
John Leeland,
John Morarity,
Daniel Maloney,
Owen McGarren,
Patrick McNally,
Thomas N. Murphy,
Thomas McGreavey,
William McClane,
David Mahoney,
James McCarthy,
Henry Myers,
Terrence McLaughlin,
Patrick Naughton,
Dennis O'Brien, No. 1,
Dennis O'Brien, No. 2,
Dennis O. Neile,
Edward Padden,
Hugh Pandergast,

THE SEVENTY-FOURTH.

Frank Farrell,
Andrew Flanigan,
John Gales,
James Gurkin,
John Glynn,
Patrick Hunt,

Molike Ryan,
Lawrence Roach,
Jacob Smith,
John Smith,
James Sullivan,
Michael Travis.

COMPANY K.

Captain Robert P. Findley,
First Lieut. Jas. H. Cochnower,
Second Lieut. Wm. H. Reed,
First Serg't Theophilus H. Barr,
John H. McRea,
Charles Rambour,
R. Ross Wallace,
James W. Partington,
Corporal Edward Proctor,
Oras Goldson.

George Lytle,
Wm. I. Holmes,
Charles L. Galligher,
Wm. Carter,
John W. Carson,
James S. McKitrick,
Fifer, Harry H. Higber,
Drummer, Napoleon B. Agy,
Wagoner, Calvin Bush,

PRIVATES.

G. Wanick Armstrong,
James Atherton,
Dorsey Ames,
Wm. Ankim,
Wm. Baird,
Henry Baker,
Robert Baker,
Robert B. Baker,
John Barker,
Thomas E. Brown,
George R. Brown,
George H. Bennett,
George W. Bush,
Jasper Babb,
James Boyd,
Wm. V. Barns,

Jackson W. Horney,
Wilson A. McKee,
Ezekiel McPeeke,
Washing Warshall,
John O. Harran,
Alphon C. Porter,
Joseph Patterson,
Andrew Pheterson,
Robert C. Parr,
Jacob H. Phillip,
Isaac C. Roberts,
Samuel Rodger,
Thomas Ralston,
Isaac Rammasour,
Andrew C. Rea,
Thomas H. Rea,

Michael Brown,
John Burk,
James Berry,
John Cargatt,
John A. Couch,
Joseph Desotell,
Wm. M. Dillon,
Wm. I. Floyd,
Joseph Faber,
Noah Guenford,
John Garthaffner,
John D. Holston,
John Horton,
Wm. Kitt,
George King,
Wm. Kent,
Pleasant A. Lemmon,
Wm. Lambert,
Henry Lyster,
Philip I. Munich,
James McMullen,
George M. May,
Wm. W. Martin,
James McCormick,
James C. May.

John Shocky,
Luke Shoemaker,
Robert Savage,
Charles Sander,
Walter S. Saull,
James A. Sleeth,
David Sleeth,
Robert C. Stewart,
Irvin Stewart,
James Stewart,
Huston Stahl,
Alexander Sankey,
Louis Sheel,
Wm. Sayner,
James Subbell,
James Thompson,
Thomas Terns,
Joseph C. Underwood,
Charles H. Underwood,
George W. Vanfassen,
James Workman,
Kinsey S. Williams,
Harris Williams,
Wm. Yates,
Wm. O. Allison.

RECRUITS FOR THREE YEARS.

COMPANY E.

Benjamin F. Cahill,
Henry Y. Cahill,
Patrick Cusic,
John S. Cosler,

Wm. Helmer,
Charles A. Kershner,
John Murphy,
Jacob Miller,

Amos Coy,
Samuel Coy,
John H. Cyphers,
Wm. K. Davis,
George B. Harshman,
Wm. Havey,
Robert Havey,

James M. Provost,
Jacob E. Swadner,
John K. Siddar,
Winfield S. Sellars,
James W. Smith,
John Truber,
Darius Wetsell.

COMPANY F.

Henry W. Allen,
Michael Bennett,
George G. Gabriel,
Joseph B. Jones,
James E. Jones,
James Jay,
John O. Kesler,

John J. Leahman,
Benjamin Lever,
Labington Norris,
Benjamin Palmer,
Charles Sprop,
Wm. I. Swallow,
John B. Wagner.

ONE-YEAR RECRUITS.

Francis Evans,
Wm. I. Gibson.

Wm. Y. Wetmore,

COMPANY G.

George Arnold,
Joseph P. Roals,
George F. Braden,
Wm. W. Branson,
Joseph B. Berry,
Wm. A. Banton,
Charles M. Blackburn,
Adam H. Barr,
Wm. H. Campbell,
John E. Caster,
Jacob C. Case,
Franklin Cartright,

Benjamin E. Furguson,
Gideon Gutchall,
Paul Grabill,
John F. Geary,
Joseph W. Cartright,
Jonas S. Gravy,
Lawrence F. Guder,
Perry Griffith,
Alexander Hammond,
Wm. A. Holmes,
Thomas A. Hall,
John Hatcher,

Thomas G. Cox,
Peter Dvalt,
Samuel Espich,
Thomas Fleming,
Wm. Furlay,
John Frazier,

Samuel R. Johnson,
George S. Krappe,
George W. Lyons,
John Liggett,
Wm. Miers,
Adam H. Mook.

COMPANY H.

John F. Powell,
James Chipman,
Laird M. Coon,
Wm. R. Coon,
David F. Coon,
Frederick Conrad,
George W. Coldwell,

Daniel Gray,
Calvin N. Hall,
Jacob Howenstein,
Albert King,
Salem Reed,
Wm. Sourbough,
Undercook, Robert Jackson.

DEATHS.

Albert Chipman,
Louis A. Gerord,

John Lutees,
Wm. Thompson.

Roster of 12th Regiment.

Colonel John W. Lowe,
Colonel Carr B. White,
Lieut. Colonel Carr B. White,
Lieut. Colonel J. D. Hines,
Major Jonathan D. Hines,
Major James D. Wallace,
Major Edward M. Carey,
Major Rigdon Williams,

Surgeon Wm. W. Holmes,
Surgeon Wm. T. Ridenhour,
Surgeon James D. Webb,
Surgeon N. F. Graham.
Ass't Surgeon, Horace P. Kay,
Ass't Surgeon, Silas T. Buck,
Chaplain Russell D. VanDusen,
Chaplain Charles L. Allen.

CAPTAINS.

James D. Wallace,
Edward M. Carey,
James Sloane,
William B. Smith,
Rigdon Williams,
Joseph L. Hilt,
Azanah W. Doane,
Watts McMurchy,
Andrew Legg,
Ferdinand Gunkle,
Henry S. Clement,
John Curtis,
Ezra Stevenson,
Wm. W. Liggett,

Daniel W. Pauley,
Wm. E. Fisher,
Henry F. Haukes,
Jonathan C. Wallace,
John Lewis,
Robert Wilson,
Aaron N. Channell,
James W. Ross,
Horatio G. Tibbals,
Jacob A. Yordy,
Jonathan Wallace,
Hiram McKay,
Ashley Brown.

FIRST LIEUTENANTS.

Henry S. Clement,
Wm. W. Liggett,

James W. Ross,
Jacob A. Yordy,

Wm. P. Coune,
George W. Goode,
Daniel W. Pauley,
Robert Wilson,
Wm. Hivling,
Alex M. Ridgway,
Jonathan C. Wallace,
Ashley Brown,
Andrew J. Roxa,
W. H. Roberts,
Wm. E. Fisher,
Henry F. Hawkes,
John Lewis,
John Wise,
Aaron N. Channell,
Calvin Goddard,

Horatio G. Tibbals,
Robert H. Shoemaker,
Hiram McKay,
John C. Campbell,
John V. O'Connor,
Michael B. Mahoney,
Wm. H. Glotfelter,
John W. Hiltz,
Thomas J. Atkinson,
Wm. B. Nesbitt,
Wm. A. Ludlum,
Frank M. Slade,
Thomas F. Hill,
John Lewis,
Harrison G. Otis,
Abraham King,

SECOND LIEUTENANTS.

Wm. E. Fisher,
John Curtis,
Ezra Stevenson,
Moses W. Trader,
James W. Ross,
Jacob A. Yordy,
Wm. H. Miller,
Alonzo M. Dimmitt,
Aaron N. Channell,
Horatio G. Tibballs,
Robert H. Shoemaker,
Hiram McKay,
John C. Campbell,
John V. O'Connor,
John W. Hiltz,
Frederick B. Schnebly,
Thomas J. Atkinson,
Edwin W. Jacoby,

Wm. H. Glotfelter,
Wm. B. Nesbitt,
Wm. A. Ludlum,
Andrew C. Miller,
Wm. Sine,
Thomas F. Hill,
Frank M. Slade,
Michael B. Mahoney,
Harrison G. Otis,
James H. Palmer,
Maurice Watkins,
Henry L. Sherwood,
Robert B. Wilson,
Jonathan H. McMillan,
Abram King,
Edward R. Grim,
Fenton L. Torrence,
John M. Busby.

COMPANY D.

Captain W. B. Smith,
George W. Goode,
Moses W. Trader,
John Lewis,
W. T. Timberlake,
W. B. Nesbitt,
John W. McMillan,
Fred B. Schebly,
Ed Bloosteman,
Wm. S. Cessna,
Hiram D. Cline,
Joseph S. Clokey,
Abram King,
John A. Snyder,
Samuel H. Nesbitt,
James I. Steen,
Charles A. McCarty,
Ephraim A. Adams,
John Alkinson,
John E. Brown,
James A. Bailey,
Henry Benser,
John H. Baker,
Francis G. Barber,
Robert K. Boggs,
Robert P. Beard,
Robert Boggs,
George W. Beard,
Wm. Butler,
Henry Boyle,
James D. Counsell,
John W. Cline,
David R. Curry,
John Cordingly,

Henry C. Huffine,
Thomas Hays,
Patrick Howard,
Wm. H. Iliff,
James H. Iliff,
Thomas W. Jenkins,
George W. King,
John W. Kirkwood,
David M. Log,
James Linton,
Lymanto McBride,
John McCreary,
John McAerleg,
Joseph D. Murry,
James W. W. Popple,
Henry Robinson,
Wm. V. Reading,
Gilbert D. Robertson,
Alfred Richardson,
James Wells,
David Wilson,
John F. Reif,
Nathan Romerne,
James Ross,
James W. Raney,
George W. Sollers,
John S. Stoops,
Nathan H. Sidwell,
Charles W. Stevenson,
Sylvester Sroufe,
James K. Smith,
John B. Scroggy,
Oliver Steviett,
James Smith,

Solon Cook,
Staunton Carter,
George Cronels,
John Davis,
·Ed S. Devine,
Wm. A. Dingess,
Adam Dingess,
David C. B. Ellis,
Thomas Ginn,
John S. Harper,
John A. Harper,
James Henry.

Wm. C. Shape,
Matimer E. Stone,
Wm. P. Taylor,
Ledwig Turner,
Alex Turnbull,
Edward S. Thomasson,
George Thompson,
J. Atkinson Thomas,
Daniel Ullery,
John White.
Cyrus Bailey,

Roster of 94th Regiment.

Colonel Joseph W. Frizell,
Colonel Stephen A. Bassford,
Lieut. Col. Stephen A. Bassford,
Lieut. Col. David King,
Lieut. Col. Rue P. Hutchins,
Major David King,
Major Rue P. Hutchins,
Major Charles C. Gibson,
Major Wm. H. Snider,

Surgeon Edwin Sinnet,
Surgeon Wm. B. Gibson,
Ass't Surgeon J. L. Sorber,
Ass't Surgeon L. C. Fouls,
Ass't Surgeon Wm. B. Gibson,
Ass't Surgeon J. Resley,
Ass't Surgeon Edwin C. Booth,
Ass't Surg. D. W. Humfreville,
Chaplain Wm. Allington.

CAPTAINS.

Perry Stewart,
John C. Drury,
Thedius W. Walton,
Rue P. Hutchins,
David Steel,
Thomas H. Workman,
Wesley Gorsuch,
Charles C. Gibson,
James Kyle,
Chauncy Riffle,
Wm. H. Snider,
James E. Edmons,

Dixon G. McLaughlin,
Charles R. Moss,
David T. Davidson,
John W. Ford,
Amaziah Winger,
Nathan G. McConkey,
Benjamin F. Coolidge,
Frank A. Hardy,
Samuel H. Sherlock,
Alex Haywood,
Andrew Gowan,
Samuel Judy.

FIRST LIEUTENANTS.

Hezekiah Kelshner,
Joshua H. Horton,
Benjamin F. Coolidge,

Frederick B. McNeal,
Amaziah Winger,
George W. Wilson,

Dixon G. McLaughlin,
James A. Petticrew,
John A. Beal,
Alfred L. Trader,
Samuel T. Arnold,
Wm. H. Snider,
George D. Farrer,
Nathan G. McConkey,
John W. Ford,
Frank A. Hardy,
Henry A. Tomlinson,
James E. Edmons,
Daniel D. Hunter,
John Kingery,
Samuel H. Sherlock,

Samuel Judy,
Alex Haywood,
Andrew Gowan,
Andrew Wiggins,
Wm. D. Putnam,
Henry C. Cushman,
James Mitchell.
John A. Hivling,
James T. Pierson,
M. Dickey,
James B. Cross,
Morrison M. Markwith,
Edward Connor,
Frank Denwiddie,
H. Newton Arnold.

SECOND LIEUTENANTS.

Amaziah Winger,
Frederick B. McNeal,
Frank A. Hardy,
Andrew Wiggins,
Henry A. Tomlinson,
Samuel Walton,
David T. Davidson,
George H. Maddox,
Charles R. Moss,
George W. Wilson,
James E. Edmon,
Wm. D. Putnam.

John Kingery,
Barton C. Mitchell,
Alexander Haywood,
John P. Patterson,
Samuel Judy,
Andrew Gowan,
Henry C. Cushman,
James Mitchell,
John A. Hivling,
James T. Pierson,
M. Dickey,

COMPANY E.

David Steel,
John A. Beal,
Samuel Walton,
Samuel H. Pierce,

John S. Perkins,
E. S. Palmer,
Milo A. Richison,
Wm. B. Richison,

John Kingery,
James Mitchell,
James W. Lucas,
David W. Surgert,
O. H. P. Knal,
Augustus Kempt,
Jacob Miller,
W. H. H. Towler,
Charles Hoffman,
Josephus Cover,
Wm. Nalan,
George H. Andrew,
Wm. F. Snediker,
E. H. Dewitt,
Henry Abey,
Simon P. Ally,
Charles Bell,
Joseph W. Beck,
Samuel A. Bowermaster,
Tilbert Browder,
Cyrus Brown,
Wm. Brannum,
Daniel Clohesey,
Abraham Coy,
Isaac Cover,
Oscar Chisty,
Adam Carnwell,
W. B. Cornwell,
D. W. Carpenter,
Christopher Cory,
Lewis Cass Cotterell,
Michael Clohesey,
Lorenzo Clark,
J. M. Cotterell,
Hiram R. Conn,
John Davis,
Solomon Dodge,
T. C. Dunn,

John Ridenhour,
John W. Steel,
Wm. Shane,
J. C. Stewart,
George M. Smith,
J. R. Stewart,
Archibald Steen,
Madison Spahr,
Wm. Smith,
John A. Steel,
Wm. N. Gilbert,
Wm. H. Goe,
James A. Gowdy,
Samuel Gowdy,
Jasper N. Greene,
John A. Hivling,
Jacob P. Harner,
Samuel Heathcook,
Finley Hopkins,
Wesley Watson,
James A. Harper,
Wm. B. Holzapple,
Andrew Jackson,
Wm. Jones,
Alfred Jones,
Patrick Jones,
John R. Jacoby,
James H. Kyle,
Isaac P. Kelley,
John C. Lovett,
Thomas Leary,
James Liddle,
Albert H. Leech,
Robert Little,
Evan B. McCord,
Hugh McQuiston,
James P. McFarland,
Isaac Martin,

George Dickerson,
John M. Eckert,
Harrison Fugale,
James M. Flanigan,
Wm. Finley,
Wm. Fogwell,
S. T. Gallen,
John A. Goe,
Henry Helmer,
Frank Haverstick,
Abel Haughey,
James M. Hames,
John Hussey,
Thomas S. Huston,
George W. Huston,
Phil C. Harshman,
Emnet Jobe,
D. A. Jones,
Addison M. Jones,
Jacob Knee,
David Kelley,
Adam G. Kershner,
John H. Koogler,
Allen Lucas,
Solomon Lucas,
Fred B. Ledbeller,
Elijah H. Lewis,
Henry I. Luty,
Joseph Lewis,
W. A. Martin,
Samuel Neal,
Robert Pratt,

John A. Miller,
Henry Oakman,
Simeon W. Oldham,
Abner W. Oldham,
John Phillips,
Harrison R. Putnam,
David Patterson,
Alfred Rader,
Frederick Steward,
Samuel Sutter,
Wm. Studevant,
Nathaniel Studevant,
George S. Sharp,
Obediah Sylvester,
John F. Shearer,
John M. Sellars,
Lassing H. Shadley,
Henry Story,
Adam Sites,
Martin Sepler,
James M. Tounsley,
Evan Tiser,
Wm. Tingley,
Michael Tobias,
Henry W. Tobias,
Harrison Truby,
John Tohos,
John M. Vancleaf,
James R. P. Weaver,
Lorenzo Williams,
Joshua Winget,
John W. Wikel.

COMPANY H.

James Kyle,
Alfred L. Trader,
David T. Davidson,

Wm. Bair,
Charles H. Thomas,
John P. Patterson,

Andrew Gowars,
Clinton C. Nickols,
John G. McPherson,
Isaac R. Lane,
James M. Thirkield,
David W. Williamson,
Philip L. McDowell,
Levi Rader,
Charles H. Miller,
George W. Pottle,
George Gillett,
Vespasian Pottle,
Wm. Foreman,
John G. Bull,
John I. Bull,
James E. Bull,
Andrew H. Black,
Daniel Buckley,
Jacob Brocias,
Wm. Clifton,
Daniel Conrad,
John N. Chisty,
Hugh M. Cooper,
Robert Cooper,
David D. Cheeney,
Wm. H. Crawford,
James Clark,
Frank Dinurddie,
Louis Duke,
James Doole,
Dennis H. Deam,
Gilbert Dehart,
Granville P. Edsall,
John Eyler,
Henry H. Eavey,
Samuel Furguson,
Lewis Gilbert,
George V. Goode,

David R. Hopping,
James Holt,
John H. Hoover,
John F. James,
James Losly,
Wm. K. McLaughlin,
Patrick H. Maley,
Albert H. Miller,
Samuel H. McMillan,
Smith Mendenhall,
Samuel Mendenhall,
John H. Noble,
Martin O. Dowel,
Christopher Peterson,
Lewis Peterson,
Wilber Peterson,
Abel F. Peterson,
Jonas Peterson, jr,
James M. Quinn,
Thomas Reid,
James R. Reid,
Anthony C. Rupell,
Wm. A. Street,
James M. Starr,
John D. M. Stewart,
Alfred Stratton,
Robert K. Stevenson,
Benjamin Short,
Wm. A. Hook,
James M. Smith,
Fenton Squire,
Jacob M. Sutton,
Samuel Thompson,
John K. Tannyhill,
John C. Thompson,
James A. Welch,
Mahlon Womble,
Joseph K. Wright,

Wm. M. Walton,
Charles E. Way,
James Staley,
Samuel Strickler,
James A. Smeigh,
Cornelius Stark,
Wm. C. Thompson,
Christian Vanhorn,

Daniel Vulty,
Jesse Wright,
Robert P. Walker,
George M. Wright,
George C. Winter,
Hugh M. Weir,
John W. Whiteman,
David M. Winter.

Roster of 110th Regiment.

Colonel J. Warren Keifer,
Lieut. Colonel Wm. N. Foster,
Lieut. Colonel Otho H. Binkley,
Major, Otho H. Binkley,
Major Wm. S. McElwaine,
Major Aaron Spangler,
Surgeon S. Pixley,
Surgeon R. McCandless,
Ass't Surgeon E. C. Owens,

Ass't Surgeon H. H. Bishop,
Ass't Surgeon A. W. Pinkerton,
Ass't Surgeon John W. Mack,
Ass't Surgeon Wm. H. Park,
Ass't Surgeon E. P. Ebersole,
Chaplain James Harvey,
Chaplain Lucius W. Chapman,
Chaplain Milton J. Miller,

COMPANY D.

Captain Wm. McElwain,
First Lieut. Daniel D. Moore,
Second Lieut. Alex. Trimble,
First Serg't Thomas S. Clark,
Second Serg't Joseph Vaneaton,
Third Serg't Wm. A. Jones,
Fourth Serg't Wm. H. Byrd,
Fifth Sergt Wm. H. Hany,
Corporal Lewis H. Beal,
Corporal Franklin H. McDaniel,
Corporal A. Pickthem,
Corporal Abraham Sheeley,
Corporal Thomas Goe,
Corporal Thomas J. Daughterly,
Corporal Wm. V. Luce,
Corporal Frederick LaRue,

James H. Clemons,
John Crites,
Jesse C. Clemons,
David Crawford,
Hiram Crumley,
Stephen Dunn,
Wm. R. Day,
James Dukin,
James C. Freeman,
Amos W. Files,
George M. Fletcher,
George W. Gano,
John Gaylor,
Wm. Gaylor,
Frederick Husker,
Christopher Hornick,

Preston Anderson,
Samuel N. Adams,
Nelson G. Adams,
Harmon Anderson,
James C. Bralton,
David Curl,

Oliver P. Heaton,
Peter Honecker,
James C. Hartsook,
A. C. Hubbard,
Joseph G. Hawkins,
James H. Harshman.

Roster of 44th Regiment.

Colonel Samuel A. Gilbert,
Lieut. Col. H. Blair Wilson,
Lieut. Col. A. O. Mitchell,
Lieut. Col. Lysander W. Tulley,
Major A. O. Mitchell,
Major Alpheus S. Moore.

Surgeon H. K. Steele,
Ass't Surgeon John H. Rodgers,
Ass't Surgeon Douglas Luce,
Ass't Surgeon Benj. F. Davis,
Chaplain Thomas P. Childs,

COMPANY D.

Lysander W. Tulley,
Nickolus D. Badger,
Samuel C. Howell,
Edward Rice,
T. B. Burkholder,
Brinton Baker,
Joseph Badger,
Milo E. Lawrence,
Wm. H. Dugdale,
O. S. Lynn,
L. M. Hageman,
Isaac N. Evans,
John W. Berth,
Caleb Paris,
M. I. Loy,
Frasser Brown,
J. M. R. Cline,
J. H. Armstrong,
Wm. Armstrong,
Joseph Baker,
Wm. Baker,
Thomas Batchelder,

James C. Brown,
Zebulon Berth,
John B. Cress,
Hamilton Cross,
Robert B. Carlisle,
Patrick Cashin,
Robert Cheeny,
Jonathan Cline,
J. F. Collier,
H. J. Confer,
John Crawford,
Charles Creighton,
Edward Cassady,
Ripley J. Davis,
Michael Dillon,
John C. Elliot,
Aaron H. Ellis,
Jacob M. Ford,
John Flatter,
Robert Farris,
Charles Field,
O. T. Hale.

Roster of 10th Ohio Battery.

COMMISSIONED OFFICERS.

Captain J. R. Crain,
First Lieut. J. B. Gage, sr. V. E.,
First Lieut. James Gilmore, jr.

Sec'd Lieut. S. A. Galbreath, sr.,
Sec'd Lieut. J. C. Bontecon, jr.,

NON-COMMISSIONED OFFICERS.

First Serg't J. W. Randall, V. E.,
Q. Master's Serg't Geo. Dasher,
R. L. White, F. S., V. E.,
W. H. Byrd, F. S., V. E.

N. Daron, F. S., V. E.,
Wm. Myers, F. S., V. E.,
George O. White, F. S., V. E.,
Joseph L. Gilmore, F. S., V. E.

CORPORALS.

Cal. Swift,
J. B. Marshall,
P. G. Clevell, V. E.,
B. C. Johnson, V. E.,
John Kauffman, V. E.,
Wells Jones, V. E.,
John Sayers,
Jacob King,
George Wentz, V. E.

Andrew Shafer,
Jacob Beemer, V. E.,
Henry Owens,
Artificer Jacob Wheeler, V. E.,
Artificer Wm. W. McFarland,
Bugler ch. John G. Trimble,
Bugler Charles Mayer,
Wagoner John W. Friend.

PRIVATES.

Wm. R. Arthur, V. E.,
John M. Armstrong,
Wm. Andrew,
Henry Boyles, V. E.,

James S. Beemes,
Daniel Buckley,
Henry Betz, 1st,
Henry Betz, 2d,

TENTH OHIO BATTERY.

Wm. Boelzner,
Anthony Boehm,
Wm. Broder, V. E.,
Herman Bolenhagen, V. E.,
Theodore Becker,
Anton Brewer,
John Bolander,
Isaiah Cook,
Wm. Cook, V. E.,
John A. Conger,
Albert Cochran, V. E.,
Andrew Crissman,
Wm. M. Daugherty,
George R. Davis,
Denis Delaney,
Frank Ditmer, V. E.,
George E. Diprey, V. E,,
Nicholas Dorn,
Lewis Dixon,
Gottfried Deckert,
Wm. H. Ditton,
Morris Davis,
John F. Droste,
John Eggert, V. E.,
Francis Ebert,
Benjamin Farnsworth, V. E.,
Augustus Fisher,
John T. Fishbaugh.
Franklin Foughty, V. E.,
Filander Ford,
Joseph Funk,
John Fieber,
Jacob Gift,
Albert Gauss,
Michael Geisel, V. E.,
Henry P. Gross,
Nevin C. M. Hill,
Herman Hayn, V. E.,

Wm. Harp, V. E.,
George Heller,
Charles Hanway,
Edward Humphreys,
Charles Hollowell,
Edwin Hollowell,
Michael Helk, V. E.,
Wm. Heineke, V. E.,
Nicholas Hertent,
John Irwin,
George F. Johnson,
Isaac Jolley, V. E.,
Henry P. Jones,
James Judy,
Peter Joute,
John S. Kirkwood, V. E.,
Walter Keith,
Frank Kauffman, V. E.,
Emil King,
Ignatz Koch,
Michael Von Kennen, V. E.,
Anthony Koenig, V. E.,
Wm. Koebler,
Frank Knauber,
Milton P. Layman,
John Lahey, V. E.,
Frederick Linderman, V. E.,
Frederick Maurer, V. E.,
Jonathan McDormond,
Myers Mitchel,
John A. Mitchel,
James C. Morgan,
Adam Markley, V. E.,
George Moore,
Frank Moline,
George Metz,
Henry Meyer,
James Nesbit.

Gustav Nolte,
Philip Ott,
Louis Philips,
George Pfeifer, V. E.,
Wm. Pritchard,
Hiram Powers,
Jeremiah Parsons, V. E.,
Charles S. Ramsey,
Levi W. Robison,
Andrew J. Rudduck, V. E.,
Levi Ringwalt,
Dempster Randall,
John W. Randall, V. E.,
George W. Randall,
John Ruhle,
Gotleib Reiner,
James Ryan,
Andrew Shimeal, V. E.,
Thomas C. Smith, V. E.,
George Smith,
Jacob B. Smith,
Henry C. Smith,
George W. Shroude, V. E.
Abraham Stout,
Christopher Schrag, V. E.,
Frederick Supper.

Joseph Shafer,
Joseph Streble,
Frank Schneider, V. E.,
Frederick Schaufert,
John T. Stephens,
John H. Simpson, V. E.,
Werner Schlumph, V. E.,
James A. Thomas, V. E.,
George Toy,
Achabees Tarrant,
George L. Townsley,
Reese Underwood,
Edward W. Vanhorn,
Wm. Volk, V. E.,
George Verhr,
George H. White,
Samuel C. Wright,
George Wehrley, V. E.,
Wm. M. Williams, V. E.,
John Wallanbauft,
Conrad Weiss, V. E.,
Jacob Witson,
Chares Weiland,
Thomas E. White,
Frederick Young,

DIED IN SERVICE.

Thomas Day,
John Fulerton,
James Guyton,
Joseph Martins,
Patrick Malone,
Ezra T. Mitchner,
Patrick Murphy.

Levi Reams,
Albert Sheldon,
Adam Seifert,
Amos Thompson,
John F. Wilson,
David Wright,

DESERTED.

Jacob Barnhard,
Solon Cook,
Richard Giligan,
Charles Hummel,
Charles C. Irwin,
Robert Morrison,

Wm. R. Kennard,
Michael Mitchel,
John Snodgrass,
John Thompson,
Frank Smith,
Louis Tuge,

DISCHARGED.

Captain H. B. White,
Captain Francis Seaman,
Lieut. Frederick W. Bardwell,
Lieut. A. A. Blount,
Lieut. Edward Grosskopff,
Lieut. Wm. T. Newcomb,
Lieut. George Kleder,
Lieut. Lanson Zane,
First Serg't Charles S. Rice,
First Serg't Wm. F. Nixon,
Q. M. Serg't Abraham Hulsizer,

Sergeant Levi Henderson,
Sergeant Jonas Tease,
Corporal Greenbury Milburn,
Corporal Francis O'Shea,
Corporal Pelegreno Tuchasey,
Artificer John S. Owens,
Artificer Mortimer Carey,
Artificer Erasmus Tulleys,
Artificer Joseph Cline,
Bugler Wm. H. Bretney,

PRIVATES.

Charles M. Adams,
Henry K. Brown,
James Brown,
Samuel A. Barr,
Isaiah L. Bottsford,
Thomas Beacham,
John Britton,
Thomas Bush,
Isaiah Cook,
Philip Demer,
John Dunson,
Robert Dunson,
Jeff. C. Davis,
John A. Davis,

Wm. H. Elwell,
Richard Ealey,
Charles Fisher,
Orlando V. Flora,
Thomas Fitzgerrald,
Thomas Fryar,
Edward Gavin,
Julius R. Gillett,
John A. Goe,
Wm. H. Grant,
Michael Hobran,
Pat. Juge,
Pat. Keating,
David Kearns,

John Kershner,
Daniel Kurtz,
Samuel J. Knott,
James Kitchen,
Wm. Leslie,
John C. Leibold,
Snow. R. Laurance,
Calvin Meachem,
Augustus Machelite,
George B. McPherson,
Michael Murphy,
Joseph J. Osborn,
Mat. Pandegrast,
B. F. Peck,
John W. Randall,
Dempster Randall,
Densmore Randall,
James Rix,
Wm. Ryan,
Richard Sparrow,
Jacob Switzer,
John W. Shumaker,
Benjamin P. Scott,
John Scott,
Batz Spicemaker,
Reuben Savage,
Philo M. Swift,
Samuel Stevens,
Emsley D. Smith,
Henry Vanmeter,
Nathan Wike,
George S. Wright,
Fred Weber,
David Wall,
Jacob Wilhelm,
James Worthington.

TRANSFERS.—Vet. Res. Corps.

George Cave,
James K. Frazier,
Joseph Hargrave,
Wm. H. Levan,
Lucius Luce,
James O. Salesbury.

UNDER-COOKS.

Edward Kenedy,
James McMillen,
James Sykes.
Ed Spencer,
Charles Helm, officer's servant,

Roster of 154th Regiment.

Colonel Robert Stevenson,
Lieut. Colonel E. Wilson,
Major Wm. A. Neil,
Surgeon George Watt,
Ass't Surgeon Leigh McClung,
Quartermaster A. J. Trader.

Adjutant J. B. Hagan,
Chaplain Robert Caslin,
Serg't Major Linus P. Bonner,
Commissary Serg't Henry Miller,
Commissary Serg't L. Paine,

COMPANY A.

Captain James B. Corry,
First Lieut. John I. Heinz,
Second Lieut. Jasper W. Reed,
Sergeant Pierce Folkerth,
Second Serg't Sam'l W. Cox, jr.,
Third Serg't Charles Shaw,
Fourth Serg't John Hume,
Fifth Serg't Joseph R. Bull,
Corporal Isaac A. Furguson,
Second Corporal Henry Cony,
Third Corporal George B. Hyde,
Fourth Corporal M. Musselman,
Fifth Corporal C. B. Lewis,
Sixth Corporal S. J. Ward,
Seventh Corporal B. R. Gass,
Eighth Corporal James Gregg,
Drum Major Julius Cone,
Fifer Alburton F. Hopkins,
Andrew Armstrong,
Robert Armstrong,

Wm. Brewer,
David R. Brewer,
Joseph Baldwin,
George Baker,
John Birch,
Newton A. Brown,
Walter Blaisdell,
Wm. Baker,
Sylvester B. Bloomfield,
John H. Barton,
James H. Baker,
George Carlisle,
Ira Collier,
James D. Currie,
Wm. R. Corey,
Cornelius Crist,
Wm. Cleveland,
Isaac H. Crowell,
Wm. B. Cornwell,
Wm. H. H. Deming,

Chauncy W. Deming,
Andrew Dodds,
Jonathan Folck,
Patrick Fogerty,
Kimball Farmer,
Cyrus Hurch,
Silas Hopping,
Moses Hopping,
John W. Hamilton,
Wm. Hafner,
Charles Harlan,
Elmer B. Hopkins,
Wilson A. Hopkins,
James Harris,
Daniel A. Jobe,
Augustus H. Jones,
Baker Jones,
David Kershner,
Nathaniel King,
Charles Knott,
Philip Kennedy,
Theodore Leonard,
Edgar Lefever,
Samuel McColloch,
James C. Miller,

James Nevins,
John Nickols,
Joel B. Record,
Andrew J. Smith,
Abram Sweny,
Wm. R. Sloane,
Russel Tulley,
Joseph M. C. Wilson,
Wm. L. Wilson,
Frank Wilder,
Daniel Wilson,
Pardon C. Wilson,
Hiatt Welliston,
James F. Lynn,
Ezra B. Lewis,
Richard McCullough,
Joel Wilder,
George Town,
Abram Pearson,
Augustus S. Hildreth,
Abraham Johnson,
Leonard Mower,
Johnson Weakly,
Frederick Mars,
James McNeal.

COMPANY B.

Captain A. C. Miller,
First Lieut. J. H. Matthews,
Second Lieut. Oscar Pool,
W. B. Smith,
P. L. McDowald,
C. Taylor,
R. F. Marshall,
J. P. Poland,
M. F. Anderson,
L. King,

P. L. Davis,
W. M. Beveridge,
George Lauman,
E. C. Hamilton,
C. I. Nesbitt,
G. R. Gibney,
J. D. Allen,
Wm. Alberger,
Wm. Anderson,
J. L. Alexander,

THE ONE HUNDRED AND FIFTY-FOURTH.

G. M. Boyd,
R. F. Buckles,
Wm. Brown,
H. E. Barlow,
B. Y. Berry,
George Beal,
Robert Boyce,
George H. Crabb,
D. M. Charters,
Nathame Collins,
A. Cross,
M. Cook,
C. E. Case,
Dan Dean,
S. C. Elwell,
J. Erwin,
J. Ewing, jr.,
B. F. Good,
D. A. Grug,
F. C. Hicks,
J. A. Harbison,
George Haliday,
James Hays,
A. Kelley,
H. B. Kepler,
O. Miller,
E. L. Moorehouse,
J. E. Martin,
O. W. Marshall,
G. W. Manor,
J. A. Miller,
R. F. Martin,
S. Marshall,
Wm. Milbourne,
D. G. Martin,
J. G. McWhirk,
H. McFadden,
Thomas Moore,

J. H. Miller,
G. W. Neville,
Samuel Newton,
A. C. Neal,
S. G. Oakley,
E. C. Paine,
G. L. Paine,
R. H. C. Parcell,
Wm. Pettigrew,
Jerry Parkhill,
Charles Robinson,
M. W. Roberts,
Joseph Slipp,
E. W. Shane,
H. B. Syeney,
Frank Sweet,
A. L. Smith,
Nat H. Stutsman,
Lon Snively,
S. L. Taylor,
J. M. Thirkield,
W. W. Torrence,
Mark Ullery,
R. B. Williams,
J. E. Wright,
D. Williams,
John Blessing,
Wm. Hamilton,
Thomas T. Harrington,
Uriah Horney,
Folger Howell,
H. B. Hopping,
John F. Hopping,
H. C. Johnson,
D. C. Laurence,
A. Lafferty,
J. M. McLane,
Alexander McLane,

J. C. McFarland,
Aaron Milburn,
Wm. M. McFarland,
Martin McClelland,
F. A. McKinney,
Martin Musselman,
J. O. McClintic,
Ira K. Minton,
Thomas Nesbett,
George B. Patterson,
Wm. Potter,
Michael Raper,
W. Sherrer,
Charles H. Srouf,

J. N. Saum,
S. I. Sanders,
George W. Shroad,
Samuel Sparrow,
Wm. Stark,
Sanford Wilson,
Leonodas Wilson,
H. D. Wise,
David J. Wise,
Samuel Wise,
George O. White,
Calvin Williams,
Martin Whalen,
Wm. H. Wright.

COMPANY D.

Captain Henry B. Guthrie,
First Lieut. George C. Canfield,
Second Lieut. Benj. F. Darst,
Silas B. Shaner,
John R. Ridenhour,
Thomas Halverstick,
A. B. Cosler,
George A. Harner,
Joseph Swaynee,
Henry C. Glotfelter,
Albert Swadner,
Harvey Helmer,
James Marshall,
John Archer,
Samuel H. Boroff,
Albert Haynes,
Cyrus Beackem,
Joseph J. Osburn,
Thomas Archer,
Isaac Ankeny,
Jacob Ankeny,

Alexander Anderson,
Henry J. Boroff,
Wilson S. Bumgardner,
David A. Brewer,
David Bopp,
Joseph Benham,
Wm. H. Brown,
John W. Benson,
Adam R. Bickett,
Edward Beal,
Harvey Bickett,
Reuben B. Carley,
Wm. G. Cory,
James W. Collins,
James M. Collins,
James Carvon,
David R. Colwell,
John Frost,
Andrew Fisher,
Harry Furguson,
John Fields,

David Fields,
George W. Gross,
Wm. H. Huston,
Samuel Harner,
John Haynes,
John H. Hyland,
Henry Harman,
Will Hayes,
George Hendrick,
John W. Haverstick,
Wm. J. Haverstick,
Hiram Irvin,
John W. Irvin,
James F. Junkins,
George W. Gerner,
Powell Lamme,
Timothy Linebaugh,
Charles Lodbetter,
Steven McClain,
Burgess Morgan.

Joel F. Needles,
Michael H. Powers,
Samuel V. Prather,
John Ritchie,
Andrew Reader,
Adolphus Stevenson,
Jacob S. Swainey,
Solomon Sheeley,
Jackson Sidensticker,
Andrew J. Sutton,
John Swaime,
Isaac Shew,
Isaac Swadner,
Jonathan Story,
W. H. Scott,
David W. Wolf,
Wm. H. Wolf,
Abram M. Wolf,
Henry Weinreich,

COMPANY E.

Captain Joseph F. Bouck,
First Lieut. Benj. H. Barney,
Second Lieut. John W. Tobias,
First Sergeant John E. Felton,
Second Serg't O. H. P. Moler,
Third Serg't Mark Newland,
Fourth Serg't Jacob L. Land,
Fifth Serg't Neal Zimmerman,
Corporal Levi T. Nagle,
Second Corp. Sam'l H. Prather,
Third Corp. Wm. Haverstick,
Fourth Corp. C. M. Galloway,
Fifth Corp. Sampson Cosad,
Sixth Corp. Paris H. Peterson,
Seventh Corp. S. H. Harshman,

Eighth Corp. Simon Gast,
Noah Aley,
Levi D. Aley,
Wesley Blessing,
David H. Baker,
Jacob L. Broadstone,
Albert T. Bush,
Aaron Cory,
Benjamin F. Cory,
Wm. S. Chany,
Joseph Cover,
Henry J. Cory,
Valentine Coy,
John Carter,
Thomas W. Carson,

James Dinwiddie,
Wm. H. Engle,
Milton Fookes,
Henry Fishenig,
Jacob Garst,
John W. Gordon,
John W. Haverstick,

Sylvester Haus,
Jacob Helmer,
John M. Hawker,
Montgomery Harshman,
John Haus,
John I. Hook,
John O. Harman.

COMPANY F.

Captain Richard King,
Daniel McMillen,
Jesse R. Marshall,
John W. Manor,
Daniel P. Jeffries,
Wm. M. North,
John S. Watts,
Joshua Jackson,
John R. Gowdy,
Chapel H. Winter,
Hugh M. Andrew,
Daniel M. Stewart,
Wm. McClelland,
James G. Stevenson,
Albert Marshall,
Albert Stratton,
Oliver Bayless,
Samuel J. Andrew,
Dan Baker,
George H. Bayless,
Ambrose Beal,
Isaac S. Bond,
Erastus Bonner,
Linus P. Bonner,
Edward M. Bonner,
Edward A. Binkley,
John H. Bratton,

John G. Brown,
James S. Buck,
Robert A. Buck,
Wm. H. Corey,
Albert Collier,
Thornton Collier,
George W. Cosby,
Jeremiah E. Cosby,
John Charters,
Michael Day,
Wm. Findley,
Henry P. Galloway,
James H. Gowdy,
Joseph C. Cartrell,
Wm. S. Galvin,
Wm. Graham,
Thomas Ginn,
James M. Hawkins,
Wm. H. Hutchison,
James Hart,
Edward Hicks,
Luther Haines,
Jacob James,
Samuel A. Kendall,
John W. King,
James B. King,
A. H. Kirkpatrick,

George McGaughey,
Isaac McElwaine,
James W. McDaniel,
Charles R. Milburn,
John Menmues,
James Menmues,
John Maxwell,
Wm. H. Pierce,
James P. Pierce,
Joseph Ray,
Orville Read,
Elijah B. Reeves,
Adam Russel,
James M. Stratton,
James R. Stewart,
Frederick Shoemaker,
David W. Shoemaker,

George Shoemaker,
Jacob Smith,
Isaac Shearer,
Jacob H. Snell,
Harrison Snyder,
Franklin B. Taylor,
Wm. C. Winter,
Alexander J. C. Wead,
James C. T. Wead,
Jackson Whiliman,
John Warnock,
Wilson H. Wilson,
John Watson,
Wm. Watson,
Steven Warwick,
Benjamin F. Jameay,
Wm. A. Robertson.

COMPANY G.

John W. Hepfard,
Ben H. Hontop,
Wm. Hawker,
Wm. John,
Douglas E. King,
Joseph H. Cable,
George C. Koogler,
Samuel B. Kelly,
Wm. Lesher,
John Lents,
David R. Lesher,
Wm. Leonard,
David Lindsey,
John Miller,
John Mallow,
John McIntosh,
Albert Owens,
John L. Peterson,

Elias Quinn,
John Reeker,
John Rohns,
Robert Richarson,
George Richarson,
David Sherman,
Francis P. Stull,
Peter Swagard,
Emance Snyder,
John A. Stewart,
Aaron Shingledecker,
James M. C. Stewart,
Samuel H. Strickle,
John Srobel,
Edward Stine,
Wm. Smith,
Wm. T. Tobias,
Harris Truber,

Wm. Troop,
Daniel F. Weaver,
John D. Yingleng,
John Yales,
J. W. Hall,
Michael Ford,
Ezra Davidson,
John A. Seiss,
D. H. Williamson,
John F. Daugherty,
George Truman,
Wm. Kirkpatrick,
Charles Gage,
Levi Ridple,
Christopher Bingaman,
Frederick Spellbring,
Jerry H. Gest,
Michael Daugherty, jr.,
Wm. Anderson,
James Stanfield,
Robert Hamilton,
Henry O. Barnett,
James R. Anderson,
Abijeuh Anderson,
Philip P. Anderson,
Charles Austin,
Nathan Anderson,
Abner Bingamon,
James Broadstone,
David Bingamon,
David Borden,
Benjamin F. Chamblis,
George W. Curvault,
George Collier,
H. W. Cheny,
Warren Chany,
Joseph Day,
Samuel L. Disbro,

Peter Dunnevant,
Joseph C. Evans,
Wm. Elam,
Josiah Elam,
Wm. S. Frazier,
Wm. D. Fowler,
Albert Gest,
Lounal Griswold,
Mathew H. Gage,
That Holland,
Hugh W. Harper,
James E. Haus,
Franklin Holt,
James Kennedy,
Tillman Loyd,
James M. Luce,
Orrin Morris,
Frank McFerrim,
W. H. McClelland, sr.,
Wm. H. McClelland, jr.,
George Maconbrie,
John Mendenhall,
Thomas P. Mendenhall,
John B. Mason,
Francis M. Moffit,
Benjamin T. Norman,
Isaac Oldham,
Thomas Pottinger,
John Power,
Wm. H. Perrine,
Cyrus Read,
Wm. B. Reige,
Robert W. Riddle.
John Ryan,
John M. Sanders,
Samuel Stanfield,
Daniel S. Stump,
Daniel Salsbury,

Ryan Saulsberry,
George R. Stiles,
Isaac Stiles,
Wm. I. Stump,
Joseph C. Sims,
Wm. Stanfield,

Benjama Speer,
James S. Talbert,
John Taylor,
George B. Talbert,
Joseph Wilds,
John M. Wright.

COMPANY II.

Joel Arey,
Lucian Smith,
James Thomas,
Jacob Simons,
Carpenter Conklin,
Isaiah Mullen,
D. I. Browder,
Hiram Powers,
Wm. Weller,
John McGregor,
Wm. Gordam,
Platte E. Mott,
George Powers,
Jacob P. Brown,
Daniel M. St. John,
James Mullen,
Wm. II. Arnold,
John Andrew,
Joshua Arnett,
Harmon Ary,
Joshua Bayliff,
I. W. Beason,
Lewis Bartin,
Levi Bortem,
Marshall Brineil,
W. C. Brinell,
Wm. D. Bone,
Peter Bun,

David Bush,
Solomon Bargdell,
Samuel Curl,
W. H. Campell,
Hiram Conklin,
Elijah S. Coat,
Isaac Cohagan,
James H. Crusew,
Samuel Devo,
Elisha Ellis,
Samuel Ellis,
John Irvin,
Allen Faulkner,
Lewis Faucett,
Nathan Fisher,
Simon H. Fudge,
Dwight K. Frost,
Henry Goram,
Wm. A. Harris,
John A. Hickmar,
Napoleon B. Harris,
David F. Flickmar,
Francis M. Harness,
James T. Hite,
James M. Linkhart,
Franklin Lucas,
Edward Linkhart,
John McElwain,

Calvin Mullem,
John March,
Harvey Murphy,
Lewis Mullin,
R. McCollough,
Joshua P. Oglesbee,
Asa R. Olehant,
James S. Peterson,
Adam H. Palmer,
Allen Powers,
Adam Powell,
John N. Peterson,
James H. Stillings,
Poley C. Siles,
Charles W. St. John,

Wesley Stevans,
Alonzo C. Smith,
Wilson St. John,
Silas Shoemaker,
John B. Spencer,
Charles Shipman,
John F. Sutton,
James Thomas,
James Wilson,
Albert Wickersham,
Clinton Williams,
George Bragg,
Henry Conklin,
John S. McGregor,
James Stipe.

Roster of 54th Regiment.

Michael Bradley,
George Marshall,
John Robinson,
John Goldsberry,
Otway Owens,
Richard Campion,

Wm. Connor,
Wm. Beall,
Charles F. Beall,
James W. Beall,
Albert Black,
L. Maddox.

Roster of 34th Regiment.

Captain S. R. S. West,
First Lieut. Albert Nesbitt,
Second Lieut: A. S. Frazer,
Orderly Serg't Frank Millward,
Sergeant I. C. Hutchins,
Sergeant N. P. Marvell,
Sergeant H. J. Marshall,
Sergeant C. L. McClure,
Corporal John Tarbox,

Corporal J. A. McNichols,
Corporal E. D. Roberts,
Corporal John H. Placke,
Corporal F. A. Austin,
Corporal John H. McCurren,
Corporal Staley F. Stemble,
Corporal James Benson,
Fifer Dwight K. Frost,
Drummer Wm. Thompson.

PRIVATES.

Wm. R. Adams,
Theodore C. Aarons,
George W. Atchley,
Wm. H. Austin,
Thomas Ball,
Dudley W. Beall,
Lewis Beall,
Matthew Bigger,
James R. Bull,
John W. Cartwright,
Edward Clevell,
Simon Cook,
Ed. M. Cordle,
Frank Curl,
Wm. Davis,
Wm. Delahunt,
Anthony Ebleheart,
George W. Ebright,

John M. Ford,
James I. Fulton,
Theodore Guggenheimer,
F. G. Hale,
Wm. Harris,
Theodore Harrison,
Morton L. Hawkins,
Wm. C. Higginson,
John F. E. Hillen,
Wm. Hitzing,
Wm. H. Hull,
Aust. M. Kelly,
Wm. H. King,
Wm. H. Kinnan,
Alex. C. Kyle,
John M. Lawrie,
Benjamin H. Likens,
John W. Logan.

George Lowe,
Wm. L. Luark,
John Mehen,
Edgar Mehen,
Wm. Meshwert,
Randolph Metcalf,
Ben. F. Mullen,
Willis D. McDonald,
Robert E. McCormick,
Napoleon McGrew,
Wm. H. Newbold,
John W. Puckham,
Wm. A. Patterson,
Valentine Percifield,
Alva L. Peters,
Jason D. Phillips,
James M. Rhodes,
Asa D. Robbins,
Milton Rogers,
Peter Rollar,
Wm. F. Rosenbarger.

John Sachs,
Permetus K. Sale,
Wesley D. Sebring,
Charles Shinkle,
John W. Shorten,
Henry S. Shue,
John W. Smith,
Ed. H. Stevens,
J. C. Stewart,
Andrew Stires,
Daniel Stratton,
Wm. Strohmeir,
A. B. Swenk,
James A. Thompson,
Innis A. Townsley,
James W. Watson,
John Williams,
James B. Winter,
John G. Winter,
J. G. Worthington,

Roster of 184th Regiment.

Colonel Henry S. Comager,
Lieut. Col. Chandler W. Carroll,
Major E. S. Dodd,
Surgeon L. G. Meyer.

Ass't Surg. Rob't A. Richardson,
Ass't Surgeon Henry H. Shaw,
Ass't Surgeon Emmet W. Price,

CAPTAINS.

Levi S. Jamison,
Joseph Allen,
Joseph W. Wise,
J. D. Moler,
George P. Davis,

Wm. J. Widener,
Luman P. P. Folkerth,
Simon Perkins,
John McNeil,
James Barrett.

FIRST LIEUTENANTS.

George A. Ells,
Alex M. Duck,
Jerome Dubois,
David A. Murphy,
John Giller,
Joseph A. Blair.

Charles W. Gerwig,
Robert Detwiler,
Joseph McCreary,
Henry C. Canfield,
Wm. H. Bettis,

SECOND LIEUTENANTS.

Harry Davis,
Hiram Reed,
Alonzo Langdon,
Charles E. Warren,
Harrison P. Taylor,

Michael Steck,
Frank Hatton,
Wm. F. Langdon,
John W. Horton,
David H. Comager.

COMPANY K.

Sam Cox,
W. A. Hopkins,
Robert Armstrong,
Andrew Armstrong,
Cyrus Hush,
Frank Wilder,
John Hume.
Wm. M. King,
James Stratton.
Isaac Stratton,
James Kershner,
David Connor,
Wm. Connor.
Nathan King,
Dan Shafer,
Jerry Shafer,
Wm. Baker,
James Caldwell.
George Carlisle,
Joseph S. Wilson,
John Huston,
Frank Shroaf,
Johnson Weakly.
Albert Kelly.

John Schulnerer,
I. T. Confer,
Abram Reed,
Wm. Dugan,
Elmer Hopkins,
J. R. Record.
Nathaniel Collins,
Frank McCreary,
James Bailey,
J. T. Collett,
Mike Bradley,
Jesse Record,
Samuel Clark.
Wm. Kiler,
George Kiler,
Charley Brewer.
John Brewer,
Thomas Toole,
Pat Abbey,
Moses Hopping,
A. Collins,
John Skellen.
Snoden Lawrence,

Roster of 3d N. Y. Calvary.

James L. Lantz,
L. H. Whiteman,
Jerry L. Whiteman,
Theodore Collier,
D. D. Barns,
W. V. Lawrence,
John T. Hogue,
W. A. Bitner,
George W. Bitner.

Harvey E. Randall,
Gustave Schilling,
James Rickets,
Andrew Hutchinson,
John Q. A. Goe,
C. C. Robinson,
Hank B. Keplar,
Joseph M. Barlow,

Roster of 1st Ohio Reg. Inf'y.

COMPANY E.

Lieutenant S. Ewing.
L. H. Roots.
Thomas Curl.
J. M. Jones.
Isaac Rudduck.
Joseph Cummings.
James Harris.
Robert Cross.
Mike Geisner.
Martin Buckly.
John Carn.

Mike Brennen.
Joshua Jones.
John Raney.
John Kisan.
Mitchel Beason.
James Sheppard.
Robert Jones.
Wm. Moses.
Levi Sleigle.
John Skellon.
James Tharpe.

ERRATA.

Officers of Company E., Seventy-Fourth Regiment, O. V. I.

The following officers were overlooked in furnishing roster to the printer, hence their appearance here:

Captain Joseph Fisher,
First Lieut. H. H. Herring,
First Lieut. B. F. Shickley.

Second Lieut. Thomas Kirby,
First Sergeant Peter O. Benham,

Anecdotes and Incidents.

PRACTICAL JOKING

Sometimes the boys would indulge in playing tricks on each other. I will give an incident or two: One time, soon after the battle of Stone River, while we were yet occupying the old Sibley tents, the boys concluded that they would have a little sport at the expense of one of their comrades; accordingly they arranged to have some singing, one evening, in one of the tents. They came in until the tent was pretty nearly full. They placed a stool near the middle of the tent, to which they invited the singer—having previously placed some cartridges under the seat. The singer took his seat, and after singing one or two songs, which were loudly encored, which was to produce the impression that there was no trick in it, one of the boys called for the song of "Reuben Wright and Phebe Brown," and at the verse where the old man shot at Reuben, which was the signal, one of the boys, set fire to the cartridges, which lifted stool, singer and all, about two feet high, singeing his hair and whiskers, and filling the tent with smoke. When it cleared away there was not a man to be seen, they having taken to their heels, leaving the poor fellow without an audience. It is unnecessary to add that the entertainment was suddenly brought to a close. The victim of the above joke was the author of this book. The boys acknowledged, however, that they carried the joke a little too far, there being more powder than they thought there was. It was a long time before I found out who ignited the cartridges. If I had known it then I would have made it pretty hot for them; but then everybody was ignorant of who did it.

Another practical joke was perpetrated on a couple of the boys who were bunking together. It was while we were on the march one evening, late. Just before we halted there was the appearance of a heavy rain coming up. We halted on the side of the hill, and commenced putting up our shelter-tents. After erecting the tents we then had to dig trenches around them to keep the water from running through them. It soon commenced raining, and rained very hard. The two boys whom I mentioned had their tent just below one of the boys, who was a very mischievous fellow, full of fun, and, by the way, a good-hearted fellow and a good soldier. Jim got up, and procuring a shovel, succeeded in turning the water into the aforesaid boys' tent, completely deluging them with water, and causing them to get up and move their tent to a drier spot, and to use expletives not very orthodox. Although the joker did it at the expense of getting completely drenched himself, when the boys emerged from their tent Jim was apparently sound asleep in his own.

Another time, while we were on the march, we had halted in the edge of the wood, by the roadside, for dinner. I think this was a forced march, and we had only time to eat a lunch. A joke was played on our captain. He was sitting on the ground, leaning against a tree, eating his lunch from his haversack. One of the boys had caught a lizard — a harmless little reptile, found in the South — and slipping up behind the captain put it into his haversack. He put his hand into the sack for a hard tack, when, feeling something cold, he withdrew his hand very suddenly, while at the same time his face became as red as a beet, and demanded, in not very soft language, 'who the perpetrator was; but no one knew anything about it — all were very busy devouring their luncheons.

Practical joking was not always very safe, as it came very near costing one man his life. One night, after the sentinels had been posted, a certain corporal thought he would scare one of the guards — who was considered not very bright — by approaching him, and trying to make him believe he was a rebel, demanding his gun. But the fellow was not so dumb as he thought he was. He halted him, but paying no attention to him kept on advancing, when the sentinel drew up his gun, and was about to let him have the contents, when he had to make himself known by giving the countersign.

Another incident happened, but not exactly of the same nature. Two soldiers concocted a plan to pass out through the lines one night. They were to get down on all fours, and root and grunt like a hog. One of them started in advance, and succeeded in passing the sentinel apparently unobserved. The other, emboldened by the success of his comrade, attempted the same feat. He had got about half way through in the same manner, when the guard suddenly whirled around, with the exclamation "that there were too many doggone hogs around," and at the same time striking our hero fairly in the side with a stone, laying him out for a few minutes. The guard became alarmed, rushing up to him, said, "Jake, I threw harder than I intended; I knew it was you all the time." Jake concluded that he was not a very good hog after all.

SHERIDAN'S RIDE.

It was the night before the battle of Cedar Creek. In the war office at Washington sat Mr. Stanton in close conversation with General Phil. Sheridan. There were some grave questions being discussed between them, for the talk lasted long after midnight. General Thomas T. Eckert, superintendent of military telegraph lines, was in an adjoining room, watching for sounds of alarm from the front, or important telegrams from any of the advancing armies in the field. A new day was fast approaching the dawn, and the war minister and the general still continued their earnest conversation. A click of the instrument caught General Eckert's ear. It was Winchester calling the war office. His skilled hand touched the key in ready response, and a moment later the words came:

"There is danger here. Hurry Sheridan to the front."

Quick as a flash the message was handed to the two men in the next room in close conversation about the campaign in the Shenandoah Valley. Sheridan went to the instrument, and there was a moment of hurried talk over the wires between him and his headquarters, when Secretary Stanton gave directions to General Eckert to telegraph the railroad authorities of the Baltimore & Ohio to clear the road, and to at once provide relays of special engines to take Sheridan to the scene of the coming battle as fast as steam could carry him. General Eckert worked the wire himself, and gave hurried directions to the railroad officials as to what to do in this emergency. While he sat with his hand on the key, perfecting the train arrangements, Stanton and Sheridan had a few hurried final words, each countenance bearing the marks of earnestness, not unmingled with anxiety. The train schedule was soon made, Sheridan left the war office, and was driven to the station with all possible speed. A panting engine had just backed in as he arrived, and jumping aboard, the engineer, instructed to make the Relay House in the shortest possible time, pulled the starting-bar, and away sped the train. It had a clear track, and reached its destination — thirty miles away — in much less than an hour. Here an engine of the main line stood waiting to take him to Harper's Ferry — seventy miles beyond. There were no obstructions all the way up. Every moving train had been side-tracked, and every other precaution taken to prevent accident to the on-rushing engine bearing Sheridan to the camp where his army lay. While this train was making its run all was anxiety in the war office. Every telegraph station reported its progress to General Eckert, and he to Secretary Stanton, who still lingered, that he might know when Sheridan reached his destination.

AT HARPER'S FERRY.

Three hours passed — dull, anxious hours to those waiting, every moment of which seemed laden with lead. Harper's Ferry at last reports Sheridan's arrival, and a fresh engine stood ready to take him to Winchester — thirty miles up the valley. Not a moment is lost at the hamlet among the rocks, when Sheridan boards the waiting messenger, and an hour later word speeds over the wires: "Sheridan just reached Winchester." The run had been made in the quickest time ever known on the road, and the worn and anxious officials at the war office breathed a sigh of relief as the click of the telegraph announced that the journey had been completed.

Eighteen, or perhaps twenty, miles of turnpike stretched away up the charming valley that had been made desolate by the torch and tramp of armies. As that charming region, clad in the garb of summer, lay between the mountains, its bright colors reflected in the rays of beautiful sunshine, it was but a sad reminder of the once great granary that for more than three years of conflict had furnished untold supplies to the Confederate army. Sheridan had laid it waste. He had clinched with and beaten Early at Winchester, and while he was being carried with all possible speed back to the scenes of his operations, the tide of battle was ebbing and flowing upon a new field, and the fate of the day hung trembling in the balance. For several weary, doubtful hours the two armies had been in deadly conflict. When Sheridan arrived at Winchester the roar of artillery and the roll of musketry could be distinctly heard from the field of carnage along Cedar Creek. Down the valley came the awful din, echoing louder and louder through the still summer air as the battle grew fiercer.

There was but short delay at Winchester, the chief town in the lower valley. There Sheridan mounted his favorite war horse, a large, beautiful, sinewy, black charger, who had borne his master through the heat of many conflicts. He is dead now, and his body has been preserved, that men yet to come may see the animal whose endurance has been recorded in verse. Through the town and out over the turnpike which leads up the Shenandoah, Sheridan rode. Who, knowing the man, or aught of his character, can not picture the restless rider urging his horse to the best to reach the field where the fate of his army was still pending in the hazard of war? He had only covered a few miles, when the moving mass of debris, that always surges to the rear of a battle-field, when the conflict is severe and doubtful, met his trained eye, and told more plainly than words what was going on in front. It was a signal of distress, and none knew it better than he. The sight fired his heart anew, and only added fresh impetus to his foaming horse. He reached the field after a sleepless night and a terrific journey, and the battle of Cedar Creek was won.

MR. MURDOCH'S LETTER.

This is the true story of Sheridan's ride — I might almost say official story. If he did not stop to gather the stragglers, as a poet's license has pictured, he did carry back the tide that was floating to the rear, because his presence had given fresh stamina to some wavering battalions. The manner of the man, his dash and courage, his reputation and successes, all combined to give heart to those who drifted back, believing the battle had been lost.

I have been sitting face to face to day, the whole afternoon, with the man who vouches for the above-written words. He is a strong, positive character, just passing three score and ten years crowded with wonderful experiences. As he told this story he warmed with the fire of the event, and his blood was hot with indignation, for he had just read a statement that Sheridan got drunk at Winchester, and did not go to the battle field, where the poet's pen has pictured him.

"Ah, but I'll put an end to all cavil about this story," said he, "what I have told you I got directly from General Eckert himself, who sat with his hand on the key, arranged and watched every stage of Sheridan's ride from Washington to Cedar Creek. He now manages the Western Union Telegraph Company, and will bear witness to these facts. But I have a letter from Sheridan. He and I were then, and are now, friends. When I heard of the ride I wrote to ask him about it, and to inquire if I had not ridden the same horse that carried him up the valley while with him at Chattanooga. Mr. Murdoch soon found among his papers the identical letter which General Sheridan wrote in reply.

"I need not tell you how highly it is prized," said the veteran, "for you will see how carefully it has been kept through all these years."

Who is there who has read this country's history that does not know James E. Murdoch — the actor, the reader, the man. It is he who tells this story and furnishes this clinching evidence of the truthful foundation of T. Buchanan Read's poem. Thousands who have watched his matchless representation of Hamlet, or sat under the spell of his dramatic readings, will be glad to know that, although he is passing seventy-three, he is still in excellent health and spirits. He is a tall, robust man, with a clean shaven face, that shows the broad, distinct lines of his strong countenance to the best advantage. His wealth of iron gray hair, and his general carriage, combine to make him a very striking character.

"Although an old man when the war was going on, he spent a great deal of time with the army, in connection with the sanitary commission and in the hospitals. He was a favorite at the head-quarters of many generals, and witnessed a great deal of the inner features of army life.

THE POEM SUGGESTED.

The story of Sheridan's ride, above written, was but a tithe of the good things he told me. The recital of this matter naturally led up to all the incidents connected with it.

"I was not with Sheridan," he said, "at this time, but was at the head-quarters of the Army of the Cumberland. Soon after the battle of Cedar Creek I came up to Cincinnati, and was visiting Mr. Cyrus Garrett, whom we called 'Old Cyclops.' He was T. Buchanan Read's brother-in-law, and with him the poet made his home. The ladies of Cincinnati had arranged to give me a reception that finally turned into an ovation. I had given a great many readings to raise funds to assist their Soldiers' Aid Society, and they were going to present me with a silk flag. Pike's Opera-house had been secured—the largest place of amusement in the city—and they had made every arrangement to have the reception a very dramatic event. The morning of the day it was to take place Read and I were, as usual, taking our breakfast late. We had just finished, but were still sitting at the table chatting. Mr. Garrett, the brother-in-law, who was a business man, and guided by business habits, came in while we were thus lounging. He wore an air of impatience, and carried a paper in his hand. He walked directly up to Read, unfolded a copy of *Harper's Weekly*, and held it up before the man so singularly gifted as both poet and painter.

"The whole front of the paper was covered with a striking picture, representing Sheridan seated on his black horse, just emerging from a cloud of dust that rolled up from the highway as he dashed along, followed by a few troopers.

"'There,' said Mr. Garrett, addressing Read, 'see what you have missed You ought to have drawn that picture yourself, and gotten the credit of it; it is just in your line. The first thing you know somebody will write a poem on that event, and then you will be beaten all around.'

"Read looked at the picture rather quizzically, a look which I interrupted by saying, 'Old Cyclops is right, Read, the subject and the circumstance are worth a poem.'

"'Oh, no,' said Read, 'that theme has been written to death. There is "Paul Revere's Ride," "Lochinvar," Tom Hood's "Wild Steed of the Plains," and half a dozen other poems of like character.'

"Filled with the idea that this was a good chance for the gifted man, I said, 'Read, you are losing a great opportunity. If I had such a poem to read at my reception to-night, it would make a great hit.'

"'But, Murdoch, you can't order a poem as you would a coat. I can't write anything in a few hours that will do either you or me any credit,' he replied rather sharply.

"I turned to him and said, 'Read, two or three thousand of the warmest hearts in Cincinnati will be in Pike's Opera-house to-night at that presentation. It will be a very significant affair. Now, you go and give me anything in rhyme, and I will give it a deliverance before that splendid audience, and you can then revise and polish it before it goes into print.' This view seemed to strike him favorably, and he finally said, "Well! Well! We'll see what can be done," and he went up-stairs to his room.

THE POET AT WORK.

"A half hour later Hattie, his wife, a brilliant woman, who is now residing in Philadelphia, came down and said:

"'He wants a pot of strong tea. He told me to get it for him, and then he would lock the door and must not be disturbed unless the house was afire.'

"Time wore on, and in our talk on other matters in the family circle we had almost forgotten the poet at work up stairs. Dinner had been announced, and we were about to sit down when Read came in and beckoned me to come. When I reached the room he said:

"'Murdoch, I think I have about what you want.'

"He read it to me, and with an enthusiasm that surprised him, I said:

"'It is just the thing.'

"We dined; and at the proper time Read and I, with the family, went to Pike's Opera-house. The building was crowded in every part. Upon the stage were sitting two hundred maimed soldiers, each with an arm or a leg off. General Joe Hooker was to present me with the flag the ladies had made, and at the time appointed we marched down the stage toward the footlights, General Hooker bearing the flag, and I with my arm in his. Such a storm of applause as greeted the appearance I never heard, before or since. Behind and each side of us were the rows of crippled soldiers; in front, the vast audience, cheering to the echo. Hooker quailed before the warm reception, and, growing nervous, said to me in an undertone:

"'I can stand the storm of battle, but this is too much for me'

"'Leave it to me,' said I; 'I am an old hand behind the footlights. I will divert the strain from you.'

"So, quickly I dropped upon my knee, took a fold of the silken flag, and pressed it to my lips. This by-play created a fresh storm of enthusiasm, but steadied Hooker, and he presented the flag very gracefully, which I accepted in fitting words.

MURDOCH'S READING.

"I then drew the poem Read had written from my pocket, and, with proper introduction, began reading it to the audience. The vast assemblage became as still as a church during prayer-time, and I read the first three lines without a pause, and then read the fourth:

"Under his spurning feet the road
Like an arrowy Alpine river flowed,
And the landscape bowed away behind,
Like an ocean dying before the wind;
And the steed, like a bark fed with furnace-ire,
Swept on, with his wild eyes full of fire;
But, lo! he is nearing his heart's desire,
He is snuffing the smoke of the roaring fray,
With Sheridan only five miles away.

"As this verse was finished the audience broke into a tumult of applause. Then I read, with all the spirit I could command:

"The first that the general saw were the groups
Of stragglers, and then the retreating troops;
What was done — what to do — a glance told him both,
And, striking his spurs with a terrible oath,
He dashed down the lines 'mid a storm of hurrahs
And the wave of retreat checked its course there, because
The sight of the master compelled it to pause.
With foam and with dust the black charger was gray;
By the flash of his eyes and his nostrils' play,
He seemed to the whole great army to say,
'I have brought you Sheridan all the way
From Winchester town to save the day.'

"The sound of my voice uttering the last word had not died away when cheer after cheer went up from the great concourse that shook the building to its very foundation. Ladies waved their handkerchiefs and men their hats, until worn out with the fervor of the hour. They then demanded the author's name, and I pointed to Read, who was sitting in a box, and he acknowledged the verses. In such a setting, and upon such an occasion as I have been able only faintly to describe to you, the poem of Sheridan's ride was given to the world. It was written in about three hours, and not a word was ever changed after I read it from the manuscript, except by the addition of the third verse, which records the fifteen mile stage of the ride:

> " But there's a road from Winchester town,
> A good, broad highway, leading down;
> And there, through the flash of the morning light,
> A steed as black as the steeds of night
> Was seen to pass as with eagle flight;
> As if he knew the terrible need,
> He stretched away with the utmost speed;
> Hills rose and fell — but his heart was gay,
> With Sheridan fifteen miles away.

"This Mr. Read wrote while on his way, shortly after I first read the poem, to attend a birthday reception to William Cullen Bryant.

"Mr. Read read the poem, thus completed, at Mr. Bryant's birthday party. The great old man listened to every line of it, and then, taking the younger poet by the hand, said, with great warmth :

"'That poem will live as long as Lochinvar.'"

THE LAST PAGEANT.

No army in history has had a more brilliant career than that commanded by General Sherman, which appeared in the closing pageant of the war. Crossing the line between loyal and rebel territory at the extreme northwestern boundary, they marched through every insurgent state and capital in the trans-Mississippi, and sweeping round like a terrible cyclone to the northeastern limits of the Confederacy, literally crushed slavery, state rights and secession before them. The tremendous enthusiasm which greeted their appearance all along the route of march, showed how greatly their countrymen appreciated their worth and services. In imagination they once more saw these stalwart braves storming the hostile works at Donelson, Vicksburg, and Chattanooga, wrestling with the foe upon the crimson fields of Pittsburg Landing, Murfreesboro, Corinth, Perryville, Iuka, and Chickamauga, and once more executing that historical campaign which resulted in the overthrow of the Richmond of the west. How vividly must a sight of the war-worn heroes recall the incidents of that eventful hundred days; the weary march from Dalton, the successful flanking of the stronghold at Dalton, the gallant dash through Buzzard Roost Gap and Allatoona Pass, the heroic but unsuccessful charge upon the beetling crags of Kenesaw, and the fierce and bloody contests south of the Chattahoochee!

COMES MARCHING HOME.

How the nation was electrified with joy by the announcement upon that memorable Saturday morning that Sherman's soldiers, after fighting by day and marching by night during nearly four months time, and over a distance of one hundred and thirty-eight miles, traversing dense thickets, surmounting rocky ledges and fording treacherous streams, had at last reached the goal of their hopes and unfurled their banners over the Gate City!

Accompanying General Sherman, whose pathway was strewn with flowers, rode the fiery Logan and the unassuming Howard, the Havelock of the war, who, after a long absence, had returned to greet his old brigade of the Second Corps, which he had led from Fair Oaks to Antietam. Following them marched the Fifteenth Corps, Sherman's original command, which won such golden laurels from Chickasaw Bayou to Jonesboro. Then came the heroes of the Seventeenth Corps, whose record from Shiloh to Bentonville is not less glorious.

Next in order followed the Twentieth, Hooker's former command, composed of the Eleventh and Twelfth corps, which made the extraordinary journey from the Rapidan to Chattanooga, when they went to the relief of Rosencranz, which afterward stormed Lookout and carried Resaca, wiping out the stain of Chancellorsville, exhibiting equal courage and skill with their western comrades all the way to Goldsboro, and furnishing commanders for both the army of Tennessee and Georgia, Howard of Maine, and Slocum of New York. Last of all came the gallant boys of the Fourteenth, who, partaking of the spirit of their corps commander — Thomas — planted themselves like a wall before the pursuers at Chickamauga, and held the impetuous foe at bay until McCook and Crittenden could rally their broken columns.

HAIL TO THE CHIEF!

As General Sherman passed the multitude of spectators sent up shouts that must have made his heart leap, and the enthusiasm increased as he approached the presidential stand. He "rode up with the light of battle in his face," holding his hat and his bridle-rein in his left hand, and saluting with the good sword in his right hand, his eyes fixed upon his commander-in-chief. His horse, decked with flowers, seemed to be inspired with the spirit of the occasion, and appeared anxious to "keep step to the music of the union."

After passing the reviewing officer, General Sherman wheeled to the left, dismounted, and joined the reviewing party, where he was greeted by Governor Dennison, of Ohio. He shook hands cordially with President Johnson and General Grant, but when Secretary Stanton advanced, with outstretched hand, he remarked, "I do not care to shake hands with clerks," and turned away. Never was there a more complete "cut direct" than was given by the central figure of that grand pageant, whose brain and hand had guided that vast multitude of stalwart braves, leading them to victory, glory, and final triumph.

The troops marched by divisions of two companies front, and the men appeared in good trim. It was generally remarked that they displayed a fine physique, and had apparently profited from their foraging among the fat turkeys of Georgia. Their faces were finely bronzed, and they marched with a firm, elastic step, that seemed capable of carrying them straight to Canada, or, by a flank movement, to Mexico, in a short space of time.

BUMMERS AND NEGROES

Any representation of Sherman's army would have been incomplete which omitted the notorious "bummers." At the end of General Blair's corps appeared the most ludicrous, and at the same time the most interesting, scene ever witnessed in connection with any army. The brigade of black servants, attended by the guards of the small baggage-train, were preceded by two diminutive donkeys, astride of which were two equally diminutive darkies, whose self-complacency was only equaled by the imperturbable animals under them.

Then came the strangest huddle of animation—canine, bovine, and human—that ever civilian beheld, but which has been common enough in Georgia — mules, asses, horses, colts, cows, sheep, pigs, goats, raccoons mounted on mules, chickens, dogs led by negroes blacker than Erebus. Every beast of burden was loaded to its capacity with tents, baggage, knapsacks, hampers, paniers, boxes, valises, kettles, pots, pans, dishes, demijohns, bird cages, cradles, mirrors, fiddles, clothing, picaninnies, and an occasional black woman.

In effect Sherman gave us a sample of his army as it appeared on the march through the Carolinas. He was, in fact, moving to another camp, and the day's display was a perfect picture of his progress, only more orderly, and no foraging. Some of the negroes appeared to have three days' rations in their ample pouches, and ten days more on the animals they led. The fraternity was complete; the goats, dogs, mules, and horses were already veterans in the field, and trudged along as if the brute world were nothing but a vast march with a daily camp. Thus we were shown how Sherman was enabled to live upon the enemy.

TECUMP'S RETORT.

The evening papers contained a letter from General Sherman which threw some light on the studied insult paid by him to Stanton. After alluding to newspaper reports about his conduct, he said, "Well, you know what importance I attach to such matters, and that I have been too long fighting with real rebels with muskets in their hands to be scared by mere non-combatants, no matter how high their civil rank or station. It is amusing to observe how brave and firm some men become when all danger is past. I have noticed on fields of battle brave men never insult the captured or mutilate the dead; but cowards and laggards always do. I can not now recall the act, but Shakespeare records how poor Falstaff, the prince of cowards and wits, rising from a figured death, stabbed again the dead Percy, and carried the carcass aloft in triumph to prove his valor. So now, when the rebellion in our land is dead, many Falstaffs appear to brandish the evidence of their valor, and seek to win applause, and to appropriate honors for deeds that never were done. As to myself, I ask no popularity, no reward; but I dare the war department to publish my official reports. I assert that my official reports have been purposely suppressed, while all the power of the press has been malignantly turned against me."

HOW JOHNNY REB HELPED CATCH A PIG.

The incident I am about to relate happened down in the wilds of West Virginia. I was a member of that glorious old Thirty-second Ohio Volunteer Infantry, which was noted for its good fighting and for its good, religious men. Now, I am not going to say whether I was very religious or not. I will leave that for some one else to say. Self-praise is worse than none; but I will say that, just before going into battle, that little prayer my mother taught me, "Now I lay me down to sleep," would come up in my mind. My face would grow long, and my mouth would open to pray; and then the Lincoln green, or tobacco, would pop from my beautiful mouth to mother earth, and I would resolve never to chew any more. About that time some comrade would say, "What's the matter, Turk?" This would break the spell, and then I would forget my praying, shut my eyes, and "go it blind." This I write for the young generation, not for the old soldiers, for they know how they felt — the same as I did, I suppose.

After the battle of Cross Keys, where General Fremont pounded old Stonewall and sent him flying down towards Richmond to lick General Mc———, General Fremont took a notion that he would cut across lots and head Stonewall off at Strawburg. Orders were very strict to "keep in ranks and not touch anything." Grub was very scarce, and I, being like the animal I was named after, always hungry, got to hankering after meat, either chicken or hog. I had a chum who was a praying man, and he could be trusted; so I told him my heart's desire. He opened his mouth and gave me very good counsel. Said he, "If you can only play off sick, and drop down, I can get leave of the captain to stay by you till the ambulances come up; and while they are coming up we will hide in the bushes and wait until they go past."

I watched my chance to get sick. Along towards evening I was taken violently sick. Down I went. My chum was left with me, and my captain took my gun. We lay there until the regiment passed us; then we hid behind some bushes until the rear guard passed; then we started for "chicken or hog." We saw a large house a mile or so off on the road, so we started for there.

We got within twenty yards of the house, when my pard said, "Turk, you go up to the house and ask for alms, while I stay and pray for the good of the mission." I told him to keep his gun in his hand and watch while he prayed. I went up to the house, and, without ceremony, opened the door. No one was in the room. Went into another room, and saw a man slide in under the bed. I said to him, "Come out, pard, and give me something to eat, or I will search the house." He said there was nothing to eat in the house. By this time he saw that I had no gun, and he got terribly bold, called me a "darned Yank," and told me to "git" or he would let his bull-dog loose, and he would eat me up, as he had a good mouth for thieves.

I told him not to do anything of that kind; that I had no gun, and was a sick soldier, and only wanted a good-sized pig or a dozen chickens. He said he had no chickens, but he had a pig I was welcome to if I could catch it. "But," said he, "remember, I will set the dog on you if you try to get the hog." Says I, "We're out of meat, and I must have that pig."

I bade him good-day, and started to where my chum was praying in the fence-corner. When I said we could have a pig if we could catch it, he said, "Glory! my prayer has been answered, and we will soon have him." He stripped for the race. I took the gun, and told chum to take a good one, and away we went. Johnny Reb saw we were after his hogs, and he let the dog loose, and it came running down, he yelling for "Bull" to "take him." I broke and ran after my chum and the hog, hallooing, "Sic! sic! whoop!" Old Bull came tearing past me and chum, and caught the largest hog by the ear and held him till chum cut his throat.

By this time old Johnny had got within fifty yards of us. He was swearing terribly at the trick we had played on him and Bull. I brought the gun up to a "ready," and told him to "halt!"—that he had given me the hog if I could get it, and now we had it. I gave the command for him to "about face" and "march," and told him if he turned his head to see which way we went I would shoot him. We gave old Bull the head and all we could not carry away, for his share.

Arriving safe in camp, chum gave the captain a good mess of meat, and reported me better. I took a large piece for my supper, and in the morning felt "like the morning star."

INTERESTING LETTER FROM AN EX-REBEL.

I was a soldier on the Confederate side, a member of Company E, Fourth Texas Regiment, Hood's Brigade, Army of Northern Virginia. I left the town with the first company that went from here to the army, and was one of the last to get back; and I was severely wounded three times.

Well, it is all over now; and here in Texas the old soldiers of both sides live side by side, trade and barter with each other, marry into each others' families, and "fight their battles o'er again" without ever a hard word or thought between them. I heard the remark made the other day, and by an ex-Confederate, too, that if there had been as many running North and South in 1861 as there are now, war between the two sections would have been impossible. His idea was that since we travel more we are better acquainted. I have never met a Union soldier who was not willing to admit that we fought well. And fight we did, for we fought for what we believed to be a righteous cause. Mothers sent their sons to battle, and wives their husbands; but our men needed no urging. They went willingly. We fought for a cause that we loved dearer than life; and we held out longer than hope lasted — held out till in reality ours was a lost cause and a conquered banner. But every true soldier fully accepts the result of the war, and desires no more conflict. Yet the beautiful lines of Father Ryan find an echo in every Confederate soldier's heart:

> "Furl that banner — furl it slowly;
> Furl it gently, it is holy,
> For it droops above the dead.
> What though conquered, we adore it,
> Love the cold, dead hands that bore it,
> Wept for those who fell before it,
> Prayed for those who trailed and tore it.
> Oh! how wildly we deplore it,
> Now to furl and fold it so."

Is there a Union soldier who would have us feel otherwise? The memory of our deeds of daring is all we have left us of the struggle. Our hardships are forgotten. Whatever bitterness we may have felt when the result of the struggle was first known has passed away, and our deeds upon the field, and the fun around the camp fire and on the march, remain as our only memories. Would any brave man who met us on the field, where we stood face to face, pouring our vollies of lead and iron into each others' ranks, begrudge us this? I know they would not.

I was a prisoner of war nine months, and, like the ghost in Hamlet, "I could a tale unfold" of hardship and suffering while in actual prison; but I do not care to do it. I would rather remember the kindness with which I was treated while in the hospital; for I was severely wounded when captured, and until I got well of my wounds I was well treated — and there let the record stop. I will contribute one anecdote, and then stop.

Upon one occasion we were near the enemy, on picket duty, and about dark we got to calling over to each other. One of our men and one of the other side got up quite a conversation, and inquired each others' names. I will call our man Jim Brown, and the Union soldier John Smith. After considerable conversation, Jim asked John if he had any coffee. He said, "Yes." Jim said, "All right. Put on a big pot, for I will be over in the morning after some." "All right," said John, "I will have the coffee ready; and you bring along some tobacco." Well, just before daylight we moved out, made a dash, and captured the whole party; and as soon as we got there Jim halloed for John, and said he had brought the tobacco and had come for his coffee. John said that was "a h—l of a time in the morning to be calling for coffee. Why didn't he wait till a man could get up and make a fire?" But they divided coffee and tobacco.

F. M. MAKEIG.

Waco, Texas.

A LITTLE GAME OF EUCHRE—AND BLUFF.

While we were on the campaign from Murfreesboro to Chattanooga, we rested for a short time on what we called University Mountain. Whether that was the real name or not, I do not know. It was in July, 1863, and there were plenty of blackberries and huckleberries inside of our lines—for a time, though, they soon disappeared, as everything generally did where there was a camp, especially eatables. One comrade of our company, James White, was a pretty good judge of commissary corn-juice; and when he had a good ration of it aboard he would lengthen his name by adding "L. J. Parsons, son of the old man."

Well, Jim and I concluded we would take a walk into the country, but had no pass, and thought one was not absolutely necessary, as I knew of a good place to get through the lines without being seen by the pickets. Taking my old musket, and a few rounds of cartridges in my pocket, off we started. After getting outside the picket-line all right, we headed for a corn-juice factory, about six miles distant. After tramping about half the distance, we discovered, on a little raise in the road, a man sitting on a horse; and from the looks of him we concluded we had gone far enough in that direction. As soon as he discovered us he fell back over the hill, out of sight. We took advantage of his movement, and retreated about a mile and a half.

The road being clear behind us, as far as we could see, we thought it was too early to return to camp; so we made a flank movement to the right, and into the brush, where we skirmished around about an hour. Then we heard an old rooster crow, a short distance ahead of us. Jim looked at me, and I looked at Jim. Then we held a council, and decided to attack the rooster at once, and accordingly ordered an advance, which was very tedious, on account of the brush being so thick. We soon came to an opening, with a road running alongside of it. On the other side of the road was fence, and just beyond the fence a house, surrounded by a few shade trees.

We kept up our advance, and just as we were climbing over the fence we discovered four men, with the butternut clothes on, playing euchre under one of the trees between us and the house; but they had no arms in sight, nor did they appear to notice us. Jim says, "What will we do?" I said we must bluff them if we could, as we had gone too far to retreat with safety. We walked up to them, apparently watching the game, but thinking of a different game from euchre. I said to Jim, "Aint it time the other boys were here?" He said he thought so. Just then a lady came to the door. I asked if she could get dinner for six of us fellows. She said she reckoned she could. I told her we would pay her what was right. In a very short time she said dinner was ready, so Jim and I marched into the house, but took our seats where we could keep an eye on the lads under the shade tree, and kept the old musket handy.

The dinner was good, but we soon got all of it that we wanted, and, paying the woman fifty cents, we assured her that the other four would be there soon, and we went back to watch the game a few minutes, asking each other, every few minutes, "why the boys didn't come!" We kept edging around until we got close to the fence, which we were not slow to get over, and into the brush; and I think we measured off about a mile before we halted, and that mile was in the opposite direction from camp, because if they followed us they would most likely hunt for us in the opposite direction from which we were. Who those fellows were we never knew. If they were not rebel soldiers they acted very strangely; and if they were, it was strange they did not take us in. But when we saw them there we gave up the idea of attacking that fellow hat was crowing.

Palmyra, Nebraska.   G. W. PETERSON.

"TO H—L MIT DE GRAND ROUNDS."

I enlisted in Company A, Fifth Michigan Cavalry, July 18, 1862. We were sent to Camp Banks, Detroit, and there drilled until October. In our regiment, the members of Company F were all Dutch, and among them were some who were very slow and backward in learning the drill; consequently the drill-master used to take them out by themselves and drill extra. Still, there were some who seemed almost dumb, and could not remember to salute the different officers according to their rank. One night there was one of them on guard duty around camp. After he had stood it as it seemed to him a long time, he began to think the relief-guard would soon be along and he would be relieved. He soon heard the clatter of sabers, and then he was sure he would soon be in his bunk for four hours' rest. Finally they came to the proper distance, and he said, "Halt! Who comes there?" The reply was, "Grand Rounds." Says he, "Advance, Grand Rounds, and give the countersign."

The officer of the day saw at once that it was one of those Dutchmen who could not remember the drill; so he motioned to the men to stay there while he advanced. As he came up, the vidette was very awkward in giving any kind of a salute, with no pretense of the right one; so he said, "Haven't you been here lately, to learn the drill, so as to know how to salute the officer of the day properly?" "Yes, I vas here." "Well," said the officer, "you don't seem to understand it. Now I propose that we change places for a short time; you be officer of the day, and I'll stand in your place. You approach, and take notice of how I present arms; then try and remember it accordingly." Poor Dutchy gave up his gun; the officer took it, ran to the guard-house, returned with an extra guard, and placed him on the vacant post. Poor Dutchy was pricked for extra duty.

Well, in a few days it came his turn to go on guard-duty again. He thought he would not be caught for anything, for he had taken pains to salute the officer of the day in the meantime. So in the night he stood a long time on post. He began to think his trick must be about up. Finally he says to himself, "It can't be more than five minutes before it is time for the relief. I guess the Grand Rounds ain't going to come." Soon afterward he heard the old, familiar jingle of sabers. Says he, "There is the relief. Halt! Who comes there?" Promptly came the answer, "The Grand Rounds." "To h—l mit de Grand Rounds! I taut it vas de relief guards."

All old soldiers will know what was done with poor Dutchy then; but let me add that when we got to the front Company F was as good a fighting company as there was in the Fifth Michigan Cavalry. For a long time afterwards, if anything went different in camp with the boys from what they expected, it would be, "To h—l mit de Grand Rounds! I taut it vas de relief-guards." A. SMITH.

A MEMORY OF WILMINGTON.

I will try and give you a history of something that I saw at Wilmington, North Carolina. As we approached the city the Johnnies were getting ready to move—I suppose to make room for us Yankees. They finally got in such a big hurry that they left a few thousand pounds of tobacco. This we took right in out of the wet, and we moved on up to the barracks. Before we had time to look around there was a detail made to hunt around and see how many of our men there were left. We found twelve men lying out in front of the barracks, who had been starved to death. They were lying in the hot sun, some with their mouths wide open, and others with eyes open, and the gray-backs crawling down their throats.

Others were found inside of the quarters, perfectly helpless. But, thank the Lord! there was a lady there who had a heart in her, for she told me she had been there all night, caring for those men. She went and begged something for them to eat, and some coffee. She was a noble lady. May the Lord bless her!

While we were on duty at this place there were some seven thousand of our men there who had been prisoners for some months. They were a horrible sight to behold—some without hats or caps, boots or shoes, some without shirts, some with pants having one leg torn off; no shirts on the half of them; dirty and ragged as could be. After starving those men in that manner, who can have the cheek to tell us "The war is over— we should forget and forgive!" I say, No; never can I forget or forgive anyone, it matters not who, who did it. We should not only remember them ourselves, but teach our children and children's children to watch them. They are not to be trusted in any way, shape, or form.

For those twelve men I spoke of, whom we found in the hot sun, we dug a grave, and put them in side by side, as best we could, spread their old blankets over them, and covered them over, and left them, without even a shingle or anything to show. But this was the best we could do for them.

J. C. P.

Salem, Ohio.

PEACH-BRANDY VALOR.

During a recent conversation, V. K. Stevenson, jr., one of our most enterprising real estate men, said:

"When the war broke out I was a small boy, and was sent to the Confederate West Point at Marietta, Georgia, where we had about six hundred cadets. My father subscribed to one hundred thousand dollars of the Confederate loan at par. He lost all his negroes, and I am glad of it. Although I was on the opposite side, I am perfectly satisfied with the result; and so is everybody else of good sense that I have talked to. Our ladies in the South were so gallant for the war that they really made me believe I could go out with a wheat straw and whip every invader across the lines. My grandfather, after the Federals got into Chattanooga, became so patriotic that he wrote my father a letter that I ought to be taken out of the the military school and sent to the battlefield. My father merely inclosed the letter to me without any remark, and thereupon I went to the commandant of the academy and asked my discharge, as I was going to enlist in the ranks to be sent to the front. I enlisted in an Irish regiment entirely composed of railroad laborers, and we started for the battlefield of Chickamauga in box-cars, every soldier being possessed of a canteen filled with New Orleans rum. You can imagine what a diabolical scene was in that car, fighting all the way along; but I was regarded as quite a young hero. We had a terrible battle, and in the excitement had no time to think. It got out, however, who my father was, and I was put on the staff of a man named Benton Smith, who was only twenty-three years old, and a general."

"Benton Smith," resumed Mr. Stevenson, "being called the boy general, concluded that he must have a staff entirely of boys. He was a prodigy of audacity and courage, but his high nervous nature at last wore him out, and not long ago he was a lunatic in a padded cell in Tennessee. He always kept his aides right up to the front, and I saw that unless something happened I should be shot. Just before the big battle at Atlanta, where McPherson was killed, Smith's brigade was re-inforced by a Georgia regiment nearly a thousand strong. I went to a hospital the morning of that battle, where I saw a pile of legs and arms amputated, and it made me sick at the stomach, being quite another lesson of the war, and finding one of our aides with several canteens of peach-brandy, I asked him to let me have some to settle my stomach, and drank the whole of it. Smith then ordered me to lead the Georgia regiment into the battle. I was blind drunk, and charged my horse right over the Federal ramparts. He had both eyes shot out and both knees broken, and as I went up the rampart I could hear the Yankees cry all down the line, 'Don't shoot that boy!' My life was really saved by my youth. It was that charge, as I have understood," said Mr. Stevenson, "which led to McPherson's death. I was twice promoted for gallantry on the battlefield, and upon my soul it was nothing but that peach-brandy."—*Gath, in New York Tribune.*

SOME OF THE AMENITIES OF CAMP LIFE.

There was a man in Company ——, of a certain Ohio regiment, who had a tremendous big nose. He was laughed at continually. On Sunday morning he would get ready to take a shave. He had a small looking-glass, which he would hang up against a tree, and then, after lathering his face, he would seize his razor in his right hand and his nose in his left. About this time fifty or more boys, who were watching, would burst out laughing, and, oh, how mad "Nosey" would get! Afterwards I was told by a soldier that he and this man were captured together. He said they were taken to the rear, and the Johnnies put our big-nosed comrade upon a stump and gathered around him. They would look and laugh, and laugh and look. Finally they said it was no use for the Yanks to deny having horns, for they had now secured a specimen—one who had a horn in the middle of his face.

Just before the battle at Nashville, Tennessee, in December, 1864, two comrades fell out—Charlie —— and Henry ——.

Both were big, stout, burly fellows. Charlie was said to be the stoutest man in the regiment, but he would rather eat than fight. It was supper-time, and Charlie was sitting down eating his supper, when Henry came round and began quarreling with him. Charlie quarreled back, but kept on eating. Quite a crowd soon collected, expecting every minute to see a champion fight. Henry abused Charlie terribly. Charlie would sit there and say, "Just go on, Henry, till I get done eating, and I'll fight you!" But the more Henry cursed him the hungrier Charlie seemed to get. The boys persuaded Henry to go off, as they wanted Charlie to get done in time to be mustered out with his regiment! It was, no doubt, a fine thing for Henry that Charlie's appetite was so good, for the writer had seen Charlie fight before then, when his appetite wasn't half so good, and he was a bad one.

There was a comrade in a certain regiment who was a one-horse preacher before the war. After getting into camp, some of his boys said he captured their coffee-pot one night The chaplain of the regiment got up a pretty big revival in the regiment, and this brother made himself very conspicuous. The boys liked their chaplain, and behaved very well till this man would begin to talk or pray; then they would yell out all over camp, "Dig him a coffee-pit!" and the poor fellow would have to quit.

CAPTURED BY A SLAVE.

During the early part of the summer of 1863 we were doing duty at Donaldsonville, Louisiana, and the rebels were scouting and firing on the passing steamers up the Mississippi River. One day a rebel lieutenant got separated from his command, and he pressed a slave as a guide through a large wooded territory in our front. Everything went along to his satisfaction until they were near our front, when the negro suddenly turned on the rebel, took his arms from him, dismounted him, and pointed for our post, threatening him with all kinds of death if he looked back. He marched him in, and delivered the prisoner up to our commanding officer.

The lieutenant was terribly frightened, but felt much better when he was safe in our hands; and the slave was elated to think he was able to do something for the suppression of the rebellion and for his own liberty. I asked the negro if he would have killed the reb. "Lor! Massa, no. I would not have hurt a hair on his wicked head, only I wanted to let him know I was boss just then." These people knew what the war was about, and they had an idea what its ending would be if the rebellion had succeeded; and I wish that they were as well treated, North and South, by all the people, as they deserve.

H. S. ARCHER.

Randolph, Massachusetts.

THE WAGON-LOAD OF BREAD.

A party of soldiers, during the late civil war, found themselves, one night, on a battlefield in charge of a great many wounded soldiers, who, by reason of the sudden retreat of the army, were left wholly without shelter or supplies. Having done their best for the poor fellows — bringing them water from a distant brook, and searching the haversacks of the dead for rations — they began to say to themselves and to one another, "These weak and wounded men must have food or they will die. The army is out of reach, and there is no village for many miles; what are we to do?"

"Pray to God to send us bread," said one.

That night, in the midst of the dead and dying, they held a little prayer-meeting, telling the Lord all about the case, and begging him to send them bread immediately; though from whence it could come they had not the most remote idea. All night long they plied their work for mercy. With the first ray of dawn the sound of an approaching wagon caught their ears; and presently, through the mists of the morning, appeared a great Dutch farm wagon, piled to the very top with loaves of bread.

On asking the driver where he came from, and who sent him, he replied: "When I went to bed last night I knew that the army was gone, and I could not sleep for thinking of the poor fellows who always have to stay behind. Something seemed to say to me: 'What will those poor fellows do for something to eat?' It came to me so strong that I waked up my old wife, and told her what was the matter. We had only a little bread in the house; and while my wife was making some more I took my team and went round to all my neighbors, making them get up and give me all the bread in their houses, telling them it was for the wounded soldiers on the battlefield. When I got home my wagon was full. My wife piled her baking on the top, and I started off to bring the bread to the boys, feeling just as if the Lord himself were sending me."—*Kind Words.*

THAT BUTTER.

I belonged to what the Third Iowa boys would call the "Butter Regiment." They will remember what a fight we had in the peach orchard at Shiloh. The Third Iowa was on our right, and the Forty-first Illinois on our left. Colonel Pugh commanded our brigade. I should like to shake hands with the boys of the old Third.

I guess they will all recollect when we were on the march from Memphis to Bolivar, Tennessee, some of the boys of the

Third captured a keg of butter; and our captain, being officer of the day, thought it his duty to recapture the butter, taking into consideration that it was something to eat, and the men were not used to such fare. But I guess the boys got the best of the joke at last; for, upon examining the butter, they found wool in it. I suppose the wool was put into the butter to hold it together, as it was in a warm country. I never found out exactly what kind of wool it was, but we can guess.

THE COLONEL HELPED.

Our regiment was introduced to the music at Fort Donelson on the morning of February 13, 1862. Late that afternoon the rain commenced falling, and we were not allowed to kindle any fire. Our colonel took a cold lunch, and said he would "rough it" with the boys. We all lay down together, and about four inches of snow fell on us that night. The next night the colonel said we would have a fire if the Johnnies did shell us, and, laying off his coat, he helped us to make a log-heap, and you can bet we were glad to have a fire to lie beside that night.

But, boys, that was not going to last long. You know how that was; and you know how it was going up that hill, over that down timber. Our colonel, with hat in one hand and sword in the other, led the way, shouting, "Come on, boys! Gad! we've got them." And so we had them; but all who went in did not come out as they went in.

W. S. Hawley.

THE DRUMMER BOY OF MISSION RIDGE.

THE SERGEANT'S STORY.

BY KATE BROWNLEE SHERWOOD.

[To John S. Kountz, Commander of the Department of Ohio, Grand Army of the Republic, this story of his experience at Mission Ridge, while serving as drummer boy of the Thirty-seventh Ohio Volunteer Infantry — the story being that of the sergeant who bore him from the field — is dedicated, as a slight testimonial to his courage on the field of battle, and his fidelity to the veteran's bond of union, "Fraternity, Charity, and Loyalty."]

Did ever you hear of the Drummer Boy of Mission Ridge, who lay
 With his face to the foe, 'neath the enemy's guns, in the charge of that terrible day?
They were firing above him and firing below, and the tempest of shot and shell
 Was raging like death, as he moaned in his pain, by the breastworks where he fell.

We had burnished our muskets and filled our canteens, as we waited for orders that morn —
Who knows when the soldier is dying of thirst, where the wounded are wailing forlorn? —
When forth from the squad that was ordered back from the burst of that furious fire,
Our Drummer Boy came, and his face was aflame with the light of a noble desire.

"Go back with your corps," our colonel had said; but he waited the moment when
He might follow the ranks and shoulder a gun with the best of us bearded men.
And so, when the signals from old Fort Wood set an army of veterans wild,
He flung down his drum, which spun down the hill like the ball of a wayward child.

And so he fell in with the foremost ranks of brave old Company G,
As we charged by the flank, with our colors ahead, and our columns
closed up like a V,
In the long, swinging lines of that splendid advance, when the flags of
our corps floated out,
Like the ribbons that dance in the jubilant lines of the march of a gala-
day rout.

He charged with the ranks, though he carried no gun, for the colonel had
said him nay, .
And he breasted the blast of the bustling guns, and the shock of the sick-
ening fray;
And when by his side they were falling like hail, he sprang to a comrade
slain,
And shouldered his musket and bore it as true as the hand that was dead
to pain.

'Twas dearly we loved him, our Drummer Boy, with a fire in his bright,
black eye,
That flashed forth a spirit too great for his form, he only was just so
high—
As tall, perhaps, as your little lad, who scarcely reaches your shoulder—
Though his heart was the heart of a veteran then, a trifle, it may be, the
bolder.

He pressed to the front, our lad so leal, and the works were almost won,
A moment more and our flags had swung, o'er the muzzle of murderous
gun ;
But a raking fire swept the van and he fell 'mid the wounded and the
slain,
With his wee, wan face turned up to Him who feeleth His children's
pain.

Again and again our lines fell back, and again with shivering shocks
They flung themselves on the rebels' works, as the fleet on the jagged
rocks ;
To be crushed and broken and scattered amain, as the wrecks of the surg-
ing storm,
Where none may rue and none may reck of aught that has human form.

So under the Ridge we were flying for the order to charge again,
And we counted our comrades missing, and we counted our comrades slain;
And one said, "Johnnie, our Drummer Boy, is grievously shot and lies
Just under the enemy's breastworks; if left on the field he dies."

Then all the blood that was in me surged up to my aching brow;
And my heart leaped up like a ball in my throat, I can feel it even now;
And I swore I would bring that boy from the field, if God would spare my breath,
If all the guns on Mission Ridge should thunder the threat of death.

I crept and crept up the ghastly Ridge, by the wounded and the dead,
With the moans of my comrades right and left, behind me and yet ahead,
Till I came to the form of our Drummer Boy, in his blouse of dusty blue,
With his face to the foe, 'neath the enemy's guns, where the blast of the battle blew.

And his gaze as he met my own, God wot, would have melted a heart of stone,
As he tried like a wounded bird to rise, and placed his hand in my own;
So wan and faint, with his ruby-red blood, drank deep by the pitiless sward,
While his breast with its fleeting, fluttering breath, throbbed painfully slow and hard.

And he said in a voice half-smothered, though its whispering thrills me yet,
"I think in a moment more that I would have stood on that parapet,
For my feet have trodden life's rugged ways, and I have been used to climb
Where some of the boys have slipped, I know, but I never missed a time.

But now I nevermore will climb, and sergeant, when you see
The men go up those breastworks there, just stoop and waken me;
For though I can not make the charge, and join the cheers that rise,
I may forget my pain to see the old flag kiss the skies."

Well, it was hard to treat him so, his poor limb shattered sore,
But I raised him to my shoulder, and to the surgeon bore,
And the boys who saw us coming each gave a shout of joy,
Though some in curses clothed their prayers for him, our Drummer Boy.

When sped the news that " Fighting Joe " had saved the Union right,
With his legions fresh from Lookout; and that Thomas massed his might
And forced the rebel center; and our cheering ran like wild;
And Sherman's heart was happy as the heart of a little child;

When Grant from his lofty outlook saw our flags by the hundred fly,
Along the shores of Mission Ridge, where'er he cast his eye;
And our Drummer Boy heard the news, and knew the mighty battle done,
The valiant contest ended, and the glorious victory won;

Then he smiled in all his agony, beneath the surgeon's steel,
And joyed that his was the blood to flow, his country's woes to heal;
And his bright, black eyes so yearning, grew strangely glad and wide;
I think that in that hour of joy he would have gladly died.

Ah, ne'er again our ranks were cheered by our little Drummer's drum,
When rub, rub, rub-a-dub, dub, we knew that our hour had come;
Beat brisk at morn, beat sharp at eve, rolled long when it called to arms,
With rub, rub, rub-a-dub, dub, 'mid the clamor of rude alarms!

Ah, ne'er again our black-eyed boy looked up in the veteran's face,
To waken thoughts of his children safe in mother love's embrace!
Oh, ne'er again with tripping feet he ran with the other boys—
His budding hopes were cast away as they were idle toys.

But ever in our hearts he dwells, with a grace that never is old,
For him the heart to duty wed can nevermore grow cold!
His heart, the hero's heart, we name the loyal, true, and brave,
The heart of the soldier hoar and gray, of the lad in his southern grave!

And when they tell of their heroes, and the laurels they have won,
Of the scars they are doomed to carry, of the deeds that they have done;
Of the horror to be biding among the ghastly dead,
The gory sod beneath them, the bursting shell o'erhead;

My heart goes back to Mission Ridge and the Drummer Boy who lay
With his face to the foe, 'neath the enemy's guns, in the charge of that
    terrible day;
And I say that the land that bears such sons is crowned and dowered
    with all
That the Lord giveth nations to stay them lest they fall.

BATTLE OF NASHVILLE.

Now Thomas came with his well-drilled command
To Nashville, on the river Cumberland,
A place of beauty in a high degree,
In state original of Tennessee,
Where, in endeavors for the public good
He militates against the aims of Hood,
Who with his army there does cogitate
That city fair to make Confederate.
His plan of battle is of simple kind,
The field uneven, yea, to hills inclined —
A feint upon the left, does quickly make
Which to the center causes him to take —
The further operations to enhance
The Sixteenth Corps was ordered to advance.

At early dawn Hood roused in much affright
At the loud firing on his distant right;
And scarcely had he time to ascertain
What it did mean, before an armed train
Came down upon him like a loosened flood,
From the united corps of Smith and Wood.
A battle this could not be truly called,
So overwhelming was the foe appall'd,
That their lines crumbled in atoms, and
The left entire was gone of Hood's command.
Thus with a single blow his left was gone,
And in confusion drove the center on —
This now let loose the nimble cavalry
Which now swept round and passed our right in glee.

Hung like avenging cloud upon the flank
And rear of rebels, as they placed their'rank
And file back on the center, sullenly,
Which Hood imperiled in a high degree.
Aroused now by the dangers imminent
Hood ordered from the right that troops be sent,

The tide reversed, of battle to sustain ;
When all around, from every hill and plain,
Could be discovered lines of infantry,
Commingled with squads of artillery
Which made the most of every joint and limb,
In gallant forward strides to rescue him.

The left is gone, the center still is held,
From which Hood is not easily expelled,
As the position is one very strong —
On lofty hills, and covered all along
With rifle-pits, well fringed with abatis,
Beyond which ordnance move — charged not to miss
As they the grape and canister did throw,
On every parcel of the land below.

Smith in command was never known to shirk,
But paused before this formidable work,
A reconnoissance of it to make,
That he successfully the same might take.
Now Wood and Schofield with their forces came
And kept all day a brisk artillery flame
Without effect ; while infantry essayed
In vain to find a spot they could invade.
But then it was not difficult
For thus, one day, to sum up the result —
Two thousand prisoners captured martially
With sixteen pieces of artillery.

Now Thomas saw the sun sink in the west,
While nature tired, inclined to sink to rest ;
Ere this, the news by telegraph does tell,
"So far, I think, we have succeeded well ;
Lest Hood decamps to-night to-morrow stead,
Will double up his right — by tactics led,
While gallant Wood endow'd with courage bold
His center most triumphantly will hold ;
And Smith and Schofield strike his left again,
While cavalry the rear work will maintain."

Hood takes a new position in the night,
The better to maintain to-morrow's fight;
And of the former is two miles in rear,
While shortened to three miles his lines appear —
So very powerful appear the whole
That at first sight they seem impregnable.
But Thomas acting on his former plan,
Commanded Steadman now to lead the van;
As yesterday, upon the rebel right.
However, now it being their design
To hold their fire, and feel the rebel line;
Till Smith and Schofield should reach the scene
Of yesterday, now passed to the serene.
The stillness of the hour now occupies
The close attention of all ears and eyes,
Like that which is precursor to the sage
Of the fierce lightning's rage,
Or like the thunderbolt's malignant fall,
When trembles earth, and skies with gloom appall.
The Union bugles, well played on, and large,
Now sound the tidings to command "the charge."
With leveled bayonets and ringing cheers
That sounded audibly in rebel ears,
They swept undauntedly, for all were brave,
Upon the rebels in one awful wave,
Wood in the center; as the sound he caught,
His regiments to a forward movement brought
And Steadman stationed on the left extreme,
Upon them charged; it was no idle dream.
Now for three miles the rebel lines became
One lively scene; ah! one vast sheet of flame.
The batteries thundred, shells screamed through the air,
The earth did tremble as a frightened hare;
Beneath our feet the ground appeared to quake,
Sulphurous clouds of smoke appearance make;
And for one hour without an intermit
It was an emblem of the burning pit.
The rebels seemed as if by whirlwinds raised,

And carried back, defeated, and amazed;
While dropping everything that would impede
The flight of one that ran for life indeed,
They sped in wild confusion o'er the land,
Who then submitted not to our command.
These words are still resounding in my ear,
Which issued from a captured brigadier;
Though at that moment I had not the time
To emphasize and place them into rhyme:
" Why, sir, it is, and ever shall be said,
The bravest act I ever witnessed;
I saw you coming, men, and held my fire —
In numbers to a full brigade entire —
Until I demonstrably could espy
The white in each and every soldier's eye;
Determined thus a bullet well to place
In each and every soldier's face;
And I supposed, when the smoke arose,
Your heels would toward us be, and not your toes.
But not thus. Each deserves a diadem;
My galling fire not even staggered them.
They came along cool, and in martial skill,
And walked up to my works upon the hill;
And ere I knew that you advance had made,
You had entire surrounded my brigade."
More than two thousand rebel prisoners we —
One major general, brigadiers just three —
Did capture in that battle with their arms,
And showed the world secession had no charms.

L. L. HANAN.

THE SOLDIER'S DEATH.

IN MEMORY OF JAMES D. SEWARD.

Who saw him fall, the noble boy?
Who whispered words of hope and joy?
Could no one pause in that sad strife,
And try to win him back to life?

Who watched beside his dying bed?
I only hear that he is dead.
I was not there to close his eyes,
Or catch his last expiring sighs.

No loved one near to soothe his pain,
Or smooth his matted locks again;
No hand to wipe the fallen tear,
Of soothe the heart of one so dear.

Were pitying angels hovering nigh
To watch my poor, lone brother die?
With pearly gates all swung ajar,
To watch his coming from afar?

His voice comes back to soothe my grief,
And give my bleeding heart relief;
His parting look, his farewell sigh —
I was not there to see him die.

I may not see his lonely grave;
He 's sleeping with his country's brave.
But though I may not mark the spot,
My heart will still forget him not.

I love to think of one so dear;
His name I'll mention with a tear,
And weep the cruel fate that gave
My brother to a soldier's grave.

C. R.

THE NINETY-FOURTH ARMY BEAN.

The following song was sung by the orphan children, at the reunion of the Ninety-fourth Regiment O. V. I., Xenia, Ohio:

[AIR—"SWEET BYE-AND-BYE."]

There's a spot that the soldiers all love,
  The mess-tent's the place that we mean,
And the dish that we like to see there,
  Is the old-fashioned white army bean.

CHORUS.

'Tis the bean, that we mean,
  And we'll eat as we ne'er ate before,
The army bean, nice and clean,
  We'll stick to our beans evermore.

Now the bean in its primitive state,
  Is a plant we have often met,
And when cooked in the old army style,
  It has charms we can never forget.

CHORUS.

The German is fond of saur-kraut,
  The potato is loved by the Mick,
But we soldiers have long since found out,
  That thro' life to our beans we should stick.

[REFRAIN—Air—"TELL AUNT RHODY."]

Beans for breakfast,
Beans for dinner,
Beans for supper,
Beans, beans, beans.

Closing Scenes of the War.

In closing this history I think it will be interesting to my readers to show how General Sherman's campaign ended. The news of the battles about Petersburg reached Sherman at Goldsboro on the 6th of April. Up to that time it was his move rapidly northward, feigning on Raleigh and striking straight for Burksville, and thus interposing his army between Johnston and Lee. The successes at Petersburg, however, changed the necessity for a junction of Sherman's army with Grant's, and the Confederate armies of Lee and Johnston became the strategic points. Grant was fully able to take care of the former, and it was Sherman's task to destroy or capture the latter. Johnston had his army well in hand about Smithfield. His infantry and artillery were estimated at thirty five thousand, and his cava'ry at from six to ten thousand. General Kilpatrick was held in reserve at Mount Olive, with orders to recruit his horses, and be ready to make a sudden and rapid march on the 10th of April.

At daybreak of the 10th all the heads of columns were in motion against the enemy. General Slocum took the two direct roads for Smithfield. General Howard was to make a circuit by the right, feigning up the Weldon road, to disconcert the enemy's cavalry; and Generals Terry and Kilpatrick moving on the west side of the Neuse River, were to aim at reaching the rear of the enemy between Smithfield and Raleigh. General Schofield followed General Slocum in support. Within six miles of Goldsboro more or less cavalry were met behind the usual rail barricades, but they were swept away by the advance, and by ten

A. M. of the 11th, Davis' Fourteenth Corps entered Smithfield, closely followed by the Twentieth Corps. Johnston had lightened up his trains by the railroad, and retreated, burning the bridge over the Neuse River, at Smithfield. Pontoons were brought up, and the crossing accomplished without resistance. It was here that the news of the surrender of Lee's army, at Appomattox Court House, Virginia, reached General Sherman, and was announced by him to the armies in orders, creating the wildest joy. The announcement was made at the head of columns, and as the joyful news was conveyed from division to division, and from regiment to regiment, each in turn took up the glad shout, making the pine forests ring with the "glad tidings of great joy." For a time all discipline was cast aside. The men seized their officers and carried them around on their shoulders, and then threw their hats or caps high in the air. Strong men wept and laughed by turns, and embraced each other in the exuberance of their joy.

While negotiations for the surrender of Johnston's army were pending at Raleigh, Jefferson Davis was making his way toward the Mississippi River, with the intention of passing into Texas, there to continue the strife. Efforts were made for his capture by the army, and, to stimulate to greater exertion, large rewards were offered for his apprehension. General Wilson, being apprised of Davis' probable route, put his whole available cavalry force in pursuit, sending squads in all directions. The Mississippi River was patrolled by gunboats, to prevent his crossing, and the coast of Georgia and Florida was watched day and night. General Wilson's report of the capture is given in the following dispatch to the Secretary of War:

MACON, GEORGIA, 9:30 A. M., May 13th.

To Hon. E. M. Stanton, Secretary of War:

Lieutenant Colonel Harden, commanding First Wisconsin, has just arrived from Irwinsville. He struck Davis' trail at Dublin, Lawrence

County, on the evening of the 7th, and followed him closely, night and day, through the pine wilderness of Alligator Creek and Green Swamp, *via* Cumberland, to Irwinsville. At Cumberland, Colonel Harden met Colonel Pritchard, with one hundred and fifty picked men and horses, of the Fourth Michigan. Harden followed the trail directly south, while Pritchard, having fresher horses, pushed down the Ocmulgee toward Hopewell, and thence by House Creek to Irwinsville, arriving there at midnight of the 9th. Jeff Davis had not arrived. From citizens Pritchard learned that his party were encamped two miles out of town. He made his dispositions, and surrounded the camp before day. Harden had encamped two miles (as he afterward learned) from Davis, the trail being too indistinct to follow. He pushed on at 3 A. M., and had gone but little more than a mile when his advance was fired upon by men of the Fourth Michigan. A fight ensued, both parties exhibiting the greatest determination. Fifteen minutes elapsed before the mistake was discovered. The firing in this skirmish was the first warning Davis received. The captors report that he hastily put on one of his wife's dresses and started for the woods, closely followed by our men, who at first thought him to be a woman, but, discovering his boots while running, suspected his sex at once. The race was a short one, and the rebel president was soon brought to bay. He brandished a bowie-knife of elegant pattern, and showed signs of battle, but yielded promptly to the persuasions of the captain's revolver, without compelling the men to fire. He expressed great indignation at the energy with which he was pursued, saying that he thought our Government was more magnanimous than to hunt down women and children. Mrs. Davis remarked to Colonel Harden after the excitement was over that "the men had better not provoke the president as he might hurt some of 'em."

       J. H. WILSON, Brevet Major General.

Davis was immediately taken to Fortress Monroe, and confined in one of the casements of the fortress prepared for him, and a strong guard placed over him to prevent escape or rescue. He was afterward bailed out by Horace Greeley, which was the cause of his political death, and doubtless his political death was the cause of his natural death.

 "O Horace Greeley, you were not the man for me;
  You went too far to bail old Jeff, and helped to set him free."

Our task, kind reader, is finished. Through more than four years of war and carnage, such as few nations have ever felt, we have tried to give a partial history of some of the regiments, and a list of Greene County s soldiers as far as we have been able to obtain them, together with some incidents and anecdotes connected with the great rebellion. From war's dark desolation and its train of human suffering and woe we have emerged into the glorious light of freedom, and universal peace now reigns throughout our land. The tramp of the soldier is no longer heard, nor the bugle-blast calling to arms; the weary march is ended; camp-fires are extinguished; the roar and din of battle is hushed. The Blue and the Gray can now meet as friends and brothers. Glorious America! the asylum of the oppressed of all nations, rising from her sackcloth and ashes, re-invigorated by the desolations of war, shall work out her glorious destiny, and teach the crumbling despotisms of the Old World that man, enlightened by the principles of free institu tions, is capable of self-government. All hail! America. Well hast thou earned the honor of being

"The land of the free and the home of the brave."

Schlesinger & Brady,

Merchant Tailors
—AND—
Gents' Furnishers.
87 East Main St., Xenia, O.

COMPLETE LINE OF READY-MADE CLOTHING

HATS, CAPS, TRUNKS, Valises, &c.

W. D. LAZIER,

Druggist.

No. 26 East Main Street, Xenia, Ohio.

A. SOWARD,

PIANOS AND ORGANS

ALSO ALL KINDS OF

MUSICAL MERCHANDISE.

WAREROOMS—No. 18 Detroit Street, - - XENIA, OHIO.

Snyder & Sons,

DEALERS IN

✦ COAL ✦

OF ALL KINDS,

AND AGRICULTURAL IMPLEMENTS.

YARDS—South End Detroit St., and W. Second St., XENIA, OHIO.

W. S. FAWCETT,
THE JEWELER,

CORNER MAIN AND DETROIT STREETS,
XENIA, OHIO.

W. M. GATCH,

Photographer.

34 and 36 E. Main St., XENIA, OHIO.

BUY YOUR GOODS OF THE

WILLIAM ALLISON

CLOTHING, HAT, GENTS' FURNISHING, BOOT AND SHOE

EMPORIUM

No. 17 and 19 Greene Street, East Side of Public Park, XENIA, OHIO.

ALLISON & STROUSS.

R. I. STEWART,
Clothing, Boots, Shoes and Rubbers

HATS, CAPS, AND GENTLEMEN'S FURNISHING GOODS.

No. 33 and 35 East Main Street, XENIA, OHIO.

www.ingramcontent.com/pod-product-compliance
Lightning Source LLC
Chambersburg PA
CBHW032055220426
43664CB00008B/1004